amazing contemporary HOMES

36 INSPIRATIONAL SELF-BUILD HOMES

365 COLOUR PHOTOS   76 COLOUR ILLUSTRATIONS

amazing contemporary HOMES

Ovolo Books
1 The Granary, Brook Farm,
Ellington, Huntingdon,
Cambridgeshire
PE28 0AE

This edition © 2010 Ovolo Books Ltd, 1 The Granary, Brook Farm,
Ellington, Cambridgeshire PE28 0AE. Original text and illustrations
© 2005-2010 Ascent Publishing Ltd, St Giles House, 50 Poland Street,
London W1F 7AX

ISBN: 9781905959198

The publishers make no representation, express or implied, with regard to the accuracy of the information contained in this publication and cannot accept any responsibility in law for any errors or omissions. The information in this publication contains general guidelines only and does not represent to be advice on any particular matter or project. No reader, purchaser or other third party should act on the basis of material or information contained in this publication without first taking professional advice appropriate to their particular circumstances.

All of the material in this book has previously appeared in Homebuilding & Renovating magazine - Britain's best selling monthly for selfbuilders and renovators (www.homebuilding.co.uk).

Design: Gill Lockhart

**This edition first published by Ovolo Books
April 2010**

Printed and bound in Great Britain by Butler Tanner & Dennis Ltd, Frome and London

For more information on books about property and home interest please visit: www.ovolobooks.co.uk

62

76

54

40

28
108

116

124

CONTENTS

174

300

200

262

316
290

270

282

FOREWORD

All too often people setting out to create a new home – either through self-build or renovation – take the conservative path. But this book celebrates those that have chosen to 'do different'. The fantastic homes in this collection don't bow to the pressure of the mainstream market or the straight-jacket of the planning regime. Neither do they conform to the notion of what a traditional house should be.

Look around any new development and what you'll see most are homes that are echoes of a nondescript period style that add nothing in terms of architectural merit and, on the whole, fail to meet the modern aspirations of their owners.

Luckily, there are a growing number of people willing to make a break from the norm and create an individual home that is truly of its time. Why do they do it? Well, they are of course keen on making an architectural statement but, more importantly, they are looking for a home that delivers the very modern requirements of being light, open-plan, with large rooms, big windows, offering simple living and energy efficiency all in one package – a contemporary one. It makes perfect sense to build a house in a contemporary style to meet contemporary needs.

Of course, the question of exactly what does make a home 'contemporary' in style is one that has puzzled critics for many years. But in our view it is a home that could only be built today. It may echo the past - Frank Lloyd Wright, the Modernist movement or almost any other period of design - but it does so with a twist that makes it of the now. Part of the reason for this may be to do with technology - big energy-efficient windows, under-floor heating and modern finishes - but ultimately it is about creating homes for the way we live today.

I hope you enjoy this fine selection of design advice and contemporary homes. They are amazing not just in their architecture but in the fact that they are so beautiful, so inspirational and so individual!

JASON ORME

Editor, Homebuilding and Renovatiing Magazine

The house faces south
for maximum solar gain.
A raised parapet runs
across the front and sides,
concealing the pitched
roof and maintaining the
Modernist look

DARE TO BE SQUARE

Allan and Carole Craigen have built a Modernist-style house full of light and space, that still retains an air of comfort and intimacy

WORDS: HAZEL DOLAN   PHOTOGRAPHY: JEREMY PHILLIPS

Few first timers would disagree that self-building presents a steep learning curve. From plotfinding and designing, to planning and the whole build process, there is so much to discover. So, once you've survived and succeeded, why stop at just one?

For Allan and Carole Craigen, project number two is a stunning Modernist glass-and-render structure in an upmarket part of Rochdale. The design follows the line of the land in a series of stepped cubes, its sharp geometry softened by imaginative landscaping and the careful use of Douglas fir window frames.

The Craigens, who run their own scaffolding company, were not initially hell-bent on following up their first self-build with a second more ambitious scheme, but the more they looked into buying a ready-built home, the more convinced they became that it would make better sense to design their own. "With the properties we were looking at, we were spending so much money already, we didn't want to then spend another £50,000 or £100,000 ripping it to pieces to make it how we wanted it," says Allan. "We felt the only way we were going to make money was to build from new."

On impulse, Allan went to check out a plot he had spotted in Bamford 12 years earlier. At the time it had planning permission for four homes and he and Carole had decided against pursuing it. Remarkably, it was still undeveloped and the site was overgrown, but the potential was clear. The builder-owner had died, leaving the land in trust for his children, planning permission had lapsed, and after a little detective work, Allan traced the builder's widow, agreed a deal and secured it.

"I have never believed in fate," he says, "but I do feel that piece of land was meant for us, because going back to it, the location was just right and we approached at the right time. The owner's daughters were about to go away to university and the trust needed a change of executor — everything fell into place."

Build one had been a fairly straightforward affair — a family house in traditional mock-Tudor style to tie in with neighbouring properties. Plans were passed before the

Craigens and their children, Jordan and Chanelle, came on board, so their input was restricted to a few key changes to the internal structure. This time, there was a chance to give full rein to their imaginations and they took it, recruiting Manchester-based architect Paula Butterfield to interpret their ideas for an Art Deco-inspired design.

"We wanted an architect with fresh vision," Allan explains. "We had an initial meeting and decided to go for it. We gave them a brief for a contemporary look. We quite like Art Deco, so wanted to incorporate some Art Deco features. We said: 'Make it modern, slightly different, south facing for as much solar gain as possible, and well insulated to keep the running costs down.'"

Paula came back with several options but a cubic-block design proved most tempting, wherein three linked cubes turn the rather awkward slope of the site to a clear advantage. A three-storey section houses a garage and basement store room, with kitchen and living space above and top-floor master suite. In the middle two-storey section, the dining room and study are at ground level, with a bedroom and bathroom above. Block three has three storeys: lounge at base level, with a bedroom, dressing room and en suite on each of the floors above. Glazed 'sunspaces' link the cubes and huge south-facing windows flood the interior with light. At the rear are slimmer, smaller, north-facing windows, with views onto the wooded slope behind the house.

One stroke of luck was that their chosen cul de sac already had a mix of house styles, including one flat-roofed design. Allan and Carole's project proved less than popular with one neighbour, but with a few compromises, including the removal of a first floor balcony, they were able to get their plans passed and set to work clearing and levelling the site. "It certainly made the plot look massive, compared to when you saw it with the trees overgrowing it," says Allan.

"MAKE IT MODERN, DIFFERENT, SOUTH FACING FOR AS MUCH SOLAR GAIN AS POSSIBLE, AND WELL INSULATED TO KEEP THE RUNNING COSTS DOWN"

A change in levels and flooring help to define the separate kitchen and sitting areas in the open plan layout

"We also had to divert a drain that ran from the adjacent house and would run right through the middle of the proposed house."

By summer 2002 the couple were ready to build, but they faced an early setback. The lack of internal walls led to their structural engineer specifying stainless steel wind posts by the windows: an expensive move, which delayed progress by two weeks.

The Craigens love the streamlined simplicity of the contemporary design, but were wary of making their new home too austere and so decided against the purists' choice of metal window frames throughout. "The natural wood softens the house and blends it with its surroundings, and Douglas fir with a light oak pigment is a good option," Allan says. "We still wanted some aluminium frames at each corner and over the sunspace. These aluminium windows give it that Modernist look, but all-aluminium could have looked more like an office building.

"THE ALUMINIUM WINDOWS GIVE IT THAT MODERNIST LOOK, BUT ALL-ALUMINIUM COULD HAVE LOOKED MORE LIKE AN OFFICE BUILDING"

We felt we got the balance right."

Practical, rather than aesthetic, concerns meant they shied away from a Modernist flat roof, too: the pitch is cleverly concealed by a low parapet. "From the front it looks as though it has a flat roof," says Allan. "The sides return at the same height but it has actually got a 60-degree sloping roof with a gutter at the back. From the front and sides people won't know there's a gutter there. It didn't aesthetically affect the look of the house — you still have the same impression of no pitch — but to me it was more of a practical issue and better from a maintenance point of view."

Their budget was inevitably stretched way beyond the initial estimate of £200,000, but they were prepared to bump up their investment to achieve the best for their prime location. "We wanted to spend more money on the infrastructure," Allan explains. "In our previous house we spent a fortune on door handles. We can swap these further down the line, but we can't put cables in once it's been plastered."

The result is spectacular — a striking exterior combined with an interior that's both light and spacious, yet thanks to its carefully planned layout and broad folding doors, also intimate and comfortable. "We built it to stay in and enjoy because it has taken a lot of our time," says Allan, "but we've also been aware that we will want to sell it on. In the meantime, we are enjoying it." ■

PROJECT NOTES

FLOORPLAN

The house is made up of three cubes. The lower ground floor of the first three-storey cube houses a garage, basement and store, kitchen and living spaces above and a master bedroom on top. In the middle two-storey section is a dining room and study at ground level with bed and bath rooms above. The final three-storey cube houses a living area, with bedroom, dressing room and en suite on each of the levels above.

FACT FILE

Names: Allan and Carole Craigen
Professions: Company director and company secretary
Area: Rochdale
House type: Five bedroom house
House size: 500m²
Build route: Self-managed with contractors
Finance: Private
Construction: Aluminium frame, dual-skin block with rendered outer skin
Build time: Jan '02 – Jan '04
Land cost: £100,000
Build cost: £450,000
Total cost: £550,000
Current value: £1,000,000
Cost/m²: £900

COST SAVING
45%

USEFUL CONTACTS

Architect Paula Butterfield at Butterfield & Macpherson: 0161 839 0222
Aluminium frames Invincible Windows: 0161 653 8900 **Bathrooms** H2O: 0161 762 9119 **Building supplies** Parrs of Rochdale: 01706 656980
Electrics and audiovisual Wired for Living: 01254 880288 **Fibre optics** Blue Beacon: 0870 241 3992 **Flooring** Build Center: 01282 842777 **Glass balustrades** Cheadle Glass: 0161 486 9333 **Joinery** David Sutcliffe: 01706 860024 **Kitchen fitting** Stuart Frazer: 0161 798 4800 **Kitchen furniture** Siematic: 01438 369327 **Lighting** Total Energy Saving Techniques: 01484 713355 **Light fittings** Genesis 1:3: 020 8845 8444 **Oak panels** Bespoke Veneers: 0161 476 3522 **Plastering** McCrea Plastering & Tiling: 01942 825444 **Screed** B & K Systems: 0113 307 9908 **Steel stair and handrails** GTS Sheet Metal: 01706 860857 **Timber frames and stair treads** Leach & Clegg: 01706 642757 **Underfloor heating** Rehau: 0161 777 7400
Windows and glass doors Interpane: 01457 837779

Ground floor

First floor

Second floor

BRICK
WORKS
Dinah and Martin Warner's striking new timber frame self-build combines cutting-edge technology with local crafts and traditional skills
WORDS: CAROLINE EDNIE
IMAGES: ANDREW LEE

"Our previous home was a fairly standard brick and block house, which we built for ourselves back in 1989," explains Martin Warner. "We brought up our two children, Tim and Becca, there and it was a very comfortable five-bedroom family home. However, building our second house was a different experience altogether, and we were able to be far more brave and experimental second-time around."

The couple had been looking for a suitable plot of land for some time and ultimately purchased a gardener's cottage, stables and a paddock just a stone's throw away from where they were living in Hertfordshire. With fabulous west-facing views, the one and- a-half-acre site overlooks Ashridge Forest — a beautiful area of ancient woodland, pasture, common land, heath and chalk downland, owned and managed by The National Trust.

As joint owner of a number of specialist brickworks, Martin wanted to demonstrate how traditional brick construction may be used in tandem with other local crafts and materials to provide beautiful, contemporary solutions.

"I really wanted to see what could be done, and push the boundaries a little," he explains. "Bricks are often perceived as being rigid and inflexible, so it was important to show that there really are no restrictions when it comes to shape. The idea was to keep the craft alive by bringing it right up to date."

Dinah and Martin contacted their architect friend David Kirkland, who specialises in designing sustainable buildings and has been involved with such diverse and curvaceous schemes as the International Terminal at Waterloo and The Eden Project in Cornwall. Dinah was very keen that the new house should be based around a curve, and David came up with a radical and organic design for a four-bedroom property which forms a sweeping crescent, 20 metres long by 11 metres wide, opening out to the rear with masses of glazing to embrace the views.

The front of the house, however, presents a far more

fortress-like façade, with the roof pulled down like a giant tea cosy of tiles over the lower walls and stopping just above the small windows. Only the very tip of the chimney is visible, and the entrance doorway stands modest and restrained, peeping out from between the brickwork.

In plan form, the ground floor of the couple's new home resembles the kind of cross-section diagrams more often found in biology text books. The central fireplace and curving walls appear more like the chambers of a heart than chambers within a building, and this unconventional layout ensures free-flowing movement between all the main living areas.

The spacious sitting/dining room is housed in a single storey drum-like structure located to the west of the plan, and is partially divided by a slim wall, which projects forward from the contemporary fireplace to create distinct seating and dining areas. "In terms of accommodation the

"THE PLANNERS WERE EXTREMELY SUPPORTIVE. WE WERE PROPOSING TO DEMOLISH THE EXISTING COTTAGE, SO IT'S TECHNICALLY A REPLACEMENT DWELLING"

house works extremely well," says Dinah. It's based on the tradition of having a fire as the home's focus, and there's a view from virtually every room."

A curving hallway of exposed brick walls and Cotswold stone flooring winds its way like a spine through the centre of the house, linking the kitchen/breakfast room at one end of the building with a ground floor bedroom, en suite

Left: The kitchen-cum-breakfast room on the ground floor has glazing one end to maximise views and solar gain
Above: The property is based around a hybrid timber structure of green and dry English oak, initially resembling an upturned boat

bathroom and study that stand to the other side of the entrance. Upstairs, the master bedroom and en suite, two further bedrooms and a bathroom are positioned in crescent formation, opening out onto an elliptical roof terrace and the planted sedum roof of the living area below.

"We already knew all of our neighbours, so we chatted to them about what we were thinking of doing and no one had any objections," recalls Martin. "The planners also proved extremely supportive of the house. We were proposing to demolish the existing cottage, so it's technically a replacement dwelling, and planning permission was approved in just eight weeks. After that, the only problem was actually building it!"

The couple remained living in their previous house while their new home was being constructed just a short distance away. They appointed a project manager to oversee the complex build, but also took an active role in employing subcontractors and sourcing materials

themselves — and they admit to being exacting about every last detail.

"We had a lot of control over every aspect of the build, and we took our time," says Dinah. "It took two and a half years to complete, but in the end it was well worth it because we haven't compromised, and the end result is exactly what we'd both hoped for."

Mini piles were required for the foundations, and the curvaceous new property is based around a skeletal timber structure which is a unique hybrid. It's built using a combination of both green and dry English oak and larch. The complex geometric frame was produced with the aid of a 3D model, and initially resembled the form of an upturned boat when it was pieced together on site. Exposed curved beams emphasise the unusual shapes of the kitchen, study, landing and upper rooms, which are further highlighted with a selection of vibrant paint colours.

"If you're building curves then everything is a problem,

and we have curved oak doors and skirtings absolutely everywhere in the house," says Martin. "Everyone working on the site found it very challenging, and the frame was particularly intricate. We certainly had a few sleepless nights, but at least when it came to the brickwork we felt far more comfortable because we were on familiar territory."

The colouring of the handmade bricks and tiles reflects the tones of the local clay, and Martin's company also provided a huge number of special bricks both inside and out — especially for the magnificent chimney, which is a dominant feature.

"The chimney itself is constructed from 12 types of specially shaped handmade bricks, individually moulded to form a tapering, curved profile," Martin explains. "This passes up 86 courses and cantilevers from the first floor level — reaching a maximum height of nine metres at its apex. We have an open fire in the living/dining room and

"IF YOU'RE BUILDING CURVES THEN EVERYTHING IS A PROBLEM, AND WE HAVE CURVED OAK DOORS AND SKIRTINGS ABSOLUTELY EVERYWHERE IN THE HOUSE"

another, back-to-back with this, in the entrance hallway which shares the same chimney."

In addition to these two woodburning fires, placed at the heart of the ground floor, underfloor heating has been laid throughout the property and is powered by an environmentally friendly ground-source heat-exchange system. Energy efficiency was a prime concern for both

Left: The streamlined shower area enjoys an uncomplicated design, with tiles in earthy tones
Above: Curves make for a complex build
Below: Woodburning fires and exposed brickwork ensure the house remains cosy in the winter months

"WE HAVE SHOWN THAT TRADITIONAL MATERIALS CAN BE USED TO CREATE A CONTEMPORARY, LOW-ENERGY HOME."

Dinah and Martin, and as a result the building is massively insulated, with high-performance glazing fitted in solid timber frames. The majority of glass is located to the rear of the property to maximise passive solar gain, with very few windows to the east — which minimises heat loss and guarantees complete privacy.

In fact, the new house is perfectly designed to fully enjoy the seasons throughout the year. Glazed elements in the kitchen and study create conservatory-style areas which are ideal for enjoying the views across the valley. During the chilly winter months, cosy fires, bright colours and exposed brick walls ensure that the house's interior feels

Above: The chimney passes up 86 courses and cantilevers from the first floor level — reaching a maximum height of nine metres
Left: Intriguing angles and cosy colour schemes make the bedroom very welcoming

pleasant and inviting. Indeed, it's the only time that Dinah and Martin turn their back on the views in order to gather around the central fireplace. "The hearth has always been the heart of a home and it just goes to prove that, despite all the technology at our fingertips, some things will never change," says Martin, who ultimately hopes to furnish the house with Arts & Crafts-style pieces. "During this project, not only have we shown that traditional materials can be used to create a contemporary, low-energy home, but the building will improve with age as these materials will weather beautifully over time. Years from now, the bricks and tiles will have mellowed and the surrounding landscape will have matured. Hopefully, it will prove to be a truly timeless design."

Not all properties make quite as much of a feature of their roof as this, but it's important not to skimp on getting the right tiles. Clay is without doubt preferable to concrete: clay mellows and improves in appearance over time, whereas concrete will appear lifeless within ten years. The type of tile itself is also a big issue. This roof used small format plain tiles, which are perfect for laying over a gently curved surface, without appearing fussy. Large-format tiles are also a great sleek choice, but can only be applied to uncomplicated roofs. Pantiles, which have an S-shaped camber are commonly seen on more traditional proper ties. The tiles' colour is also of paramount importance. Monotones can look good on contemporary roofs, but blends of different shades usually look better on large expanses and period homes. ■

PROJECT NOTES

FACT FILE

Name: Martin and Dinah Warner
Profession: MD of Michelmersh Brick holdings and voluntary worker
House Type: Four-bedroom
House Size: 450m²
Finance: Private
Build route: Self-managed subcontractors
Construction system: Timber frame, brick and tile
Region: East of England
County: Hertfordshire

Build Time: Nov 03 – May 06
Build Cost: £100,0000
Current Value: £200,0000
Cost /m²: £2222

FLOORPLAN

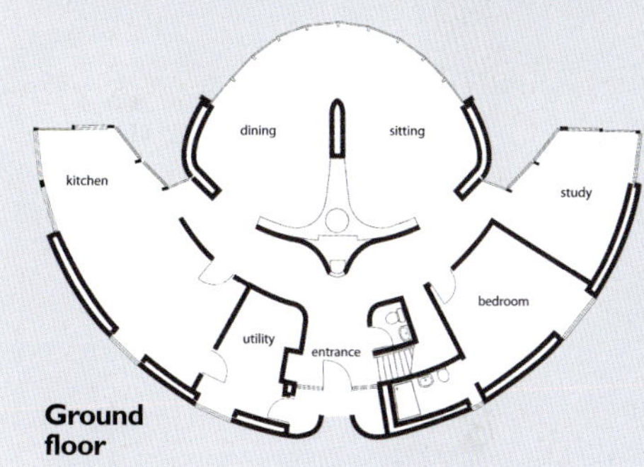

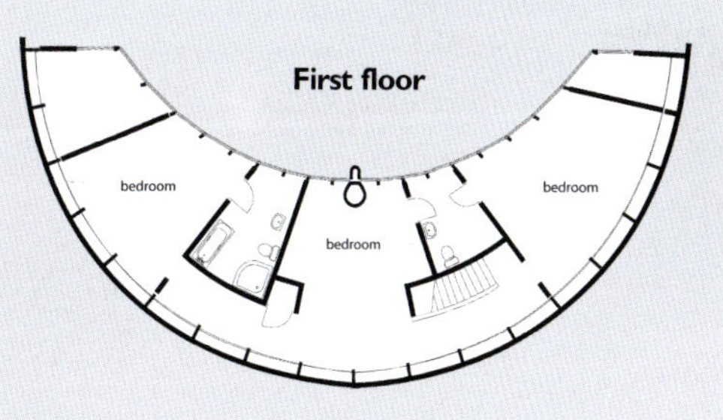

USEFUL CONTACTS

Architect Kirkland Fraser Moor 020 7247 7172 **Structural engineers** David Dexter Associates 020 7247 7172 **Environmental engineers** Arup 020 7636 1531 **Piled foundations** Abbey Pynford 0870 085 8400 **Timber frame** Carpenter Oak & Woodland 01225 743089 **Sanitaryware** Kohler UK 0870 850 5551 **Bricks/ tiles/ paving** Michelmersh Brick & Tile Company 01794 368506 **Windows** Rationel Windows (UK) Ltd 01869 248181 **Ground-source heating** EarthEnergy Limited 01326 310650 **Kitchen/ utility room** Fine Fitted Interiors 01582 794444.

LIGHT
FANTASTIC
Michael Lewis – with more than a little help from architect
Simon Reid – has transformed a modest cottage into an
extraordinary contemporary retreat
WORDS: JASON ORME PHOTOGRAPHY: JEREMY PHILLIPS

What type of home would you create if money were no object and you didn't have to squeeze in as many bedrooms as possible? And what if you didn't have to worry about the property market or re-sale values, or having to accommodate play spaces and sensible storage, or compromising with your partner on the interior fittings?

For Manchester-based property developer Michael Lewis — quite obviously single nor short of a bob or two — the result was Willow House, a remarkable fantasy home set in one of the prime areas of real estate in one of the leafiest upmarket corners of Cheshire.

Rather brilliant, too, that in one of the most cripplingly expensive corners of the UK property market, Willow

Above: The entrance hall uses the same slatted oak cladding as the front elevation. The floor is an elegant grey limestone
Left: Etched glass separates the bathroom from the landing area. Glass balustrades and an oak staircase continue the theme in the entrance hall

House displays a bewitching ignorance of the 'let's get it valued' culture that is a fact of life for 90% of the rest of the UK's self-build population.

"I'm obviously very much involved with the property industry," says owner Michael, "but I took this project on out of a general interest in seeing what we could create

without the usual business concerns. I wanted something that would give me the opportunity to explore my growing interest in innovative and contemporary design without the normal worries of trying to second-guess commercial property market trends."

Despite looking like a brand new home, Willow House

Left: The en suite presents great views, a pop-up flat-screen television at the foot of the bath, and twin shower heads situated in a service bar in the roof structure
Above: The reception area leads through to the dinning hall that features a magnificent glass-topped, gnarled wood table

is actually a rather significant remodelling and extension of a traditional cottage-style house. Yet rather than add bedrooms and bathrooms for all that it's worth, Michael decided that he wanted to create great big spaces instead. Enormous, self-indulgent spaces. For this, he enlisted the help of Manchester-based architect Simon Reid, with whom he had worked on several more commercially orientated projects. "Simon has always shown a high level of creativity and intensive thinking in his designs, regardless of what they were," says Michael.

"We were instructed at the outset to design a modest — in local terms — scheme of alteration and refurbishment," explains Simon. "This was based on the fact that when Michael acquired the property it had only recently been comprehensively refurbished and enlarged. The quantum leap in the brief — the moment it became much more than a simple refurbishment — came with the

discovery that a significant part of the existing house was in such poor structural condition that demolition was the only viable option."

At this stage, Simon explains, Michael began to drive the project and push it forward in ways hitherto unseen. "Michael's view is that some of the best creative thinking comes from the need to address constrained and complex issues," he explains. At this stage, of course, for most ordinary souls, panic would have ensued and financial factors would have either resulted in a consideration to a) knock the whole thing down and start again, at the very least having the consolation of being able to salvage 17.5% VAT; b) scaling down the project to rectify the structural problems and compromising on the amount of work elsewhere; or c) selling up. For Michael, the only option was d) scaling up.

"Getting back the VAT was not really a consideration," he says. The major work was to completely remove the middle section of the building and replace it with a double-height pitched section with glazed gable ends.

So with the work now taking on a whole new scale and impetus, and Michael's own team of contractors busy working away — one of the many added benefits of the

project for Michael was that it helped to build the skills of his company working with contemporary interiors — work progressed rapidly and straightforwardly. The whole project took around 18 months from start to finish, with Michael and Simon spending a considerable amount of time on site, monitoring progress.

This is a house that makes you feel a million dollars. Even the four world-weary, car-tired, shirts-creased-from-too-many-nights-in-a-Travelodge judges of H&R's Best New Homes in Britain competition felt instantly re-cast into a Beverly Hills-type fantasy drama, upon carefully manoeuvring their hire car through the automated gates and up the drive to get the first glimpse of it. It's like something from MTV's Cribs show — right up there with Mariah Carey showing you round her "floor for people who visit occasionally — it's where I keep my hair salon, complete with three permanent stylists. When they don't work on me they just sit around and work on themselves." Willow House is in that fine tradition — it's fun and indulgent but, unlike most of the houses on Cribs, incredibly stylish.

The first thing that hits you is the massive glazed oversized American-influenced elevations. With a lighting

scheme of the highest order — all controlled from a range of wall-mounted keypads throughout the house — the main focus is immediately on an astonishing double-height entrance hall overlooked by a balcony. Oak cladding, cut into minimal slats, creates an unusual but very successful textured feel to the exterior. There's also a remarkably reassuring farmhouse feel to the whole place, thanks to the retention of much of the original cottage structure.

A walk around the gardens confirms the sense that, for all its contemporary stylings, this is a home that doesn't seem out of place in its wooded setting. It enjoys fantastic private views over to the Peak District with 100% privacy and a water-based landscaping scheme that at night reflects the colourful lights shining both inside and out.

The side entrance to the house brings visitors into a large traditional kitchen and TV room that's all very nice but presents a slight surprise for those expecting

"I TOOK THE OPPORTUNITY TO EXPLORE
MY INTEREST IN INNOVATIVE AND
CONTEMPORARY DESIGN WITHOUT THE
NORMAL WORRIES OF TRYING TO SECOND-
GUESS PROPERTY MARKET TRENDS"

a modern kitchen. Simon explains that for his many extravagances, even Michael couldn't contemplate trashing a £40,000 kitchen that was brand new and had been installed just before he bought the property — even though Simon would have preferred to have had it replaced with something more in keeping with the rest of the interior scheme.

Elsewhere the interior spaces are more contemporary, playful and indulgent. There's an envy-inducing snooker room, an informal relaxation area that benefits from an outstanding lighting design, and an entrance hall dominated by a vast wall of frameless glazing on the front gable end.

At the rear of the hall, conventional doors are replaced by seamless sliding panels that are so smooth and precise they hold works of art on each side which disappear into recesses, allowing the flexible space to be opened up or closed down as required.

It's upstairs that the real fun begins, however. A 'family' bathroom is separated from the landing by a green-tinged etched-glass wall, creating a beautiful light effect when illuminated. There's a token spare bedroom or two and a large master bedroom overlooking the garden. So far, so impressive. But it is the en suite that really takes your

breath away. The centrally located infinity bath's spectacular views to the Peak District through huge frameless glass can only be obstructed by the pop-up LCD TV that emerges at the touch of a button at the foot of the bath. The bath itself is filled by a unique overhead service bar that looks like part of the A-frame roof structure but which, in addition, houses two shower heads (one each side of the bath). The mind boggles at what goes on in here, but either way it's an astonishing piece of interior design and a real standard bearer for bathroom luxury.

After that it's all a blur of polished concrete walls, grey limestone floors, climate and lighting controls, seamless design and great attention to detail.

What Simon has created here for a very accommodating client is, without question, remarkable. It's everything that domestic architecture should be in an ideal world: indulgent, fun, stylish and ground-breaking. It's also worth noting that, for all its paeans to satisfying the private rather than the public, Michael, who is hardly naïve when it comes to making money out of property, believes his investment in Willow House will be a highly profitable one. For some people, it seems, it is possible to have your cake and eat it. ■

PROJECT NOTES

FACT FILE

Name: Michael Lewis
Profession: Property developer
Area: Cheshire
house type: Remodelled detached
House size: 355m²

+ 85m² garage
Build route: Architect, self as main contractor
Finance: Private
Build time: Nov '04 – April '06
House cost: £1.25m
Build cost: £1.25m

Total cost: £2.5m
Current value: £3.5m
Cost/m²: £2,840

COST SAVING
28%

FLOORPLAN

The ground floor has a number of living areas, with the main reception walls consisting of sliding doors that can be opened up to make the whole floor open plan. Upstairs, the large master bedroom suite dominates, with just two guest bedrooms.

USEFUL CONTACTS

Architect Simon Reid at Reid Architects: 0161 234 0991 www.reid-architects.com **Timber/joinery/ staircase** Openshaw Joinery: 0161 231 4795 **Zinc roofing/cladding** Longworth Metal Roofing: 0161 973 8398 **Sliding door ironmongery** Centor UK Ltd: 0121 782 5400 **Etched/sculpted glass (bathroom)** Andrew Moor Associates: 020 7586 8181 **Feature fireplace** The Platonic Fireplace Company: 020 8891 5904 **Stone flooring** DAR Marble and Granite: 0161 834 3989 **Oak cladding** Timbmet: 01865 862223 **Home entertainment** Sensory International Ltd: 0870 350 2244 **En suite wall panels** Cast Advanced Concretes Ltd: 0870 241 8171 **Ironmongery** Joseph Giles: 020 8680 2602 **Lighting** Cameron Peters: 01235 835000 **Furniture** Ferrious: 0161 228 6880; Stocktons: 0161 273 5331

ON A ROLL

The rolling green roof of Roger and Linda Brown's unusual self-built eco house is almost as striking as the sheer amount of work that went into getting the whole thing built

WORDS: DEBBIE JEFFERY
PHOTOGRAPHY: NIGEL RIGDEN

Local Yorkshire stone has been used for the main body of the building, with the first floor clad in Canadian red cedar, sourced from sustainable forests. A sedum-covered roof curves to reflect the rolling hills around

O n a hilltop, overlooking the small market town of Penistone in Yorkshire, stands a brand new addition to the landscape which has been causing quite a stir. With very little modern architecture in the area, passers-by often stop to gape at Roger and Linda Brown's newly completed house.

Its walls may be of traditional local stone, but this is the only similarity between 'Highfield' and its more conventional neighbours — for vertical red cedar cladding and grey aluminium-framed windows shelter beneath a distinctive curved roof planted with colourful sedum.

The unusual new building manages to span three generations: self-built by the Browns as a home for their retirement, it was designed by the couple's architect son, Andrew, and built on the one-acre site of a 1940s bungalow which previously belonged to Roger's father, who lived there for 45 years.

"I also lived there myself until I married," explains Roger, now 62, "and when I recently inherited the bungalow we decided to extend and renovate the property for our own retirement."

However, failing foundations meant that demolition was inevitable and the project became a new build instead. The unique form of the replacement house was generated from the footprint of the original bungalow, with the addition of side and first floor extensions which enlarge the overall property and garage to 200m².

A sweeping double-curved roof knits together these various elements, and its form has been continued throughout the building in details such as the curving stainless steel door handles and staircase balustrade.

"We asked Andrew to come up with a design and, other than listing the rooms we wanted, gave him a free hand," says Linda. "The site is on the edge of a Conservation Area, and we were concerned that the planners might not approve a modern house, but they were very open to the idea."

One of the only changes made to Andrew's original design involved using locally quarried Yorkshire stone instead of the proposed white-rendered blockwork. This inevitably impacted on the final budget, particularly as the stone slabs, which form the outer leaf of the house, are of finely polished ashlar.

A generous insulated cavity and an inner skin of dense concrete blockwork complete the extremely thick external walls, and their high thermal mass helps to regulate the temperature of the rooms.

Internally, the layout has been inverted so that the three bedrooms are positioned on the ground floor with the main living space upstairs — taking full advantage of wonderful views over the town through a large picture window. This living space also gives access to a decked south-facing terrace above the garage, opening the entire first floor to the outside when the folding sliding doors are open.

The open plan layout fully expresses the sweep of the roof, with its exposed glulam beams, and permits

views down into the double-height kitchen/diner from the first floor study space, behind which a delicately suspended oak and sycamore staircase rises up to form the centrepiece of the house.

"I knew from the start that this would be a hands-on project," says Roger, an engineer by trade who had never previously undertaken a new build. Helped by Linda and several good friends, he was responsible for virtually every aspect of the build — from pouring the foundations to laying the sedum on the roof.

"We sold our old farmhouse on the other side of town and moved into a caravan on site," Linda recalls. "It was difficult to keep warm in winter, and cost a fortune in gas and electricity, but we managed there for two years during the build."

"ONE OF THE MOST DIFFICULT JOBS WAS LAYING THE SEDUM BUT THE COLOURS ARE INCREDIBLE — A MIXTURE OFGREEN, YELLOW AND PINK"

Demolishing his father's old bungalow proved a tough call for Roger, but with the rubble carted away and new standard strip foundations in place, building work began in earnest. Once the substantial blockwork and stone walls had been constructed, the 9.5-metre-long glulam beams for the roof structure were craned into position — which caused passing traffic to slow to a virtual standstill.

"One of the most difficult jobs was laying the sedum, because the roof is such an unusual angle and it was extremely windy in February," recalls Roger, "but the colours are incredible — a mixture of green, yellow and pink hues which tie the house into the landscape."

The house also boasts a rainwater recycling system which stores water from hard standing, the roof and terrace, to be used in the garden.

"WE RESEARCHED ECO-FRIENDLY PRODUCTS AND PRICES ONLINE AND BOUGHT EVERYTHING AS LOCALLY AS POSSIBLE"

The double curve of the super-insulated roof falls away to the north elevation – reducing heat loss to the cold face and opening out the southern elevation to make the most of solar gain. The south-facing glazing is shaded from high-summer sun by a large overhang of translucent sheet, which also creates an all-weather outside area on the upper terrace (above).

High levels of insulation and thermal mass, combined with a heat recovery ventilation system and an airtight fabric, help to combat rising fuel bills and dwindling fossil fuel supplies. In fact, the house has proved so easy to keep warm that the couple have only needed to turn on their underfloor heating once since moving in, and also have a pre-heat hot-water system designed to minimise water wastage.

The couple chose locally sourced oak floors, doors and mouldings with European whitewood roof beams and red cedar external cladding from sustainable forests. "We researched eco-friendly products and prices online and bought everything as locally as possible," says Roger.

Linda and Roger's new home was designed with the future in mind, keeping its carbon footprint as low as possible throughout the build and reducing their reliance on traditional energy sources. The house has even begun to change the way people think about the sustainability of homes in the area — becoming a talking point and grabbing the attention of the local press.

Building an eco-friendly house hasn't prevented the couple from adding some fun and frivolous touches, however. For 20 years they ran their own business making copper lights for gardens, so lighting inevitably plays an important role in the overall design of their new home. Strips of blue LEDs illuminate the oak and sycamore treads of the feature staircase, with red LED lights positioned behind an opaque acrylic sheet beneath the oak breakfast bar in the kitchen.

"Building this house has been a once-in-a-lifetime adventure," says Linda, "and a self-build project was the perfect way to ease us into retirement. We've both developed muscles from so much hard physical labour, but now that the house is finished we're definitely planning to have a much more relaxed pace of life." ∎

PROJECT NOTES

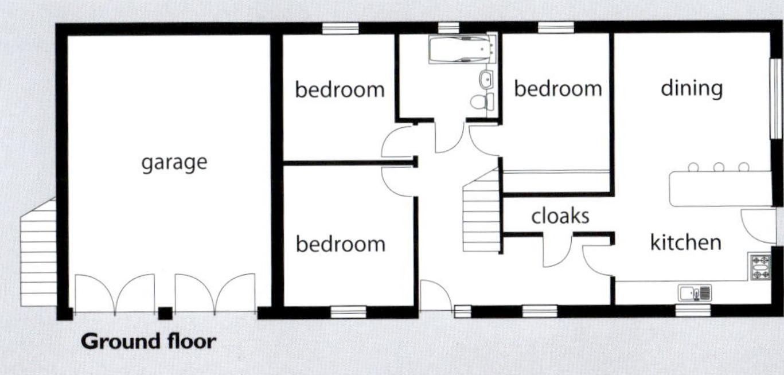

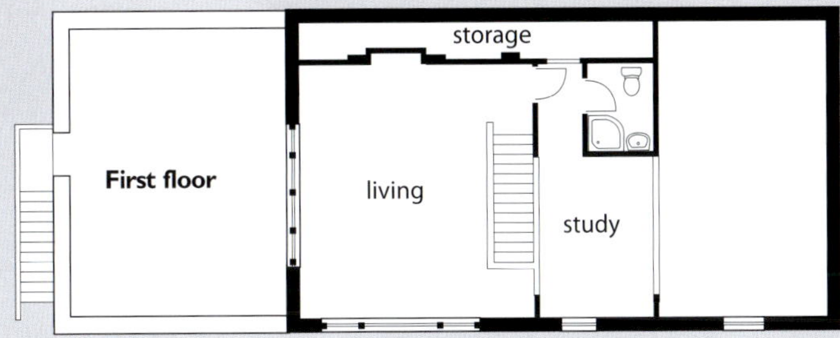

AN UPSIDE-DOWN LAYOUT

A double-height kitchen/dining room, three bedrooms and bathroom are positioned on the ground floor. The majority of the first floor is used as a living room, with open plan study positioned to overlook the kitchen/dining room below. A narrow storage room runs behind the fireplace and bathroom to compensate for lack of loft space

FACT FILE

Names: Roger and Linda Brown
Professions: Retired
Area: Yorkshire
House type: Three bedroom contemporary eco house
House size: 200m²
Build route: DIY and subcontractors
Finance: Private
Construction: Blockwork, stone, cedar cladding, sedum roof
Build time: Feb '06 – Jan '08
Land value: £150,000
Build cost: £175,000
Total cost: £325,000
Value on completion: £500,000
Cost/m²: £875

COST SAVING
35%

THE MECHANICS OF MODERN STAIRS

Roger and Linda's staircase appears to be held up by fine steel wires, practically floating in the air. However, this is just an illusion, as the treads are actually completely supported at the other end by the wall. This is known as cantilevering. In order for the wall to be able to safely hold the weight of the treads, supporting steelwork is built into the wall. The treads span several inches in depth internally. Roger constructed the staircase using sycamore sandwiched between oak for the treads, with stainless steel handrails. Due to Building Regulations, staircases cannot be open-sided, although the issue of disrupted vision is dealt with here by using fine wires which do not impact on the view of the stairs.

USEFUL CONTACTS

Architect Andrew Brown, Design Space Architects: 01937 558213 **Underfloor heating** Nu-Heat: 0800 731 1976 **Insulation** Kingspan Insulation: 0870 850 8555 **Aluminium windows** AM Profiles: 01246 856000 **Glulam roof beams** Lamisell: 01409 220333 **Sedum roof** Evergreen Roof Gardens: 01903 600122 **Ashlar stone** Johnsons Wellfield Quarries: 01484 652311 **Folding sliding doors** Folding Sliding Door Co: 0845 644 6630 **Ventilation** Rega Ventilation: 01767 600499 **Bathrooms, wall and floor tiles** Crown Tiles & Bathrooms: 01226 380116 **Internal doors** Howdens Joinery: 01226 321514 **Electrics** JMS Electrical: 01226 763628 **Cedar cladding** Palmer Timber: 0121 559 5511 **Structural engineers** Richard Rhodes & Partners: 0161 427 8388

A DREAM COME TRUE

Teresa and Garry Elcock endured 13 years in an asbestos shack and a battle with the planners to fulfil their long-term ambition to build a new home in the New Forest

WORDS: DEBBIE JEFFERY   PHOTOGRAPHY: NIGEL RIGDEN

t was a relief when we were eventually able to demolish our home of 13 years," says Garry Elcock. "We had planned to replace it with a new house for so long and finally it was happening. Neither of us had any building experience, but we were both fully involved with every area of the project. Building our own home had been a lifelong dream, and we overcame all the pressures and difficulties to fulfil our ambition."

Garry and his wife, Teresa – known as Terry – are both police officers who purchased a run-down asbestos bungalow on a prime Dorset site with the sole intention of knocking it down. In 1990 the couple paid £140,000 for the property, where they lived for a number of years with their children — during which time they planned and saved for their first and only self-build project.

"Everyone referred to our bungalow as 'the shack', but we always knew one day we'd replace it with something far better," Terry explains. "Our one-and-a-half-acre site is elevated and the views are so spectacular we were prepared to wait for as long as it took. Eventually, once our children had grown up, we were financially ready to begin. By then the shack was literally falling down and water was dripping through the kitchen ceiling."

The Elcocks were determined that their new house would be worthy of its spectacular location on the edge of a small village in the New Forest. They wanted a low-maintenance, energy-efficient property which would complement the site and take full advantage of the sunlight and far-reaching views across surrounding farmland towards Bournemouth.

They approached Dorset architect, David Underhill, at an exhibition and asked him to visit their site, finding him approachable and interested. "We found we'd only be allowed to enlarge the footprint of the existing bungalow by 30%, but we were keen to build a two storey house for maximum space," Garry explains. "The planning authority insisted on a single-storey property, so we had to go to appeal which we eventually won — allowing us to build rooms in the roof space. Compromises had to be made though. We'd have liked a fourth bedroom and a basement, for example, and we wasted the opportunity to gain a better view from the master bedroom, but overall we're happy with the layout."

The rooms in the roof have intimate sloping ceilings and skylight windows, with triangular sections of glazing in the gable ends

Terry and Garry both love to cook, so a large kitchen with an informal dining area was high on their list of priorities. They also wanted a formal dining room on the ground floor, and this has been achieved by creating a spacious dining hall which leads down two steps into the separate sitting room. A study is located to the other end of the house, with three additional bedrooms and two bathrooms tucked into the roof space.

With the nearest property more than one mile away privacy was not an issue, and the couple wanted to introduce as much glass into the design as possible, with panels of floor-to-ceiling glazing leading out onto a large paved patio. Upstairs, roof lights and triangular dormer windows combine with glazed gable ends to create bright, airy interiors.

The Elcocks remained living in their old bungalow throughout the build, with the new house literally abutting the existing property. "We realised early on that building the house was not going to be as straightforward as

we'd imagined," admits Garry. "Most suppliers didn't even respond to our letters and calls, and we had real problems finding suitable materials in this country. We found it was actually cheaper to import items from abroad."

The Elcocks wanted to project manage individual subcontractors rather than employ a single contractor, and believed that paying their tradesmen a day rate would offer them the best value for money. Apart from the bricklayer and landscape gardener, however, every one of the tradesmen let the couple down.

The design would have been complex and ambitious for an experienced builder, but for self-builders with no previous knowledge, it was a minefield of problems. Undeterred, Garry and Terry spent every spare moment on site and – apart from the facing brickwork – were physically involved in all parts of the build, from digging the foundations to laying the underfloor heating and fitting the kitchen.

Substantial oak trees border the site and necessitated sinking the sitting room down into the ground — enabling views out beneath the canopy of branches which would otherwise have blocked out the light. This involved tanking much of the ground floor to prevent the ingress of water. Brick and block external walls have a 100mm cavity, and the entire structure has been highly insulated to compensate for heat losses through the numerous steel-framed windows, which were installed by the Elcocks with the help of friends.

"We engaged carpenters who came with excellent references, but were still unable to construct the

"WE ENGAGED CARPENTERS WHO CAME WITH EXCELLENT REFERENCES, BUT WERE STILL UNABLE TO CONSTRUCT THE COMPLEX, OVERHANGING ROOF STRUCTURE ACCORDING TO OUR PLANS"

complex, overhanging roof structure according to our plans," says Terry. "In the end we dismissed them, took down their work and started from scratch.

"Garry and I had no experience, and it was definitely the most challenging part of the entire build but we did it ourselves while still working full time. It was the one thing that really got us down and took months to complete, but financially we had no other choice."

Once the new house was finished, Terry and Garry decided to undertake the demolition of the old bungalow themselves, taking great care when dealing with the asbestos. They took out licenses with the local authority, which was involved in removing the asbestos from site, and found this final stage of the project a huge relief.

When the bungalow had been removed, the new house could finally open up to the full vista of light and views which had previously been blocked by the neighbouring building.

"We do have one or two regrets about the finished house," says Garry. "The taps were chosen because of their attractive smooth design, but we soon realised that they could not be fully turned off with wet hands. It was also unnecessary to install underfloor heating upstairs, because the overall energy efficiency of the house means that we only ever use the bathroom towel rails."

"People frequently ask us whether we will build again, but why should we when we have such an idyllic site right here?" says Terry.

"It was Garry's lifelong ambition to build his own home, and we thoroughly enjoyed the process. We're also much fitter after all our building work. In September 2006 we'll both retire from the police service, and hope to fulfil another dream by running our own ski chalet in France or Austria, which would involve renting the house out for six months each winter. But we will certainly look forward to returning every summer to relax and enjoy the fruits of our labour."

PROJECT NOTES

FACT FILE

Name: Teresa and Garry Elcock
Profession: Police officers
Area: Dorset
House type: Three bedroom house
House size: 170m²
Build route: Selves and subcontractors
Warranty: NHBC Solo for Self Build
Finance: Private
Construction: Brick and block, clay roof tiles
Build time: Jan '00 – Dec '02

Land cost: £140,000
Build cost: £173,000
Total cost: £313,000
Current value: £800,000
Cost/m²: £1,018

COST SAVING
61%

COST BREAKDOWN

Demolition and landscaping	£32,000
Materials, & VAT	£123,661
Labour	£17,800
TOTAL	**£173,461**

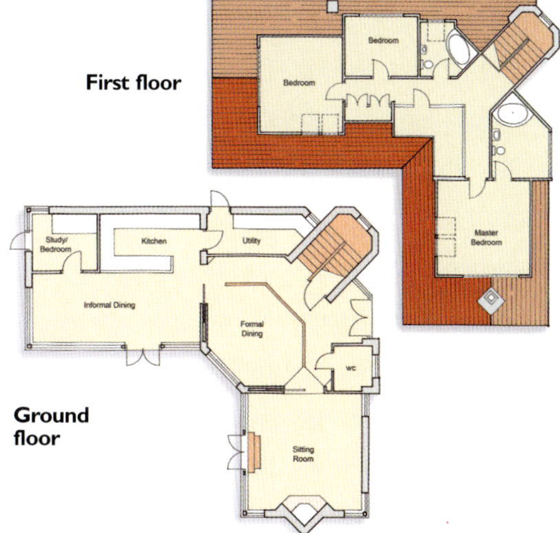

USEFUL CONTACTS

Architect David Underhill, DUA Architecture LLP: 01425 278252 **Bricks and roof tiles** Michelmersh Brick & Tile Co. Ltd: 01794 368506 **Andersen Windows** Meon Developments: 01730 825032 **Worktops** Cobb Bros Ltd: 01202 631007 **Staircase** Dibben Joinery: 01425 652807 **Plumbing and heating supplies** Plumb Center: 01202 499344; **Timber** Sydenhams Timber Merchants: 01202 674461 **Wall, floor and roof insulation** Sheffield Insulation: 02380 740074 **Plumbing and heating** Paul Yeatman: 01258 857834 **Landscaping and driveway** Steve Blake, Landscaping & Building Contractor: 01202 822845 **Electrics and lighting** Screwfix Direct: 0500 414141

SHAPE SHIFTERS

Claire and Paul Hearson have combined contemporary and traditional style by reusing and extending a dilapidated farm steading, transforming it into a striking family home

WORDS: CAROLINE EDNIE
PHOTOGRAPHY: ANDREW LEE

After almost 30 years of spending summers holidaying in Morayshire, Claire Hearson decided that it was high time the family owned a home there. Two years after coming to that decision, the Hearson family had not only managed to find a prime site within what's now the Cairngorms National Park, but had also completed a hugely ambitious and highly successful conversion and extension project, transforming a series of unpromising run-down farm buildings into Midport Steading, a clever mix of traditional single-storey living spaces and contemporary two-storey accommodation.

Paul Hearson readily admits that the project was largely driven by his wife, Claire: "To begin with I was dead against it, but now I think it was absolutely the right thing to do. The lovely thing is that the location is remote in many respects, yet is only a couple of miles from the main town, with its supermarket and amenities. It's also convenient for the airport at Inverness. We live a pretty hectic life, so the seclusion has a huge appeal."

Once the couple decided to go ahead with plans for a Highland home, Claire approached an Edinburgh-based home search company and within months they had found a run-down cottage and farmstead building in Morayshire. Having bought the site and an accompanying acre of land, the original thought was to convert the cottage building; however, following discussions with Inverness-based HRI Architects, Claire decided that the dilapidated L-shaped steading, which occupied an elevated position on the site, would be the best option for re-development.

The architects prepared a number of options and after some consideration, Paul admits that "we decided that we'd go for probably the most ambitious plans. It suddenly seemed stupid not to be ambitious given what we had." The final plan involved re-using the existing single-storey steading building and augmenting this with an additional two-storey accommodation wing to the south-east of the site. The architects wanted the old building to follow the traditional style, with the new building having a contemporary slant to it. "We didn't believe that there was any point in trying to make something new

look like something old, so we made the extension look like a modern piece of architecture," explains project co-ordinator Mark Williams.

Following a relatively painless planning application, construction began in the summer of 2004. "The steading building was completely rotten. The only thing that stayed up were the stone walls," explains Paul. The roof was removed by specialists as it partly contained asbestos. The design of the new traditional roof structure refers very strongly to the original roof, using its pattern to dramatic effect in the interiors.

"The old roof had stood there for well over 100 years, yet when it came to re-building it, the engineers maintained that it could never stand up if it were based on the original construction," explains Mark. "Our argument was that the roof had already stood in its original form, come hell or high water; however, modern structural standards are very different, so we put in tie bracings in the form of stainless steel rods."

Only one small section of the steading had to be rebuilt, the rest of the fabric of the old part of the building is original. All of the original openings have been retained and only one additional window has been inserted. In terms of living space, the converted steading comprises a garage situated in the rough-sawn larch-clad south gable and a utility area, with a shower room and boiler room. This leads to an open-plan kitchen, dining and living area; the lounge then in turn leads to the entrance lobby, where the end of the old steading building cleverly dovetails via a glazed insertion into the new modern extension.

The two-storey extension is essentially a bespoke timber-frame kit with polyurethane CFC-free insulation to the pitched roof, followed by sheathing ply; a breather paper (to avoid the problem of condensation); rockwool ventilated cavity batts to the wall; and 100mm of blockwork with STO render and horizontal dressed larch cladding elements. The roof is finished with slate

"WE DECIDED WE'D GO FOR PROBABLY THE MOST AMBITIOUS PLANS. IT SEEMED STUPID NOT TO BE AMBITIOUS GIVEN WHAT WE HAD"

"THE IDEA OF THE EXTENSION WAS TO TWIST THE BUILDING TOWARDS THE VIEWS OF THE CAIRNGORMS"

from the Alfred McAlpine quarry in Wales.

In order to give the new build a bit of a twist, a strong diagonal wall has been inserted. This follows the line directly from the main hall staircase and punctures through the outer fabric of the building (next to the hot tub). The four en suite bedrooms on the ground floor and the upper-level living area follow the line of this wall, which continues into the external works and forms the basis for the angle of the lower-level larch decking and upper-level galvanised steel balcony. "The idea of the extension was to twist the building towards the views of the Cairngorms," explains Mark.

The Hearsons' main concern was to bring as much light into the building as possible and this has been achieved using NorDan windows on the old part of the building and aluminium framed windows and doors in the extensively glazed south-facing extension. In addition to solar gain, underfloor oil-fired heating from Invisible Heating Systems and a woodburning stove situated on the upper-level living area provide heat in the Highland winters. The stove is recessed into a blockwork wall — a device designed purely to take the weight of the chimney. Other features in the extension include the bespoke central staircase, made by McGarry & Sons of Perth.

Taking the spirit of innovation even further, the master en suite bathroom also boasts heated panels set into the recessed wall that function as a heated towel rail. But, undoubtedly, the pièce de résistance is a bespoke concrete bath. The one-and-a-half-ton bath, which was manufactured by Concreations of London, was installed by a forklift truck.

Midport Steading manages to achieve a canny balance of cool contemporary and cosy traditional luxury, seamlessly under two roofs. Paul admits that despite his initial reservations he is now hugely enamoured with the house. "I can't believe the transformation. I had zero imagination but Claire has always had great creativity and, together with the architects, she has put together a wonderful combination of old and new, which I love." ■

PROJECT NOTES

FACT FILE

Names: Paul and Claire Hearson
Professions: Chairman of engineering firm and homemaker
Area: Strathspey, Morayshire
House type: Converted and extended farm steading
House size: 220m²
Build route: Main contractor
Finance: Private
Construction: Stone with timber frame extension
Build time: 10 months
Land cost: Undisclosed
Build cost: £550,000
Total cost: N/A
Current value: Unknown
Cost/m²: £2,500

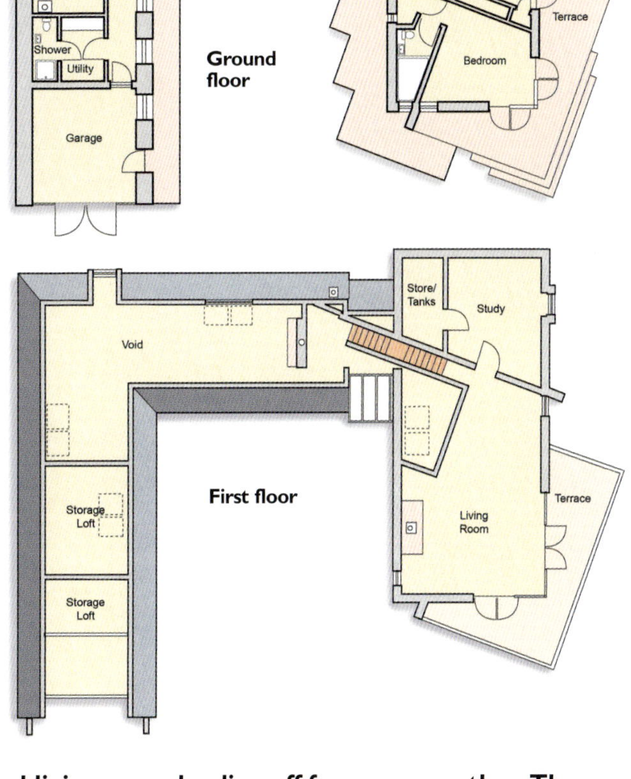

The single storey steading conversion is largely open plan, with the kitchen, dining and living areas leading off from one another. The new section is set at an angle, with the two ground floor bedrooms and entrance hall following the line of a diagonal wall, leading out to a terrace. The new living room is on the first floor to make the most of the stunning views.

USEFUL CONTACTS

Architect HRI Architects: 01463 240066 www.hri-architects.com **Main building contractor** Robertson Construction: 01343 548621 **Larch joinery and oak flooring** Russwood Ltd: 01540 673648 **NorDan windows** Aberdeen Window & Door Systems: 01224 633174 **Aluminium framed windows** AC Yule: 01224 230000 **Underfloor oil-fired heating** Invisible Heating Systems: 01854 613161 **Kitchen manufacturer** Alaris, Inverness: 01463 663340 **Lava stone worktops, woodburning stove, bathroom tiles, Caithness flagstones and slate, and shower trays** Marble Granite & Fire, Inverness: 01463 234844 **Bath** Concreations: 020 8408 3000 **Internal doors** Vicaima: 01793 532333 **Hot tub** Terete Hot Tubs: 01609 883103 **Stair and balustrades** McGarrie & Son of Perth: 01738 624158

The kitchen features red lacquered units, a Corian worktop and a lino floor over underfloor heating

IT'S HIP TO BE SQUARE

WORDS: ANGELA PERTUSINI PHOTOGRAPHY: TIMOTHY SOAR

Above: Despite the unashamedly contemporary appearance of the house, located in a street of 19th century terraces, planning permission wasn't a problem for the house, which was built on a site previously used for industrial storage

My wife wanted a Victorian place," sighs architect Richard Dudzicki, looking around his bright and spacious modern home. Being a loyal husband, his face remains deadpan as he explains: "She'd grown up with Victorian houses. It was what she was comfortable with. But, after a little gentle persuasion, she agreed to this instead."

The house that Richard eventually built for himself and his lawyer wife, Eva has about as much in common with Victoriana as an iPod. An appealing slab of modernity in an otherwise unremarkable street of plain 19th century terraces, the house makes no attempt to ally itself to its neighbours — Richard thoughtfully provided the door number but there's little doubt which house is his. "As it's the first house in the road, it's OK to do something different," he says. "It's a punctuation mark."

Quite how the house came into being is a slightly meandering tale which combines the two great driving forces in London property ownership: spiralling rents and a growing family. Richard would have us believe the house is almost accidental but this seems a little disingenuous. Nonetheless, the opportunity that he grabbed in 1999 was to buy a former light industrial, two- storey building on a Dulwich side-street. He applied for, and received, consent to convert it into a residential unit, only to decide, almost immediately, to move his architectural practice there from Clerkenwell, then the capital of the UK's dot.com boom and subsequently an area of increasingly greedy landlords.

Almost inevitably the unit became too cramped as both the Dudzicki practice and the Dudzicki family expanded. In 2003, with the arrival of his daughter, Richard began to cast around for a solution and, more in the spirit of hope than expectation, applied for permission to demolish a pair of garages in front of the unit and build a home.

The land had a planning history of stock car racing and, Richard claims, was such a scrappy and unattractive piece of fly-tipped suburban decay, that building on it hadn't occurred to him before. The council was supportive as were most of the local residents — as a new house, even

"IT WAS A SENSATIONALLY CHEAP BUILD — THE LAND WAS MORE OR LESS FREE AND THE HOUSE COST £148,570"

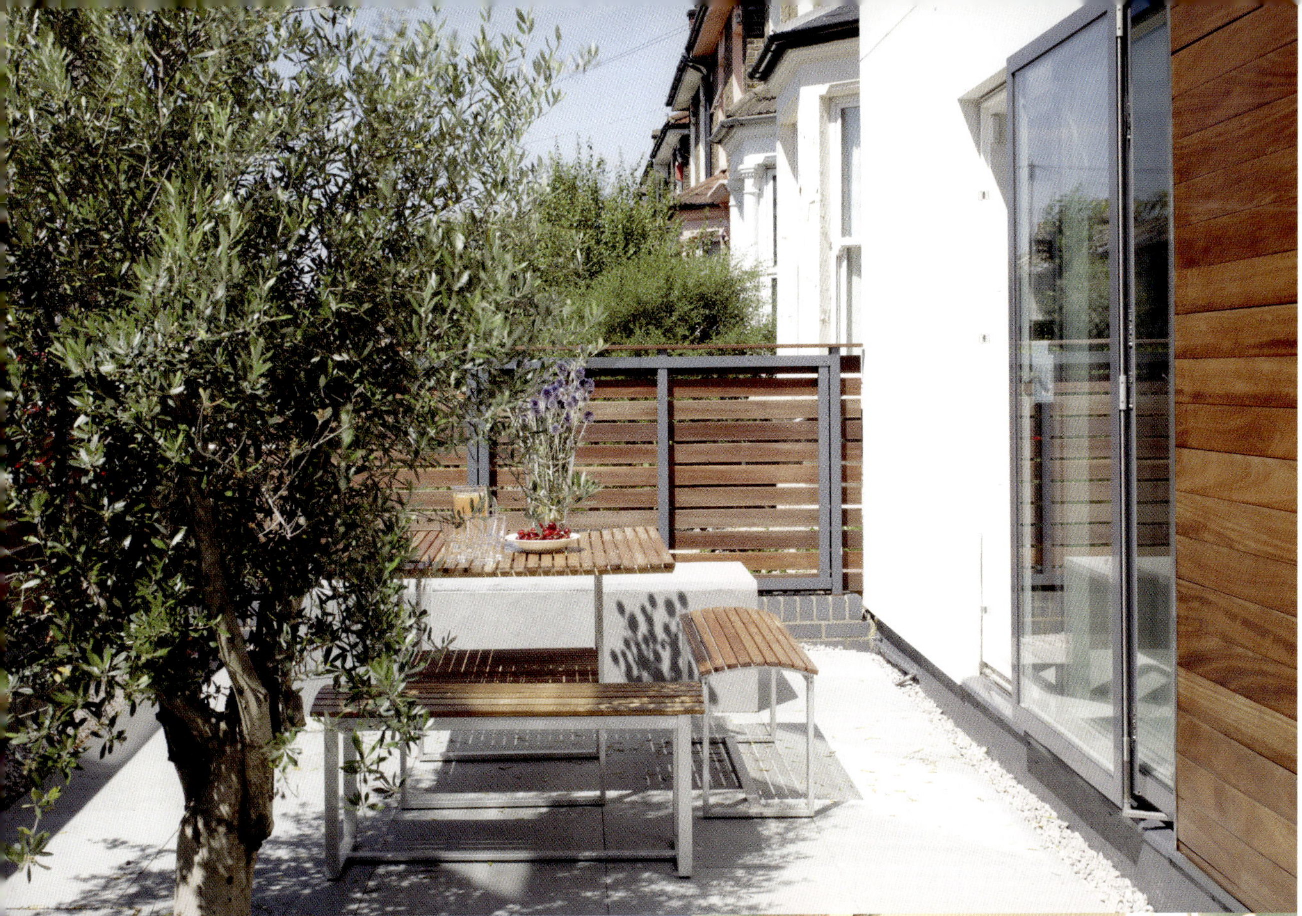

Above: Sliding doors lead to a private courtyard area, complete with a mature olive tree
Right: The clutter-free wet room not only makes the most of available space, but also increases the feeling of it too, through clever the use of glass, mirrors and built-in sanitaryware

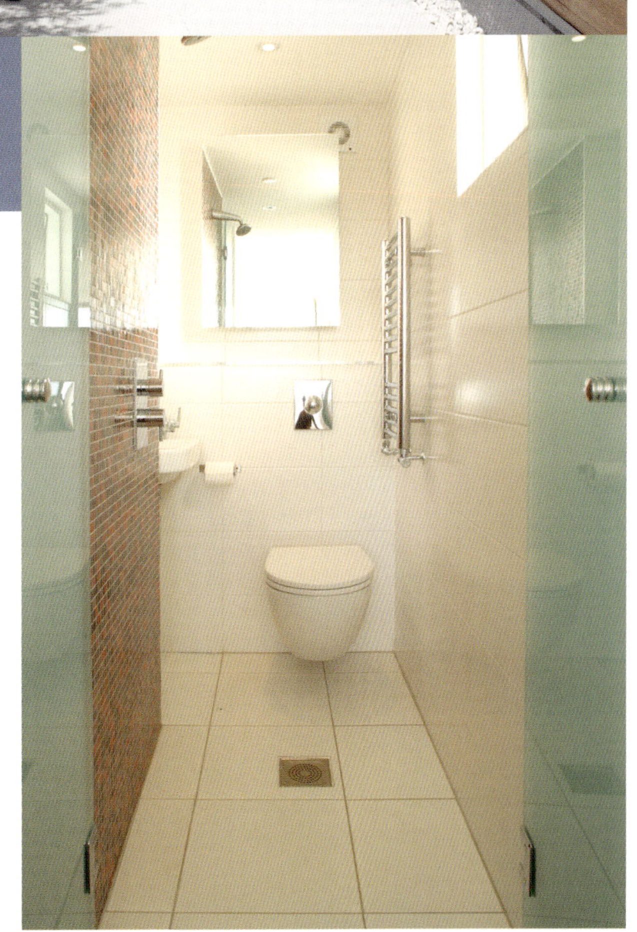

a scary, contemporary one, has to be a lot more desirable than the ramshackle garages and festering mattresses that were already there. In property value terms, the perennial refuge of the nimby, it could only improve matters.

"One neighbour was very difficult about party wall consents," says Richard, "but he doesn't even live here — he rents out the property. I think everyone else was just relieved that something was going to be done with this horrible eyesore."

And so, in terms of appearance, once he had dismissed his wife's wishlist of sash windows and London stock bricks, Richard had a pretty free hand and took advantage of that to create a sleek, three storey box which soars out of an unpromisingly small footprint.

Ah yes, the footprint. Hemmed in by an electrical sub-station at the rear and the street's building line to the fore, the house isn't as generously proportioned as most self-builders would hope for. Richard's open plan designs usually rely on a bit more space to be open in. Once Building

Control got on board and demanded the necessary but irksome ground floor WC, a wall separating the entrance from the living area and a door on the kitchen, the available space had dwindled even more. But, by using an extremely simple palette of glass, bold red kitchen units and white everything else, together with a crafty layout, the feeling of space is generous.

Upstairs there are two bedrooms and bathrooms and, on the top floor, a wonderful eyrie of a chill-out zone (ready to be dragooned, together with the adjacent utility room, into service as the master bedroom and en suite when the couple's second baby arrives shortly). Huge, full-length windows dominate one wall and a large balcony wraps around two sides of the room, giving superb rooftop views.

"AS IT'S THE FIRST HOUSE IN THE ROAD, IT'S OK TO DO SOMETHING DIFFERENT, IT'S A PUNCTUATION MARK"

Having spent almost two years planning the build, the actual construction in 2005 went remarkably smoothly, taking less than nine months from breaking ground to moving in. Environmental concerns led Richard to opt for SIPs (Structural Insulated Panels) which create walls from super-efficient insulation sandwiched between sheets of ply. Although his contractor had never built using SIPs before, he had worked with Richard in the past, who was impressed enough to pay for him and his team to attend a two-day course to learn more about the method. A few weeks later, the walls of the house arrived on two pallets and were up in less than a fortnight.

As well as being relatively problem-free, it was also a sensationally cheap build — the land came more or less free with the old factory unit he bought for £40,000, and the house cost only £148,570 to build. On such a tight budget, Richard has done a fabulous job of sourcing cheap but chic finishes for the home and the only thing that makes him really groan is the £8,000 he had to pay a utility company with a local monopoly to connect the house to the water mains a couple of metres away.

Anyone would struggle to make a loss with those numbers but Richard also hit pay dirt by buying into East Dulwich in the first place, a suburb of increasingly high falutin' prices and aspirations.

By anyone's standards this house is a success. The fact that it fits so much into so little is extremely impressive and it does so while maintaining an admirable appearance of calm and simplicity. But it may not remain a small house for too much longer. Despite a serendipitous beginning, Richard is beginning to display imperialist tendencies towards his immediate neighbourhood: having converted the light industrial unit and built over the garages, he has now bought up the plot next door, a former single-storey gallery building.

Plans are still hazy at this stage but another residential project is in the offing, possibly a similar house but faced in brick rather than cool white render and iroko cladding. He could just sell it on of course but the Dudzickis are toying with the idea of linking the two properties via a bridge in order to grab a little more living space.

It's a thrillingly daring idea and it would be wonderful if it happened. But Richard Dudzicki's neighbours might begin to feel a bit nervous about where he will cast his net next... ■

The sun-drenched 'chill out' room leads on to a large balcony – the perfect place to unwind

PROJECT NOTES

FLOORPLAN

The three-storey home features an open-plan kitchen/ dining area at ground level with the main living accommodation making the most of the balcony space.

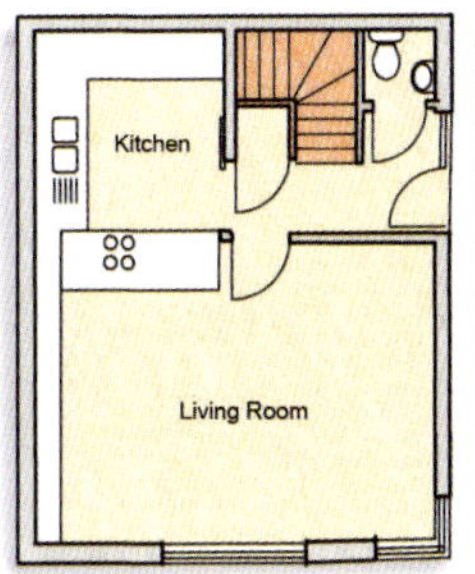

Ground floor

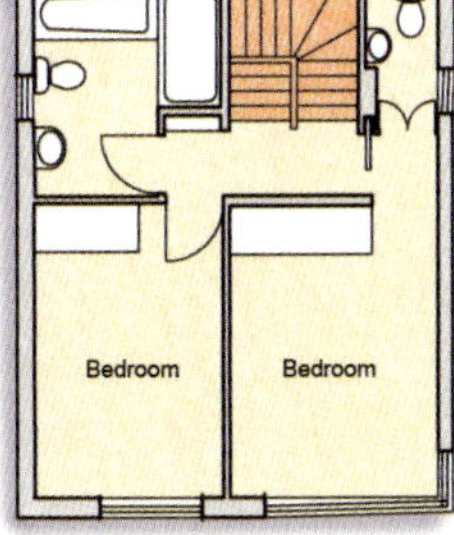

First floor

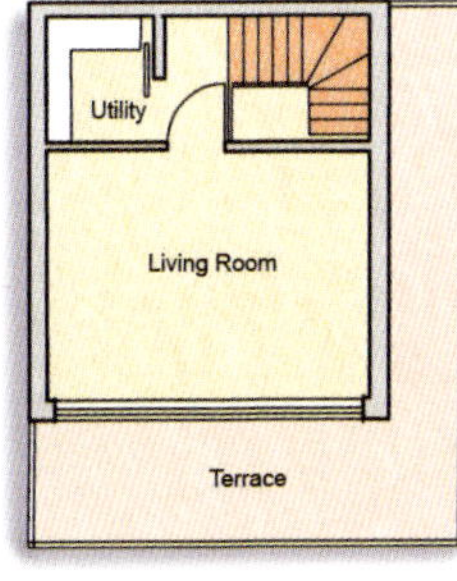

Second floor

URBAN IDEAL

Richard and Eva's new home would be a remarkable achievement on its merits – brave, radical architecture that perfectly adds to the street scene; use of eco-friendly Structural Insulated Panels that mean super-fast build times and lower energy bills to boot; re-use of a grotty urban site; a build budget to make any self-builder in the UK jealous – but when combined with the clever use of the most modest of footprints to create a home that not only comfortably meets their family's needs but also provides bags of open, light, indulgent living spaces, it's a clear blueprint for how best to build affordable, clever, small homes that feel anything but pinched.

FACT FILE

Names: Richard Dudzicki and Eva Edohen
Professions: Architect and lawyer
Area: Dulwich
House type: Two bed, three-storey contemporary home
House size: 98m²
Build route: Main contractor
Finance: Private
Construction: SIPs, with STO render
Build time: Feb '05 – Oct '05
Land cost: £40,000
Build cost: £148,570
Total cost: £188,570
Current value: £400,000
Cost/m²: £1,516

COST SAVING
53%

COST BREAKDOWN

Demolition and site clearance:	£3,600
Substructure:	£12,800
Superstructure:	£74,000
Finishes:	£15,400
Fittings and furnishings:	£18,200
Services:	£8,470
External works:	£15,300
TOTAL	**£148,570**

USEFUL CONTACTS

Architect RDA UK: 020 8299 2222 **Main Contractor** DKBS Ltd: 0207 267 7567 **Builders** JCP Builders: 07957 296928 **Structural Engineer** CEC Engineers: 0208 679 5621 **Building Control** MLM Building Control: 0207 613 7500 **Roofing** CU.TECH: 01732 822064 **Windows and doors** Velfac: 01223 897100 **SIPs** Kingspan TEK: 01544 387361 **Render** STO-Render: 0208 554 7937 **Landscape Designer** James Lee Landscape & Garden Design: 0208 693 9391

Built within the walls of
an old herb garden, the
house is reminiscent
of an elegant lean-to
greenhouse

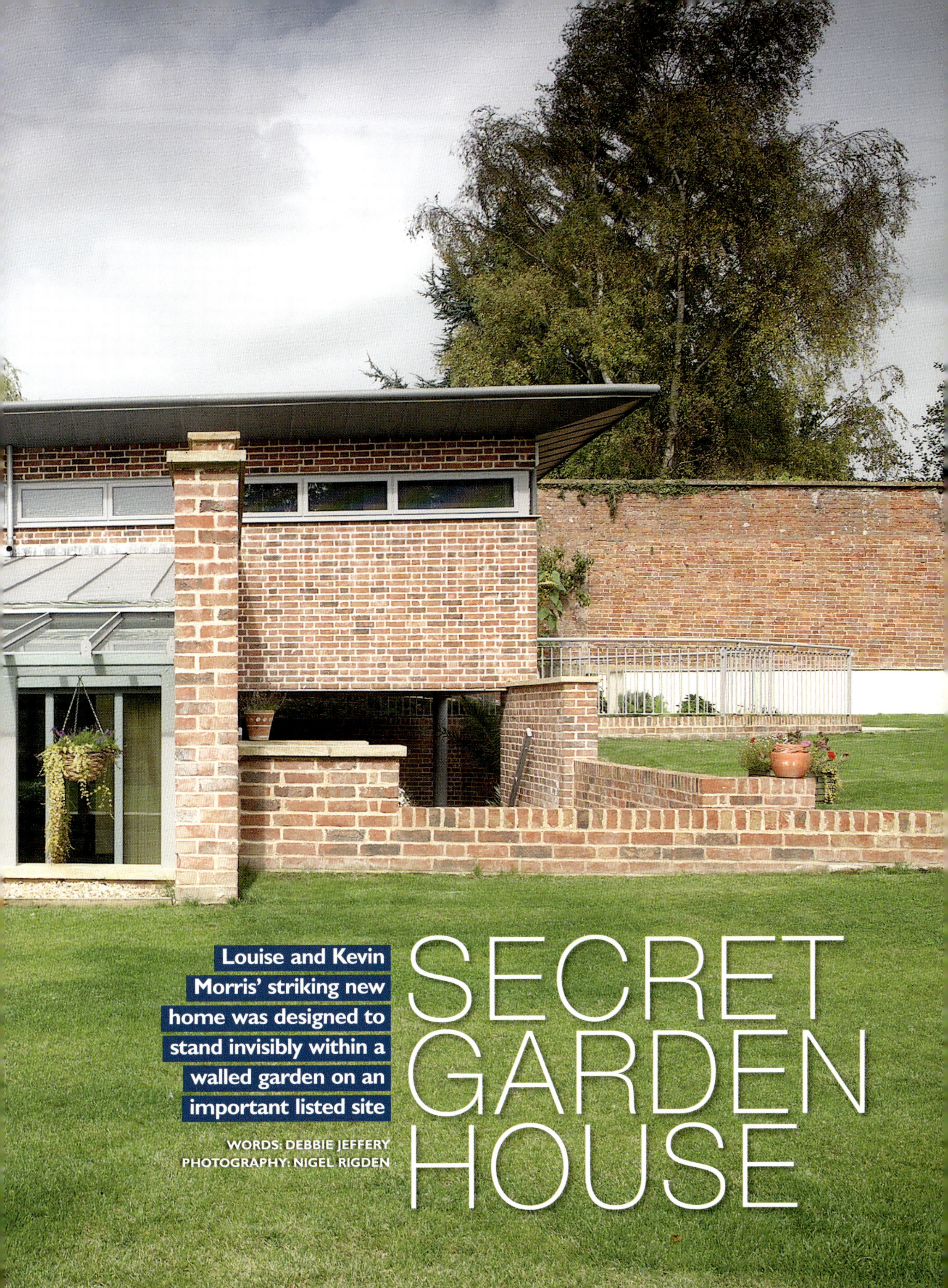

Louise and Kevin
Morris' striking new
home was designed to
stand invisibly within a
walled garden on an
important listed site

WORDS: DEBBIE JEFFERY
PHOTOGRAPHY: NIGEL RIGDEN

SECRET
GARDEN
HOUSE

The planners told us that we would need to design 'an invisible building' for our site within a listed walled garden," says Kevin Morris of his new home. "They would not allow our house to rise above the height of the old garden wall, which meant that we had to sink the structure into the ground. There was to be no compromise, and the result is that passers-by really can't tell there's a house inside the garden wall at all."

When Kevin and his wife, Louise, first walked through a wooden door into the overgrown garden, tucked away in a quiet Somerset village, they were spellbound by its tranquil atmosphere. Formerly a nursery, the half-acre site had once belonged to the neighbouring listed coach house and was occupied by four tumbledown greenhouses.

"We found the plot through word of mouth, and agreed to buy it from the two sisters who owned it on the condition that we could obtain planning permission," says Louise. "Although we realised that building in such a sensitive location would prove difficult, we sold our house and moved into rented accommodation with our daughters, Olivia and Rebecca. It took over a year to gain planning consent and a further 12 months to build the house, but we were prepared to wait for such a perfect setting."

Louise and Kevin briefed Yeovil-based architects, Boon Brown, wrongly believing that the planners would be sympathetic to a traditional house on such an historic site. "The planners had warned us that they were looking

"THE PARISH COUNCIL WAS OPPOSED TO ANYTHING WHICH WOULD OBSCURE VIEWS OF THE LOCAL CHURCH OR IMPACT ON THE MANOR HOUSE, AND REQUESTED A SINGLE-STOREY DWELLING"

The lounge measures 10.5 x 7m and leads into the dining area, decorated in Farrow & Ball's New White

for something special, but we were surprised when we realised that they seemed to be pushing for a modern design," says Kevin. "We wanted a two storey house with four bedrooms, but the parish council was opposed to anything which would obscure views of the local church or impact on the neighbouring manor house, and requested a single-storey dwelling."

Architect Justin Paterson suggested a clever compromise — proposing to sink a contemporary two-storey dwelling into the site, completely hiding it from

view behind the wall. A glass frontage and veranda walkways connect the house with the garden, and are reminiscent of the greenhouses which once occupied the plot. Inside, the lounge and dining room are open plan, and a wall of glass blocks in the main hallway draws additional light into the kitchen.

A builder by profession, Kevin, now 36, had built his own house at the age of 20 and is a director of the family's building firm, Bradlook Homes. He went on to construct his second house in a traditional style, undertaking much of the work himself with the help of subcontractors. He duly decided to take a similar route with the new house.

The site was cleared in readiness for the deep excavation, which took two weeks to complete and resulted in over 100 lorry loads of spoil. "Access onto the site was difficult because we were only allowed to make minor alterations to widen the narrow opening in the wall. The weather was terrible, and we were hindered by continuous rain for about three months, which was filling

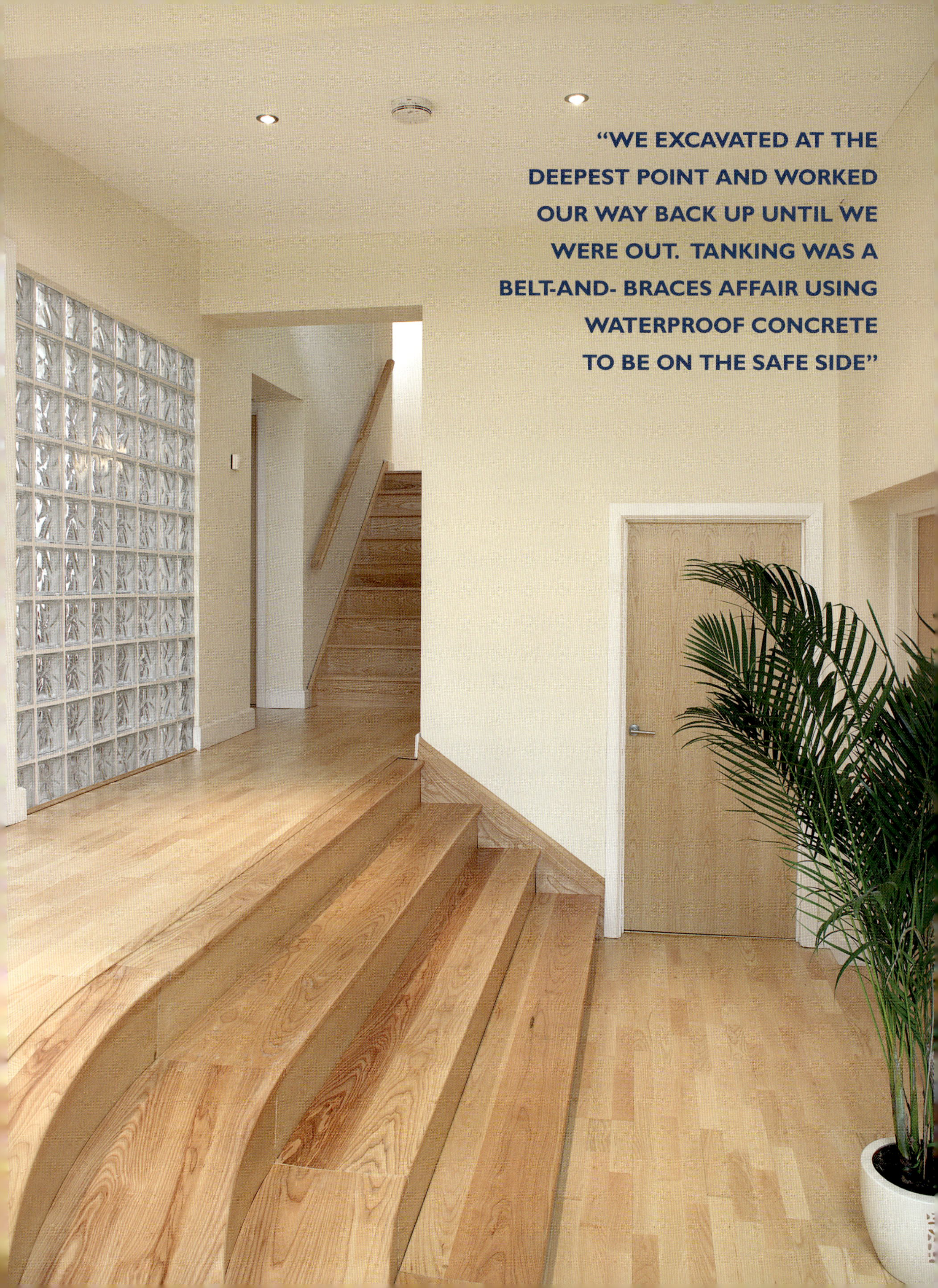

"WE EXCAVATED AT THE DEEPEST POINT AND WORKED OUR WAY BACK UP UNTIL WE WERE OUT. TANKING WAS A BELT-AND- BRACES AFFAIR USING WATERPROOF CONCRETE TO BE ON THE SAFE SIDE"

Left: The entrance is at ground floor height with the living spaces on a lower basement level
Above: The kitchen has oak units, black granite worktops and a stainless steel range-style cooker

the hole like a swimming pool and meant that we needed to use a pump to try and dry it out," explains Kevin, who was working on site every day.

"We began excavating at the deepest point, concreting the different floor levels, and worked our way back up a ramp until we were out. Tanking was a belt-and-braces affair, using waterproof concrete to be on the safe side."

Structural steelwork supports and strengthens the building, and the entire first floor is constructed around a steel frame — which Kevin likens to an industrial unit. Brick and blockwork was built up to infill between each steel column, and Kevin made up several test panels of bricks to illustrate to the planners the bond and lime mortar he wanted to use in order to match the existing garden wall.

Specialist firm Mansbridge Roofing installed the flat roofs, which were designed to minimise the roof line and remain invisible beyond the wall. Grey powder-coated aluminium windows were chosen to match the zinc roof covering, which has weathered to a dull grey, and the overall impression is reminiscent of an elegant lean-to conservatory standing against a brick wall.

"When people saw how much south-facing glass we were going to have in the house they warned us that we would bake," says Louise. "Originally we had wanted glazing in the dining room which could fold right back and open up this space to the veranda, but this proved too expensive. The design was well thought out, though, and thanks to high levels of insulation and the fact that it is partially earth sheltered, the building is actually quite cool in the summer."

Louise and Kevin read magazines to inspire them with ideas for the interiors, preferring minimal, modern finishes which they felt would complement the style of the house, and replacing much of their old furniture with more contemporary pieces. The kitchen has been fitted with oak units, black granite worktops and a stainless steel range cooker and extractor hood. Zoned underfloor heating was laid throughout the building, which is constructed over three different levels, and practical ash flooring was chosen for the ground floor living rooms, with the unusual curved steps in the hallway

"WITHOUT THE PLANNERS' STRICT BRIEF WE WOULD NEVER HAVE ATTEMPTED SUCH AN UNUSUAL DESIGN"

Top: A sunken, private terrace adds another element of space to the floorplan
Above left: The unusual curved steps in the hallway were made by a specialist company
Above: Louise and Kevin read magazines to inspire them with ideas for the interiors, preferring minimal, modern finishes which they felt would complement the style of the house

made by a specialist company.

Twins Olivia and Rebecca, now aged seven, have chosen pink and purple colour schemes for their bedrooms on the first floor, where they also have a playroom lit by internal glass-block windows. Small square windows line the long corridor on this level, leading to the master bedroom and en suite bathroom.

"We have a jacuzzi bath in the main bathroom, and a power shower with body jets downstairs," says Kevin, who employed a plumber and electrician, completing all of the decorating himself at weekends. "We chose modern white sanitaryware, with marble-effect panels instead of tiles in the showers, which were quick to fit and are easy to keep clean. Everything in the house is low maintenance and was chosen to suit family life."

The couple have named their house The Herb Garden to mark the site's origins, and were able to save several of the original shrubs and fruit trees. A door leads through the wall into the former potting shed on the other side, which Kevin has made into a suitably quirky garden shed.

"Without the planners' strict brief we would never have attempted such an unusual design," says Louise. "At times it was a nightmare because of the number of level changes, but this has given the house character, and allowed us to have a variety of different ceiling heights which make it feel even more spacious. Having so much glass means we are now very good friends with our window cleaner, but we are totally private thanks to the garden wall. It's very easy to forget about the rest of the world when you're living in such a secluded, peaceful place." ■

PROJECT NOTES

FACT FILE

Names: Kevin and Louise Morris
Professions: Director of building company and housewife
Area: Somerset
House type: Four bedroom, two-storey house
House size: 239m² + 32m² garage
Build route: Bradlook Homes and subcontractors
Construction: Steel frame, brick and block, zinc roof
Warranty: Architect's Certificate
Finance: Private and stage payment mortgage through Cheltenham & Gloucester
Build time: May '03 - May '04
Land cost: £100,000
Build cost: £312,000
Total cost: £412,000
House value: £685,000
Cost/m²: £1,151

COST SAVING
40%

COST BREAKDOWN

Surveying	£3,000
Substructure, groundworks and superstructure	£204,000
Carpenters	£8,000
Steel fabrication	£4,900
Plastering	£4,500
Electrics	£5,600
Zinc roofing	£37,000
Glazing and tiling	£3,000
Windows	£27,000
Welding, railings etc	£3,000
Heating and plumbing	£8,000
Sprinklers	£2,000
Blinds	£2,000
TOTAL	**£312,000**

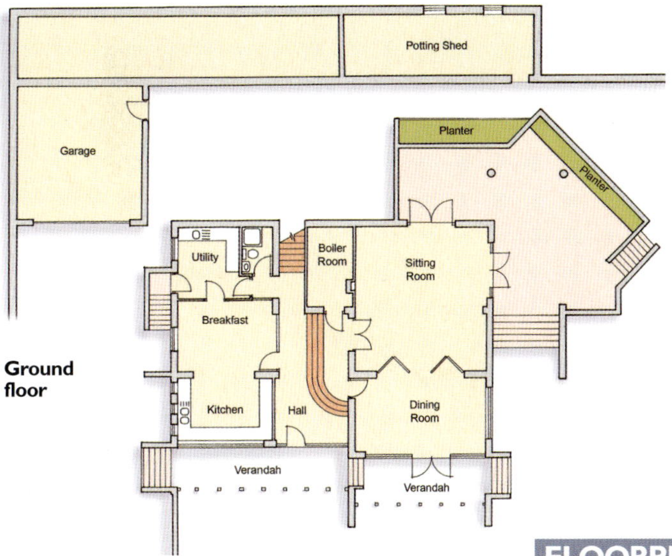

Ground floor

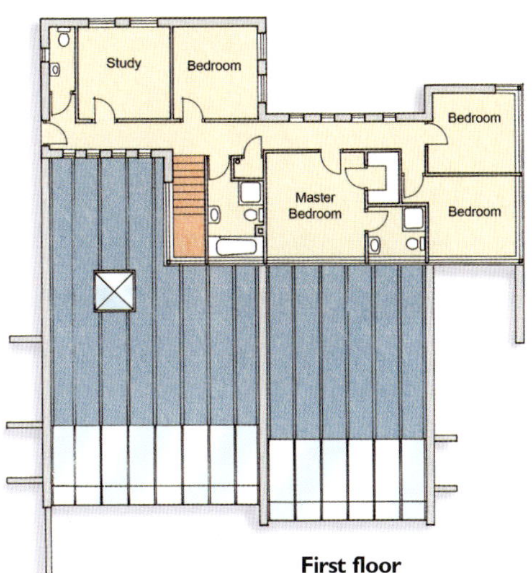

First floor

FLOORPLAN

The house has been partially earth sheltered with the kitchen, utility, study, shower room and open-plan lounge and dining room on the ground floor. Upstairs, four bedrooms, a playroom, family bathroom and en suite lead off from the long corridor.

USEFUL CONTACTS

Substructure, groundworks, superstructure Bradlook Homes: 01460 240815 **Surveyor** Slade and Parry, Yeovil: 01935 422298 **Architect** Boon Brown Architects: 01935 420803 **Roofers** Mansbridge Roofing Ltd: 02380 811900 **Plumbing and underfloor heating** Mr Payne: 07966 362898 **Glazing** Westcraft Ltd: 07836 314366 **Carpentry and kitchen fitting** Peppercroft Ltd: 07767 765888 **Steel fabrication** Steel Fabrications of Martock: 01935 824450 **Plastering** Pete Smart: 07970 680392 **Electrics** R. Manning: 07767 790958 **Floor tiling** D Stenner & Son: 01460 723323 **Railings** STL Welding & Fabrications: 01935 826729 **Machinery and equipment** Yeovil Hire Centre: 07971 054903 **Materials, kitchen and sanitaryware planning** Bradfords Building Supplies: 01935 845245 **Timber** Palgrave Brown: 01935 420901 **Materials** Jewsons: 01935 427411 **Bricks** –Terca Bricks: 07778 817567 **Sand and aggregate** S. Morris Ltd: 07970 958401 **Ready-mix and waterproof concrete** Hansons: 07966 499175 **Floor reinforcement and retaining walls** KB Reinforcement Ltd: 01626 833861 **Blinds** Hillarys: 0800 916 6524

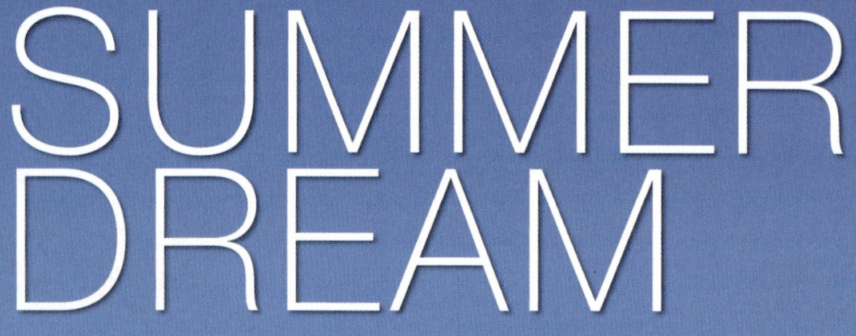

SUMMER DREAM

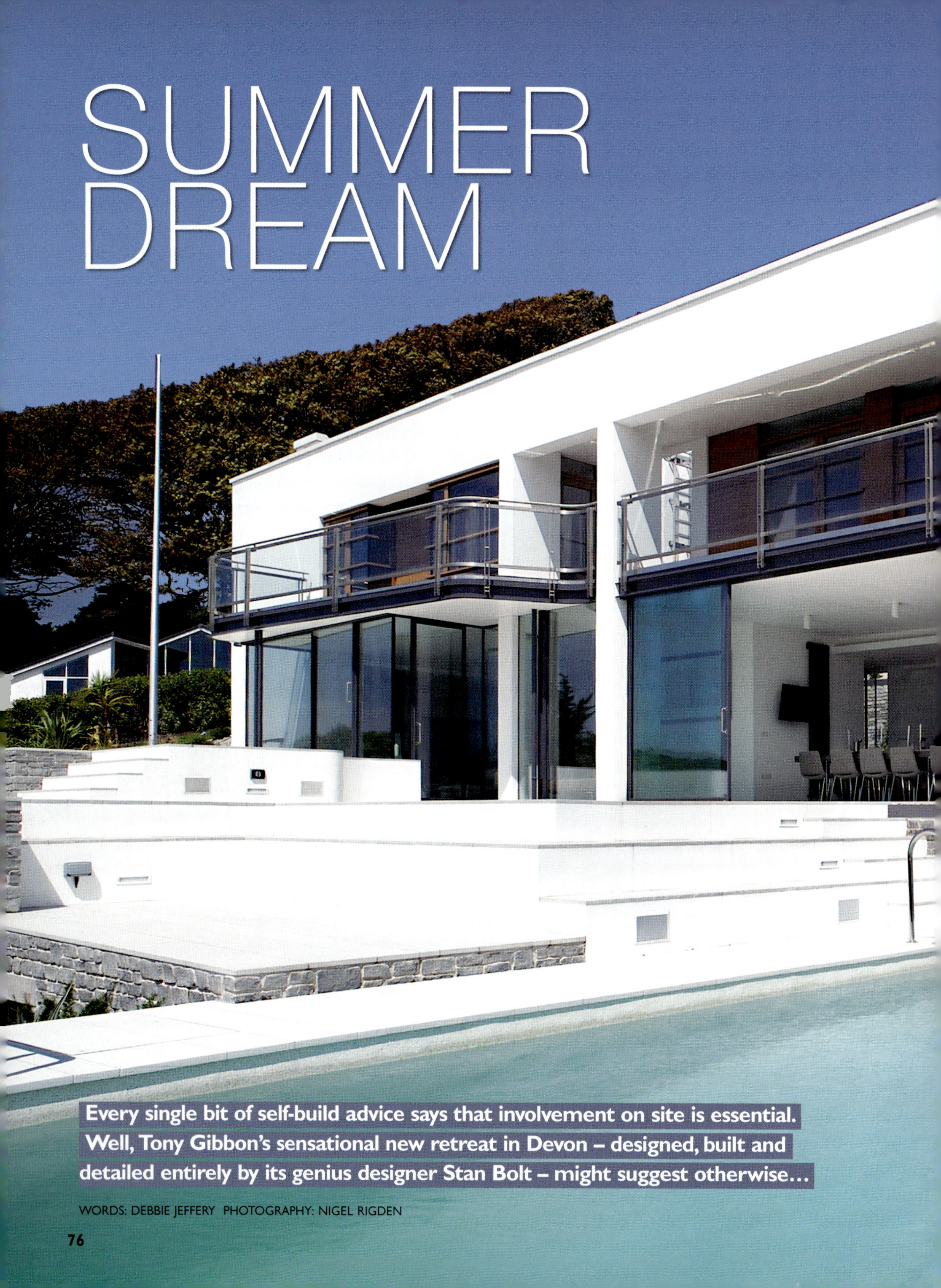

Every single bit of self-build advice says that involvement on site is essential. Well, Tony Gibbon's sensational new retreat in Devon – designed, built and detailed entirely by its genius designer Stan Bolt – might suggest otherwise…

WORDS: DEBBIE JEFFERY PHOTOGRAPHY: NIGEL RIGDEN

Most architects must secretly dream of a wealthy client who arrives with no brief, asks few questions and sets no budget — so when Tony Gibbon first approached his Devon-based architect, Stan Bolt, it must have seemed to Stan as if all his Christmases had come at once. "I felt incredibly privileged to be involved in such a project," he says. "Very few architects ever get this kind of opportunity."

Tony had recently purchased a large 1960s house on a dramatic site in Salcombe, with panoramic vistas of wooded landscape, beaches, the mouth of the estuary and an open seascape beyond. It was this setting that was to form the blank canvas for his new house, which replaces the original property while still retaining a similar sized footprint.

"At first I considered renovating and improving the existing house, and spent two years going down that route. However, costs were prohibitive compared to a new build and the site is so fantastic that I felt it deserved something special," explains Tony. "I'd never built a house before, so finding the right architect was vital — particularly as I'm so busy and knew my input would be minimal. I had to work with someone I could absolutely trust."

A friend had recommended Stan Bolt, who is well known for his striking contemporary designs — many

"I'D NEVER BUILT A HOUSE BEFORE, SO FINDING THE RIGHT ARCHITECT WAS VITAL — PARTICULARLY AS I'M SO BUSY AND KNEW MY INPUT WOULD BE MINIMAL"

"I SIMPLY ASKED HIM TO DESIGN HIS OWN DREAM HOME. WE HAD AN INITIAL 15-MINUTE MEETING AND I THINK I SAID SOMETHING ALONG THE LINES OF: 'IT HAS TO BE AN AWARD WINNER, STAN!'"

of which are situated close to the sea. Impressed by his portfolio, Tony determined that Stan would take charge of building a replacement dwelling for his site, which is most prominent when viewed from the estuary below.

"I felt very comfortable with Stan," says Tony. "He's honest, and I knew that he and my contractor, Ian, wouldn't let me down. No formal budget was set and there was no real brief. I simply asked him to design his own dream home. We had an initial 15-minute meeting and I think I said something along the lines of: 'It has to be an award winner, Stan!'"

For many architects such a brief would have been a licence to go berserk, but Stan took the opposite approach, paring everything down to create a stripped-back, minimal design blurring the divide between inside and outside and virtually dragging the landscape into the building. Adopting such an approach demanded finesse when it came to completing the structure and finishes.

"We could have been totally outrageous and taken advantage of the situation, but I think we actually went the other way," says Stan. "After working for so long with Tony on plans to redesign the original house, he was understandably impatient to start building, so keeping things simple also helped to speed up the process."

Gaining planning permission for the new house was fraught with potential pitfalls — not least because the site stands within an Area of Outstanding Natural Beauty and a Coastal Preservation Area. Carving the building into the contours of the hillside and bounding the site with walls and mature planting has ensured that it looks

The aluminium sliding doors are from Fineline Aluminium. The material is very strong and lightweight, meaning that the frames can be much thinner than when using other materials — perfect for creating a minimalist look

discrete, and remains private from neighbours.

"Excavating the ground floor into the site significantly reduces its impact on the landscape," says Stan. "We retained the established building lines, but the new house has flat roofs and is far more transparent than the previous two storey 1960s property, which had a higher pitched roof."

The planners concluded that the proposed design presented 'a good contemporary solution', and the application was passed. Tony, content to remain detached from the overall process, visited the site only twice during the build. Ian, his contractor, landscape designer and an interior designer – who had previously worked on Tony's New York loft apartment and was responsible for choosing items of furniture – joined the team to complete the property, which was then duly unveiled to its owner.

"I thought it was fantastic," Tony recalls. "Stan had incorporated many of his trademarks, such as a pivoting

entrance door, glass floors, bridges and balconies. The fact that somebody else designed everything right down to the colour of the kitchen really wasn't a problem for me, because the end result is perfect."

In fact, Tony's only slight concern about the entire building related to increasing the storage areas. Despite the jaw-dropping features, integrated gadgets and inviting outdoor swimming pool, it is still, however, the view which gets him every time.

"I'm happy to hang out up here and enjoy the peace and quiet, standing staring out to sea," he explains. "Family and friends come to stay, and they're also amazed by the view and the way the house opens up so completely to the surroundings."

Frameless glazing, large areas of external walling and a continuation of floor, wall and ceiling finishes serve to visually and physically link the landscape and gradient of the coastal slope through the house, which is virtually transparent from front to rear on the predominantly open plan ground floor.

Upstairs, the accommodation is more cellular, set back from the front façade of the property. Glazed walls, lightweight oak-faced panels, terraces and balustrades shield and frame elements of the seascape beyond. To the rear, slot views of the northern courtyard, landscaped garden and sky offer privacy and contrast strongly with the front elevation.

"Orientating the lightweight glazed façade to face

"STAN HAD INCORPORATED HIS TRADEMARKS: A PIVOTING ENTRANCE DOOR, GLASS FLOORS, BRIDGES AND BALCONIES"

south-west also maximises the benefits of passive solar heating," says Stan, "and the predominant use of stone flooring and masonry walls creates a heat sink. In fact, the majority of the solid elements of the building, such as the flat roof, approach super-insulation levels."

Areas of glass sliding wall provide plenty of natural ventilation, and the house has also been designed with a sophisticated heat-management control system, which is co-ordinated by a network of zoned thermostatic valves, all relating to external temperature sensors that fine-tune the high-efficiency gas boiler. An open woodburner serves the main living space, alongside underfloor heating throughout.

"It's possible to operate virtually everything remotely on the internet, so that I can control the heating, lighting and security while I'm away," says Tony.

For Stan Bolt and his team – particularly project architect, Annie Martin – the great reveal was understandably a tense moment. "We did wonder whether Tony would like what we'd done," she says. "It's an exciting brief to be asked to design your own dream home, and means that we're all extremely attached to the house — as we are with all our projects."

In fact, when Tony began introducing his own artwork, Stan and Annie did tentatively suggest that hanging paintings of Paul Weller on the stone wall running through the building and out into the grounds might somewhat spoil the 'inside-outside' illusion. "Tough," says Tony, "I need him around me at all times!"

For some, the concept of allowing your architect such a free reign would be unthinkable, but Tony's trust has undoubtedly paid off. His new house responds directly to the nature of the site and its exposed marine environment. It is distinctly masculine, simple in form, and evokes a sense of robust durability. This is a house which will age gracefully and engages sympathetically and fully with its surroundings. ■

PROJECT NOTES

LINKING TO THE LANDSCAPE

The predominantly open plan ground floor incorporates a kitchen/dining/living area which opens directly onto outdoor terraces and a rear courtyard through walls of glass. There are two bathrooms and two store rooms on this level, with an open plan staircase rising up behind the kitchen to bridge-style landings which lead to four bedrooms, a study, a bathroom and two en suites upstairs.

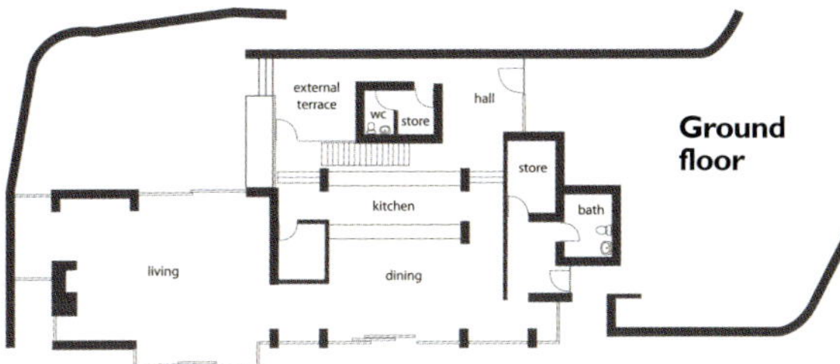

Ground floor

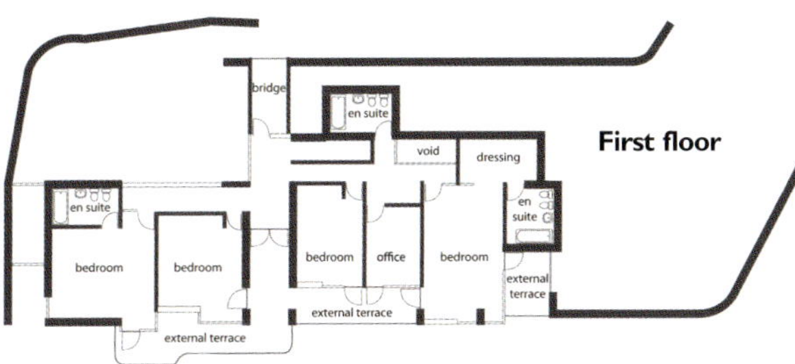

First floor

The house stands on a dramatic coastal site looking out to sea and has been carved into the contours of the hillside

Architect Stan Bolt

FACT FILE

Name: Tony Gibbon
Area: Salcombe, Devon
House type: Four bedroom detached house
House size: 370m²
Build route: Building contractor and specialist subcontractors
Construction: Rendered blockwork
Build time: June '05 – March '07

The infinity pool seems at one with the seascape

USEFUL CONTACTS

Architect Stan Bolt Architect: 01803 852588 **Building contractor and joinery** Heron Building Contractors: 01548 559121 **Structural engineer** John Grimes Partnership: 01753 690533 **Service engineer** DCL Consulting Engineers: 01752 253559 **Quantity surveyor** Davis Langdon: 01752 827444 **Landscape designer** Stopher Design Partnership: 01548 853844 **Client consultant** Taiga Design: 07913 329635 **Taps, basin** Lefroy Brooks: 01992 708316 **WC** CP Hart: 0845 600 1950 **Bath** Kaldewei: 020 8337 1441 **Aluminium glazed sliding doors** Fineline Aluminium: 01934 429922 **Iberian stone floor** Architectural Ceramics: 0121 706 6456 **Stone walling** Ham & Doulton Stone Company: 01458 223166 **Flat roofing** Roofkrete System 4: 01647 277320 **D-Line ironmongery** Allgood: 0121 359 4415 **Steel frame windows** Monk Metal Windows: 0121 351 4411 **Swimming pool contractor** Young Leisure: 01626 333103 **Lighting** Amos Lighting: 01392 677030; Bega: 020 8589 1830 **Zinc cladding** Rheinzink: 01276 686725 **Flushglaze fixed rooflight** Glazing Vision: 01842 815581 **Towel radiators** Bisque: 01276 605800 **Radiators** Hudevad: 01932 247835 **Underfloor heating** Rehau: 0121 344 2300

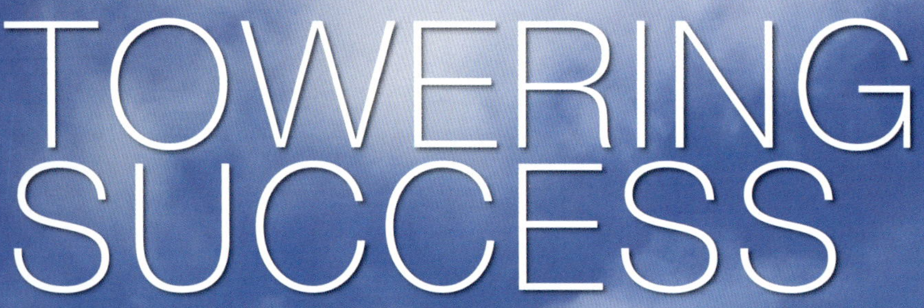

TOWERING SUCCESS

Harry and Christine Sharp have built a contemporary cedar-clad tower house on a small island in Essex

WORDS: DEBBIE JEFFERY PHOTOGRAPHY: JASON BYE

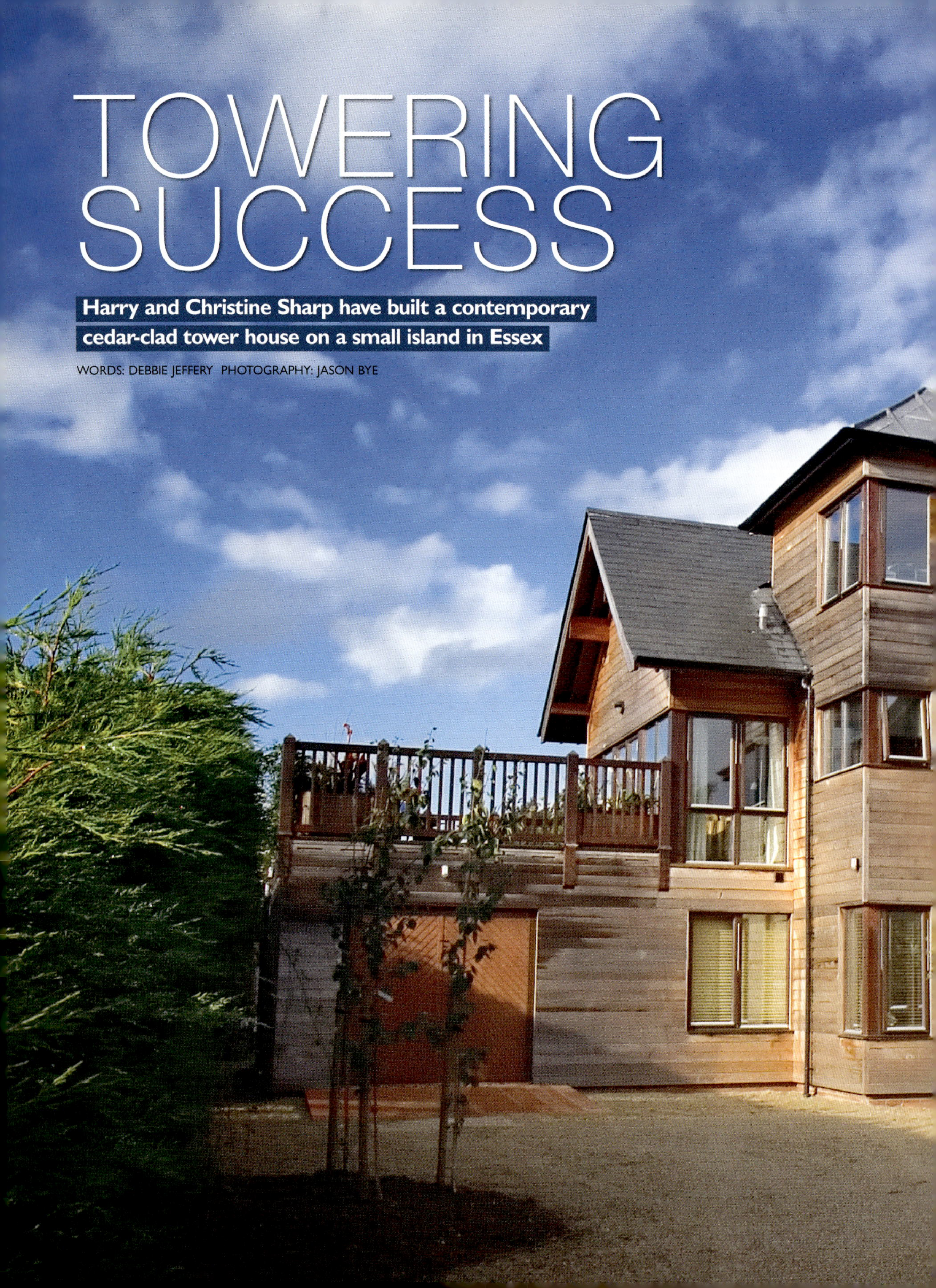

The idea of living on a desert island may be an idyllic dream for those exhausted by the stresses of city life, but relaxed island living might not be that unattainable — for just off the east coast of Essex lies the most easterly inhabited island in the UK – Mersea Island, with a resident population of around 6,500. It's linked to the mainland by The Strood: an artificial causeway about half a mile long which forms part of the B1025 road to Colchester. During high tides The Strood is covered by the sea and becomes almost impassable — catching out many unsuspecting visitors. The islanders are regularly brought together by a host of events ranging from the Christmas pantomime to the Mersea Island Regatta, ensuring a close-knit community reminiscent of village life.

Opposite: Granite worktops have been chosen for the open-plan kitchen, which features units from Inspired Kitchens
Above: The kitchen and living spaces are divided by a fireplace containing a double-sided woodburner
Left: Swedhouse supplied the tall windows

Christine and Harry Sharp had often dreamed of living on Mersea, but could not find a property on the island which suited their requirements. "We viewed a rather unattractive bungalow on Mersea Island which had a two-storey extension. The rooms were poorly organised, so we actually rejected it out of hand and continued to view other properties."

Harry is a building surveyor by profession, working freelance as a building estimator and project manager for large commercial projects. Some years ago the couple had built a timber-framed holiday home for Harry's mother but, even with this pedigree, they had never considered building their own home from scratch due to the lack of affordable plots of land. This was until they attended a self-build show and realised that it might be possible to replace the tatty bungalow they had viewed with a new house designed for their own requirements.

"We enjoy sailing and wanted to live close to the water, so the island location was ideal with the sea just a 15-minute walk from the front gate," says Harry. "The bungalow also had a lovely two-thirds-of-an-acre garden overlooking agricultural land to the west, so we bought it — but didn't have the heart to tell the elderly owners about our plans. We had spoken to the planning officer and knew that we could build something to replace it, and we were well fired up by then!"

Harry and Christine went to see three architects before meeting Robin Matthews of Stanley Bragg Architects in Colchester. They explained that they wanted to build a timber-framed house with the living rooms positioned upstairs to take advantage of the views, and despite the fact that the planners preferred a more traditional design, with a detached garage, planning permission was granted for a contemporary cedar-clad property formed around a central three-storey tower.

Building began in January 2003 with the demolition of the existing brick bungalow. Piled foundations were constructed to compensate for the clay soil and the couple commissioned Southern Timber Frame in Southampton to provide and erect the frame and cedar cladding. Harry acted as overall project manager with Christine sourcing materials, and their youngest son, Matt, worked on site and helped to co-ordinate the various subcontractors. Corner windows and an

"THE HOUSE HAS BECOME A LOCAL LANDMARK… TO KNOW THAT OTHERS ADMIRE IT MAKES IT REALLY SPECIAL"

"BUILDING A PROMINENT HOUSE ON A SMALL ISLAND WAS ALWAYS GOING TO CAUSE A STIR"

intricate roof ensured that the house proved complex to build, but was still completed in just under a year — despite the need to check tide times prior to organising deliveries from the mainland!

"Building a prominent contemporary house on a small island was always going to cause a stir, particularly as our plot is situated in a Countryside Conservation Area," says Christine, a former teacher who now volunteers for the charity Home-Start. "We kept our neighbours and the local Parish Council informed of our plans, and were delighted by their positive reaction."

It has taken Harry and Christine time to adapt to living in a reverse-level house, but they both enjoy having a kitchen which is totally open plan to the living and dining rooms. The first floor kitchen stands within the tower and has a standard-height ceiling, but the dining and living areas are open to the apex of the roof and feature exposed Douglas fir structural timbers.

The dining area leads out onto a spacious terrace, built on the roof of the integral garage, and is partially divided from the living room by a monolithic tapering brick fireplace, open on two sides, which was designed by Harry and Christine themselves.

Swedhouse supplied the windows and four sets of double doors for the house, but the company only offers outward-opening units, which are ideal for accessing a balcony or decking but can prove impractical for entrance doors in this country. The Sharps decided to commission a pair of triple-glazed inward-opening double doors from local company Essex Woodcraft, which match the windows perfectly and — at 2.3m high — make an imposing entrance into the glazed atrium.

Christine and Harry love the attention that building such an unusual house has attracted. "Holidaymakers come to the island to walk the nearby local footpaths, often stopping at our gate for a look," says Harry. "The house has become quite a local landmark. We love it for its location and overall design, and to know that other people admire it does make it really special. ■

PROJECT NOTES

FACT FILE

Names: Harry and Christine Sharp
Professions: Building estimator/project manager and charity volunteer for Home-Start
Area: Essex
House type: Five bedroom house with three-storey tower
House size: 282m²
Build route: Kit supplier, subcontractors and selves
Finance: Private
Construction: Cedar-clad timber frame, Spanish slate and lead roofs
Build time: Jan – Dec '03
Land Value: £220,000
Build cost: £285,000
Total cost: £505,000
Current value: £850,000
Cost/m²: £1,011

COST SAVING
41%

COST BREAKDOWN

Preliminaries	£2,500
Demolition and groundworks	£25,100
Piling	£6,100
Drainage	£16,600
General building	£5,500
External works	£7,200
Timber frame and external joinery	£65,600
Insulation	£8,300
Roofing	£16,700
Joinery	£43,200
Kitchen and utility units and appliances	£12,000
Dry-lining, plastering and screeding	£8,400
Tiling	£4,900
Flooring	£5,000
Decorating	£1,100
Plumbing and heating	£18,600
Vacuum installation	£1,000
Electrical installation	£10,000
Fees and general expenses	£26,200

UPSIDE-DOWN LIVING

Four bedrooms, three bathrooms, a store, cloakroom, utility room and garage are located on the ground floor, with an open-plan living/dining room/kitchen on the first floor leading onto a large balcony. A central three-storey tower provides a second floor bedroom and study with sea views.

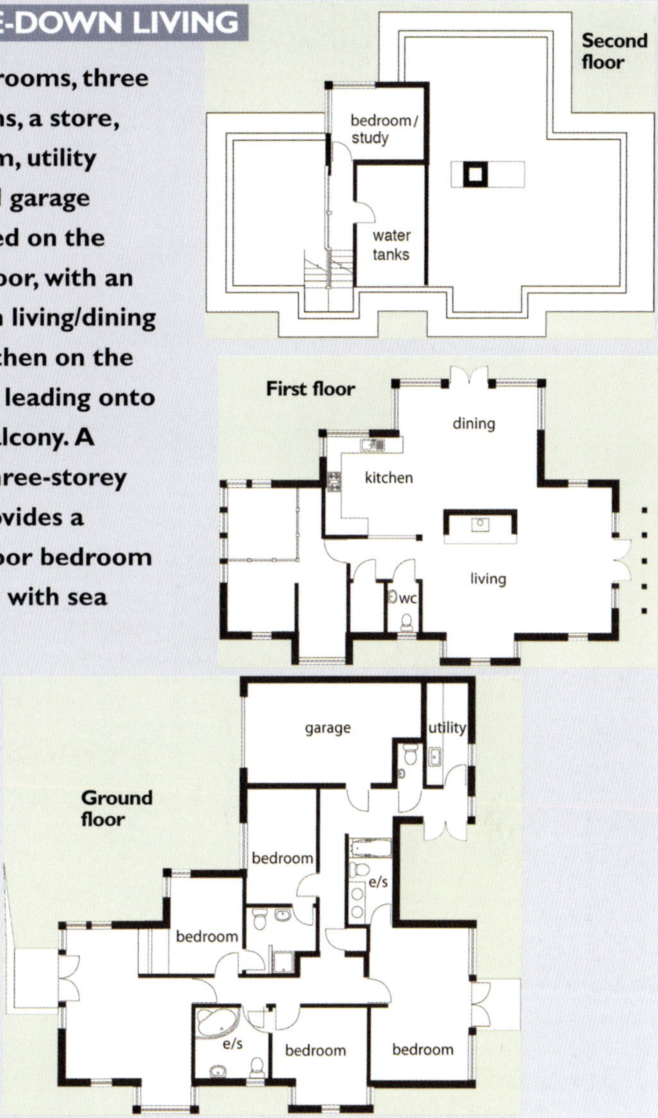

USEFUL CONTACTS

Architect The Stanley Bragg Partnership: 01206 571371 **Piling Central Piling:** 01787 474000 **Block and beam concrete floor** Milbank Floors: 01787 223931 **Timber frame and cedar cladding** Southern Timber Frame: 023 8029 3062 **Roof** Brown Roofing: 01255 862511 **Windows** Swedhouse: 01905 791090 **Heating** Chelmer Heating Services: 01245 471111 **External doors and internal staircases** Essex Woodcraft: 01206 795464 **Internal doors and skirtings** Peter Howe WinDors Limited: 0115 854 7622 **Slate, floor and wall tiles** Topps Tiles: 0800 783 6262 **Wood flooring** Kahrs: 01243 778747 **Woodburning stove** Opie's The Stove Shop: 01245 380471 **Central vacuum system** DuoVac UK: 01233 664244 **Kitchen units** Inspired Kitchens: 01206 547779 **Granite** RC Coppin: 01376 550009 **Sanitaryware and taps** Falcon Plumbing & Heating Supplies: 01206 767366 **Sanitaryware** B&Q: 0845 609 6688 **Glass and mirrors** Taylor Brown: 0845 130 7474 **Decking** DM Hull: 01621 810779 **Lightning conductor** Straker Tech UK: 01376 556449

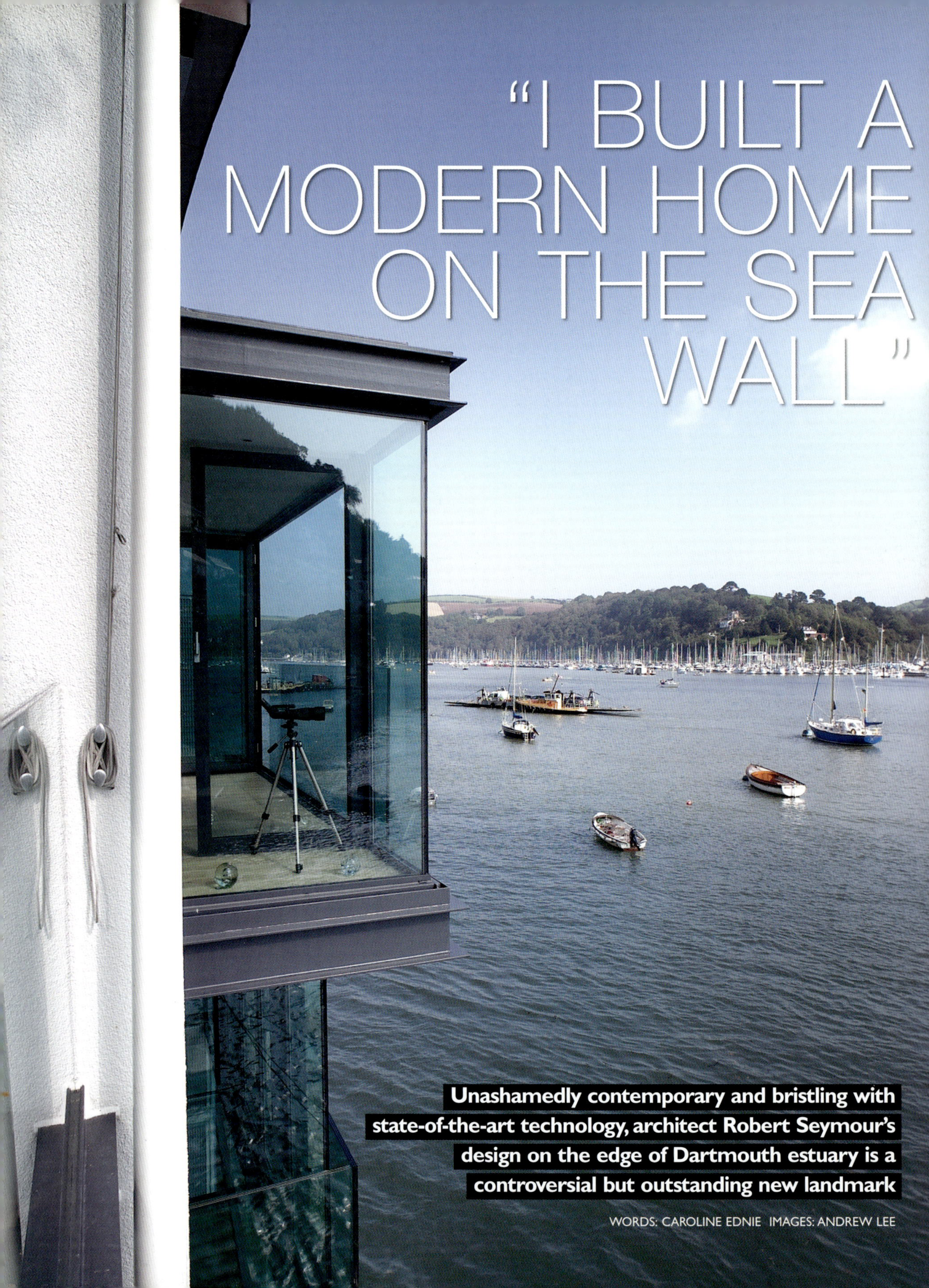

"I BUILT A MODERN HOME ON THE SEA WALL"

Unashamedly contemporary and bristling with state-of-the-art technology, architect Robert Seymour's design on the edge of Dartmouth estuary is a controversial but outstanding new landmark

WORDS: CAROLINE EDNIE IMAGES: ANDREW LEE

Sandwiched between traditional riverside houses, the newly completed Riverhouse stands within an Area of Outstanding Natural Beauty in the historic town of Dartmouth, where it quite literally hugs the bank of the River Dart. For Devon architect Robert Seymour, this uncompromisingly modern house has proved to be both a dream job and a logistical nightmare. Nothing about the project was straightforward — from gaining planning consent to constructing the technically demanding contemporary home — and stressful new challenges arose around every corner.

"When I was first invited to visit the site I already knew the place extremely well," says Robert, a long-term resident of Dartmouth. "Ten years ago, I was also responsible for designing the L-shaped house which stands right next door, and this gave me a real insight into some of the challenges which lay ahead."

Situated at the base of a 20 metre-high cliff and perched directly on the water's edge, the setting for this breathtakingly contemporary property is both magnificent and daunting. The ancient town and deepwater port of Dartmouth is in a truly picturesque location on the River Dart, with steep wooded hills rising up on either side.

"My client is a London businessman who enjoys sailing, and would often visit the area with his wife for that reason," Robert explains, "so when the opportunity arose to buy a house in the town they jumped at the chance, mainly due to the amazing location right beside the water and the fantastic sweeping views."

Robert was initially invited to come up with suggestions to alter and improve the existing timber-framed house which stood here. However, it soon became clear that his clients' dreams of an unashamedly contemporary, sustainable home could only be met by designing a brand new replacement house for the site.

Inspired by the spectacular natural setting, Robert worked with a team of experts to develop his clients' wish list into an ambitious two-storey 600m² design, incorporating glass walls, floors and folding sliding doors in order to maximise the glorious estuary views beyond and

Gentle overhead light suffuses the living space, passing through a ring of clerestory windows. Far-reaching views of the estuary can be enjoyed from the living-cum-dining area through folding sliding doors and from the bay window which lies directly above the river

reflect the water lapping directly below the building —
casting dappled reflections around the interior walls.

"It's quite a long, narrow site, which is hemmed in by
the cliff and high boundary walls, so one of the main
concerns was bringing natural light into all the rooms,"
explains Robert, who solved this potential problem
by effectively splitting the floorplan in two and linking
these halves with a narrow courtyard, while introducing
skylights to many of the rooms.

A copper barrel-vaulted roof appears to float above the
white rendered walls, supported on an upstand of glazing
which drops natural light down into the L-shaped living-
cum-dining room and kitchen, located on the first floor.
Here, the free-standing polished plaster fireplace and its
suspended stainless steel flue act as a low room divider,
and a projecting bay window draws you towards the water
and its magnificent view.

The house has been designed as a reverse-level affair,
with four en suite bedrooms located on the ground
floor. The master bedroom has its own projecting glass
bay overlooking the estuary with a glazed floor panel
positioned directly above the water. A simple, clear glass
partition is all that stands between the egg-shaped bath

and the bedroom itself, allowing the bather to enjoy views of passing boats outside the window.

Unprepared to compromise, Robert also realised that such an overtly contemporary proposal would meet with widespread disapproval from residents of the town. "The site's in an extremely sensitive setting — on the edge of a Conservation Area — and we knew from the very start that gaining planning permission would be a battle," he recalls. "But it was never the intention that the house should simply 'fit in' — we wanted its design to stand out and rely on its own merits."

Even so, the barrage of local protest still came as rather a shock to Robert, who admits that he takes such criticism extremely personally. Fortunately, the local council were more enlightened, and ultimately approved the plans following 18 months of detailed negotiations.

"One of the many planning conditions of the build

involved bringing all of the materials to site over the water rather than by road, to avoid clogging up the traffic," Robert explains. "This meant that the main contractor, Midas Construction, needed to build a temporary crane platform in the water and then deliver everything by barge from the other side of the estuary."

Another potential hazard was the fact that Riverhouse stands on part of the shoreline designated by the Environment Agency as high risk in terms of flooding.

"ONE OF THE PLANNING CONDITIONS INVOLVED BRINGING ALL THE MATERIALS TO SITE OVER THE WATER, RATHER THAN BY ROAD. IT MEANT THE CONTRACTOR HAD TO BUILD A CRANE"

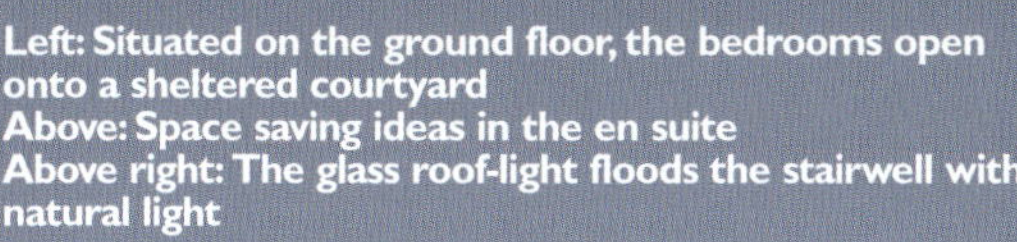

Determined to insure against future climate change, Robert designed a robust but attractive bund wall to wrap around the site. This rises more than one metre above the lowest floor level, appearing as triple-glazed balustrades in places, and was constructed using a combination of water-resistant concrete and stonework, with bonded sheets of clear laminated glass to ensure that the building effectively sits in an impervious dish.

"The house was designed to be built using a limited palette of high-quality materials: glass, stainless steel, painted metal, copper, render and natural wood," Robert explains. "There are none of the usual details — no skirting boards or window frames — because everything has been pared down into its simplest form."

To achieve such minimalism took far longer than constructing a standard house. Time-consuming shadow gaps were created, whilst window frames are concealed within walls and electrically operated blinds are cleverly hidden from view when not in use. Staircase balustrades are made from frameless glazing, without even a handrail to spoil the unfussy lines of the house.

The latest technology has also been incorporated throughout the property. The house boasts a sophisticated multi-room music system, a TV which rises out from the fireplace feature at the touch of a button and a glass screen which slides across the main living space — acting as a room divider to separate it from the rest of the house as and when required.

Making the best use of environmentally friendly technology was also a priority for Robert's clients and the decision was taken to sink pipes into the Dart so that heat could be extracted from the river by means of a heat

"THE HOUSE WAS DESIGNED USING A LIMITED PALETTE OF MATERIALS: GLASS, STAINLESS STEEL, PAINTED METAL, COPPER, RENDER AND NATURAL WOOD"

The ground floor master bedroom offers unparalleled views through a projecting glass bay complete with a glazed floor for views of the water lapping below

"IT WAS NEVER THE INTENTION THAT THE HOUSE SHOULD SIMPLY 'FIT IN' — WE WANTED ITS DESIGN TO STAND OUT AND RELY ON ITS OWN MERITS"

exchanger — a process which required special permission from the Duchy of Cornwall. "It seemed the obvious solution and it means that the underfloor heating costs virtually nothing to run," says Robert. "Rainwater is also harvested then stored in an underground tank, and there are areas of sedum-planted roof space too."

Building such a technologically advanced new home cost more than initially anticipated, with work grinding to a halt part way through the project when the local water supplier insisted that the waterside platform would have to be removed as it stood in the way of an underwater sewer which was being built at the same time. "This meant that I needed to go back to the planning committee and ask for special dispensation to make a limited number of deliveries by road," recalls Robert. "It held up the build by around six months, and all the time costs were escalating and the builders were becoming more disgruntled. Even now, the snagging list has only just been completed almost two years after work first began on site, and we're still experiencing certain problems with the lift."

Surrounded by Victorian and Edwardian villas in brick and stone, the controversial Riverhouse has undoubtedly made its mark on the town. Standing on the edge of the beautiful estuary, it has been designed from the inside out to take full advantage of its spectacular setting, and only upon entering the house does the extent of this concept become fully apparent.

To the casual passer-by the building may appear to be a rather jumbled collection of features, with its flat and curved roofs, skylights, parapets, balconies, terraces, flowing courtyards, planted roofs and external staircases. To its owners, however, Riverhouse is first and foremost a light-filled window onto the water and an ever-changing vista of river life. ∎

PROJECT NOTES

Architect Robert Seymour

FACT FILE

Area: Dartmouth, Devon
House type: Five bedroom detached
House size: 600m²
Build route: Building contractor
Finance: Private
Construction: Rendered blockwork, steel, copper and planted roofs
Build time: Sept '06 – Sept '08
Land cost: £1,000,000
Build cost: £2,500,000
Total cost: £3,500,000
Value on completion: £5,000,000
Cost/m²: £4,167

COST SAVING
30%

REVERSE-LEVEL LIVING

The upstairs/downstairs design places bedrooms and bathrooms on the ground floor, where the master suite features a free-standing bath behind a glass screen, with separate en suite shower room, WC and dressing area. There are three further en suite bedrooms on this level in addition to a utility room, plant room and lift. The first floor is predominantly open plan, with a living/dining/kitchen leading out onto the exterior terrace.

To the other side of the link there is a separate study, fifth bedroom and bathroom.

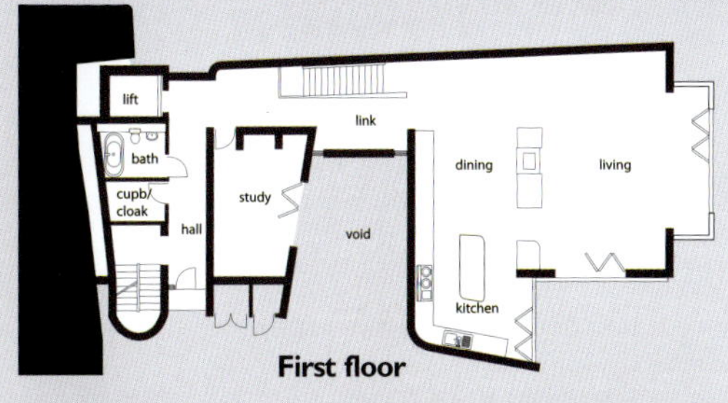

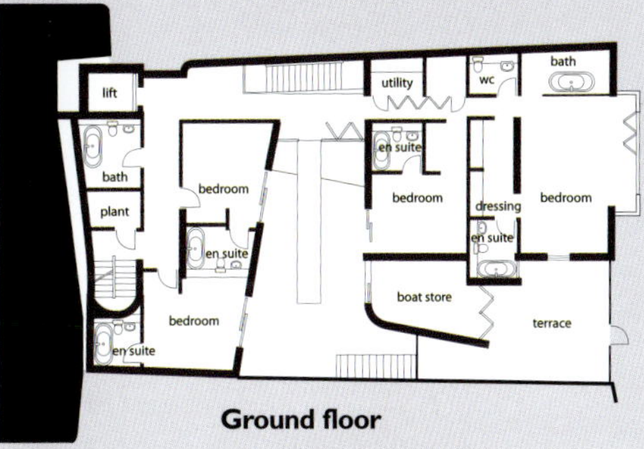

EXTRACTING HEAT FROM THE RIVER

The Riverhouse's innovative use of a heat pump in the River Dart is explained by Robert Seymour Architects: "We considered using an air heat exchanger, but this wouldn't have been as efficient as the most prominent resource: the river. Pipes have been sunk into the estuary that pump out water, extract the retained heat with a heat exchanger and then flow the water back into the river again. It works in the same way as a borehole ground-source heat pump that takes heat from the water in the ground, except that it takes it from the Dart instead. Before the water gets to the exchanger it passes through a series of filters to ensure that the system doesn't get clogged up.

"Though an effective solution, it is not without its drawbacks. A system like this is expensive, around £10,000, and it is also very big. In the Riverhouse, an area has been specifically designed on the patio area to bury it beneath the ground, with access created for annual maintenance. Although the system places low demands on electricity, it does require a constant trickle, and a full-size gas-fired boiler has been installed as a back-up in emergencies. Also, because the Duchy of Cornwall owned the water source, we had to get special permission — a long, drawn-out process."

USEFUL CONTACTS

Architect Robert Seymour & Associates: 01803 834722 **Main contractor** Midas Construction: 01752 603456 **Structural engineer** Chris Wright Associates: 01803 865500 **Quantity surveyor** Davis Langdon: 01752 827444 **Service engineers** Scott Wilson Ltd: 01752 676700 **Copper roof** JE Gibbings & Sons Ltd: 01454 776622 **Balustrade and rooflights** Glass UK: 01753 231250 **Windows** Solaglas: 0117 902 1000 **Slate** Stone Age: 0117 923 8180 **Steel staircases** Bfec Ltd: 01752 581281 **Flooring** Walking on Wood: 020 7352 7311 **Doors** EIC Ltd: 01752 345040 **Render** Sto Ltd: 0141 892 8000 **Kitchen/bathroom design** Artichoke Ltd: 01934 863840 **Sound system** Bose: 0800 085 9021 **Egg bath and sanitaryware** Capitol Ceramics: 020 7736 7468

RUNAWAY SUCCESS

Calum and Alison MacCalman responded to their sloping site by creating a multi-level home, complete with an expansive deck to take full advantage of the stunning views

WORDS: CAROLINE EDNIE
PHOTOGRAPHY: ANDREW LEE

Calum and Alison MacCalman have, for the past 15 years, been building up to this: the pinnacle of their self-build career. After a number of property redevelopments and conversions in Glasgow's West End, the couple now have the house they've always wanted, and to top it all, it sits on an impressive elevated site in one of Glasgow's leafy suburbs that takes full advantage of some wonderful south-facing views.

The new MacCalman House actually rose from the ashes – or rather the demolished remains – of a flat-roofed 1970s bungalow. When the couple bought the site at the beginning of 2002, they admit that it was the elevated third-of-an-acre site, rather than the quintessential 1970s house and garage on it, that attracted them in the first place. "The house we bought, and which we actually lived in for two years, was a bit dark and claustrophobic. We always thought how amazing the views would be if we built up and lived in the roof space — exploiting the potential of the elevated south-west-facing site," explains Calum who, as a director of Glasgow-based Davis Duncan Architects, has been at the forefront of many cutting-edge housing projects in Scotland's Central Belt.

"We originally thought about a remodelling and extension project but then, because of the costs, we thought that it would be more cost-effective to build a new house from scratch. This worked out well in terms of planning, as the house is outside the local designated Conservation Area. In fact, the planning authorities were actually quite excited about the whole thing," says Calum who, along with wife Alison and a fellow practice director at Davis Duncan Architects, also set up a property development company the very same year, called Box Property Developments Ltd.

"THIS AREA IS JUST A BIG LIVING ROOM WITHOUT A ROOF. WE LIVE OUT THERE IN THE SUMMER"

The couple's new detached villa doesn't immediately present itself from the road in any kind of full-on way. It's only after a short climb up a flight of stairs that it looms upon you — the whole house area is just over 465m². As a result it packs quite a contemporary Modernist punch in an area defined more by quaintness and conservatism. The structure is essentially timber frame incorporating some steel framework, with extensive south-facing glazing at the front of the house, and finished with a white rendered façade. Built over three levels, the four-bedroom home has allowed the slope of the site to dictate its design — therefore the south-east entrance corner features a strong vertical elevation, while the south-west elevation, which occupies higher ground, is arranged horizontally over two levels.

In terms of the interior plans, the ground floor entrance features a striking double-height and light-filled hall. Concealed rooms to the back of the house include a WC, utility area and office/study. Beyond this, to the north, is a large area, as yet undeveloped and which currently contains the gas-fired condensing boiler with unvented hot water cylinders. Eventually Calum would like to turn this space into a darkroom-cum-studio. The entrance sets the tone of minimalist luxury that characterises the whole building. As light pours into the extensive glazing in this south-east corner, the area has no sense of overheating due to the fact that the south-facing glass is solar-controlled, thanks to a coating on the Nordan windows.

A solid oak staircase leads to the first-level living area, which is located in the south-east corner of the house and which accommodates a games/music room. This is essentially a lounge and the hub of Calum's Bang & Olufsen music system — wired throughout the house and controlled by dinky control panels. From this area a sliding door, which could alternatively function as a wall when closed, features the house's chill-out area, or more specifi-cally, Alison's yoga room.

The pièce de résistance of the whole house is probably the huge decking area in the south-western wing. "This area is just a big living room without a roof. We live out there in the summer," explains Calum. There are covered

The MacCalmans admit they'd have liked to include underfloor heating in the bathrooms, as well as in the entrance hall, but this was a budgetary sacrifice they just had to make

"THE SUN TRACKS ROUND THE BUILDING… IT SWEEPS INTO OUR EN SUITE FIRST THING — WHAT A GREAT WAKE-UP CALL!"

areas for the barbecue, sauna and shower room that Calum is currently finishing off, yet mostly the terrace is a larch-decked open-air lounge complete with hot tub, trees and great views. "The roof terrace cost a lot of money but it's what the house is all about — being able to live outside and take as much advantage of the location as possible," insists Calum. "The most costly element was the massive amount of steel in the structure used to support the back wall. This terrace and the flat roof (finished in Protan, a single polymer membrane) cantilevers front and back. In addition, the gutter lines are located in such a way that they can pour out with the building lines. There's a lot of safety built into the design, but features like this cost more."

Construction began with demolition of the previous property followed by extensive groundworks, then finally the building – all of which took a year, more or less.

The project involved a full design team of architect, quantity surveyor and engineer. "You need to have a full design team on a job like this if you're going to have control over the costs," explains Calum. "Otherwise you're offering the contractors a blank cheque. We had a tight grip on the project, and although we lived off site while the house was being built, we still managed to inspect the work almost daily. You need to keep a close eye over the process."

Calum and Alison have also been hands-on in terms of the finishes. The couple laid the garden: "We barrowed four tons of sand and then the turf bales," winces Calum; and they also spent around three months painting the house as a cost-cutting exercise. Another money-saving measure involved forsaking the corner windows, as this would have involved further costly structural steelwork.

Apart from these few little compromises the couple conclude that "we would change nothing about this house. Our understanding of the building was helped by living on the site first. So, now we have a building that the sun tracks round. It shines in the dining room at night and blasts into the kitchen in the morning. It also sweeps into our en suite first thing — what a great wake-up call! And we love spending our time up at the top of the house — it's like standing on the deck of an ocean liner." ■

PROJECT NOTES

FLOORPLAN

The sloping site dictated a split-level layout, with a functional living area on the ground floor, bedrooms on the first and the main living areas making the most of the deck on the second floor.

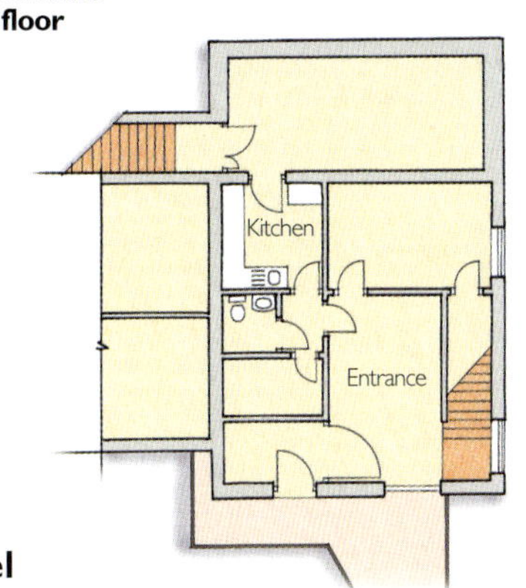

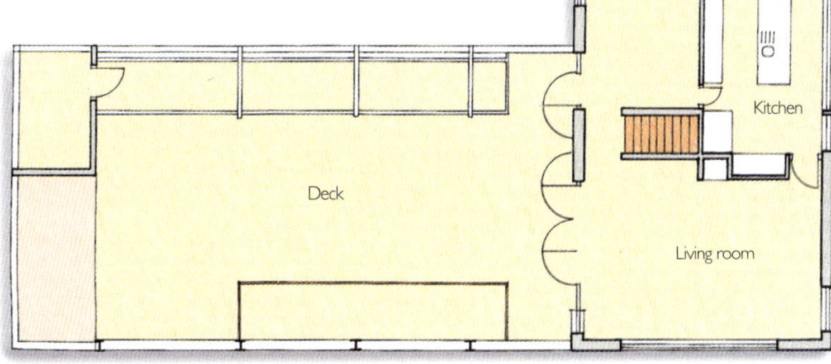

DECKING

Over the past ten years many of the nation's gardens have been transformed into useable outdoor living spaces by the introduction of decking. There are, however, a range of considerations for self-builders and renovators looking to introduce this type of feature, such as orientation, type of timber and the type of foundations. Simple installations are not beyond the competencies of the DIYer — larger installations, especially on sloping sites, will need a professional. Budget between £3000-10,000 for a decking area covering more than one side of a house. Visit www.tda.org.uk for more information.

FACT FILE

Names: Calum and Alison MacCalman
Professions: Architectural practice director and office manager
Area: Bearsden
House type: Detached villa
House size: 465m²
Build route: Selves plus contractors
Construction: Timber frame
Finance: Private
Build time: Nov '03 – Nov '04
Land cost: £150,000
Build cost: Approx. £500,000
Total cost: £650,000
House value: Unknown
Cost/m²: Approx. £1,075

USEFUL CONTACTS

Architects Davis Duncan Architects: 0141 333 0594 **Structural engineer** The Structural Partnership: 0141 331 2280 **Quantity surveyor** Neilson Binnie McKenzie: 0141 221 7170 **Main contractor** JG Henry Builders: 0141 347 4330 **Roof** Protan: 01252 338378 **Windows** Nordan: 01452 883131 **Bathroom** Scope: www.scope-bathrooms.co.uk; CP Hart: www.cphart.co.uk **Tiles** Porcelanosa: 0141 552 8110 www.porcelanosa.co.uk **Flooring** Oak by Partnership Flooring: 0141 946 3030 **Doors:** Doors By Design: 0141 812 1212 **Insulation** Kingspan: 0870 850 8555 **Gas fire** Gibson & Goold: 0141 429 7997 **Extractor ventilation** NuAire: 029 2088 5911 **Hot tub** Hindhead Hot Tubs: 01428 605894

LIFE'S A BREEZE

WORDS: VICTORIA JENKINS   PHOTOGRAPHY: NICK YARSLEY

The ground floor hallway leads to all five bedrooms and bathrooms and also to the basement via a discreet door under the stairs

There were two major flaws in Ben White's plan to build a modern beach house on the site of his old one. Firstly, Britain's only known colony of termites was discovered to be living on site and, secondly, architect Philip Domville-Musters of pdm Design found he would have to design a structure that would stand up on sand, some 15 metres deep.

The site was very close to Saunton Sands in North Devon and so the insects quickly became known as the 'Saunton termites'. "The termites were a serious issue," says Philip, who had been asked to design the replacement beach house for Ben and his extended family. "Someone between the wars may have unwittingly imported them along with lots of new plants from North Africa and they had taken hold of the terrain and become a sub-species. Just getting rid of them held building work up for a year!"

First the Building Research Establishment and the Forestry Commission were consulted before a termite specialist, Dr Robert Verkerk from South Africa, was asked to exterminate them. "He did this by using a growth-inhibitor hormone," explains Philip. "Essentially this means their bodies get too big for their encasements."

There are now no longer any termites in Britain as far as anyone knows, but while this was being investigated, the Forestry Commission placed a restriction of movement order on the four acres of land and its surroundings. "They created an exclusion zone of one kilometre in diameter — apparently this restriction order has only ever been imposed twice before in Britain," says Philip. "This caused delays as initially we couldn't clear the land of its wilderness of bracken and nettles, nor level the ground to begin building. Otherwise we could have been shovelling up termites too and spreading them into landfill sites."

However, Philip managed to negotiate with the golf club — which also fell within the exclusion zone — and they were happy to accept the spoil from the site to create new

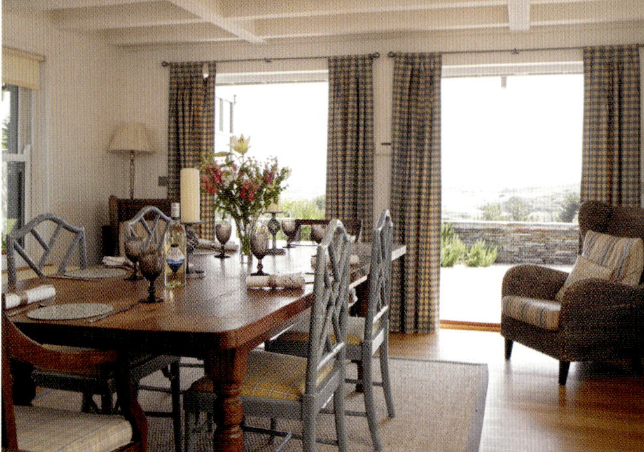

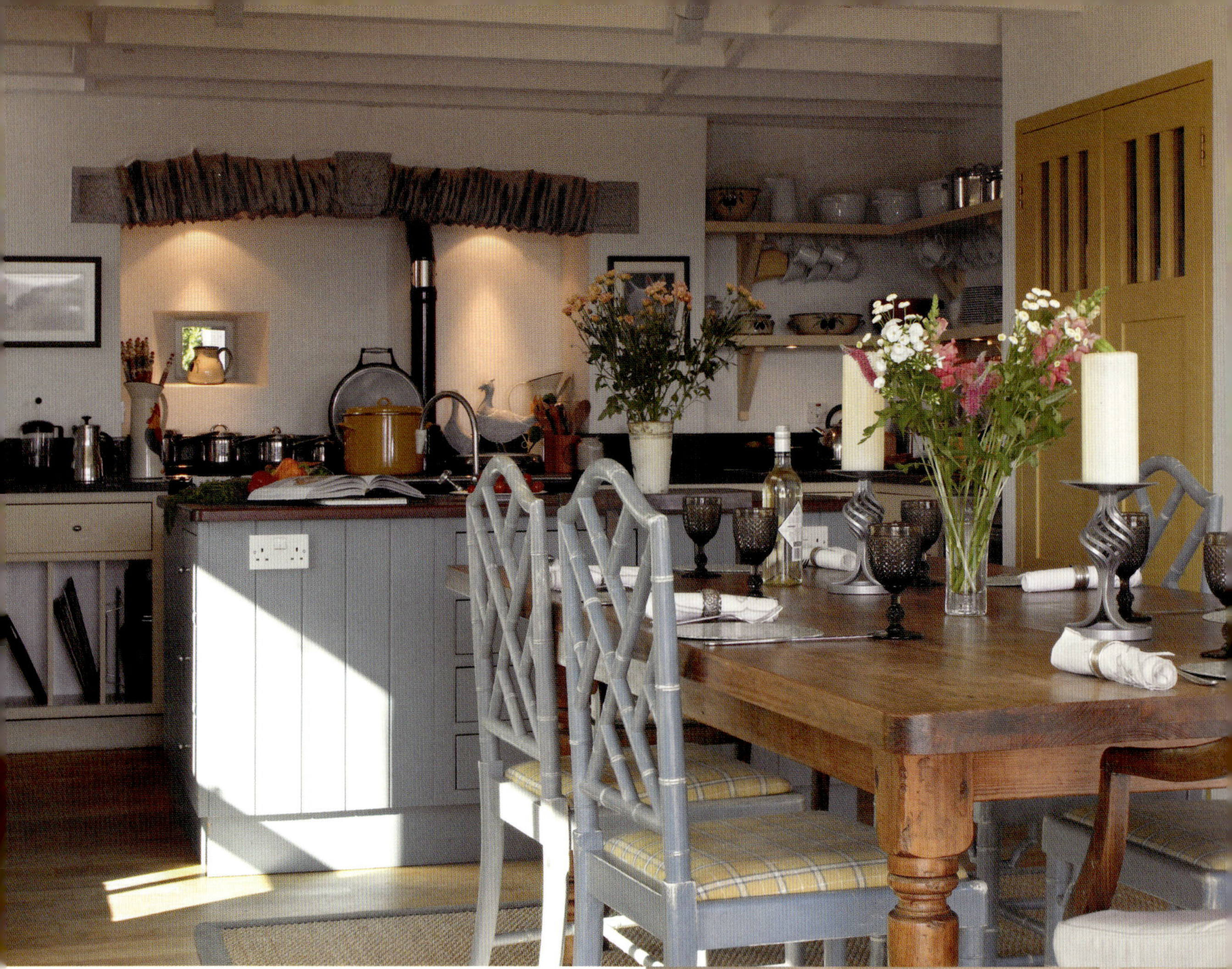

bunkers. Work could finally begin.

There was already a rather insubstantial beach chalet house on site which dated from the 1930s and was clad with asbestos. However, Ben wanted something rather more solid than the existing place he likened to a 'Nissen hut'. "We spoke to three different architects — all of whom had experience with beach-style properties in places like South Africa and California — and gave them a free hand," he says. "We picked the one who best understood our lifestyle and came up with an inspired design using a lot of slate, glass and timber. This was Philip Domville-Musters, and he did an amazing job — beyond our expectations."

"Ben said the family wanted something bungalow-style and I said that Frank Lloyd Wright was the best inspiration for that," says Philip. "The family knew his work and told me to base the new house on his designs."

However, next came the second major problem — the house was to be built on sand 15 metres deep. "This called for a piled solution, using interlocking sheet piles which

Top: The kitchen features worktops of Delabole slate and a Kohler double Belfast ceramic sink. The dining area overlooks stunning beach views. The area is floored with oak from Exmoor
Left: Airy living spaces echo their woodland setting.
Right: The sitting room was planned to be on the first floor with a balcony to make the most of the stunning, if windswept, views over the sea

extended some 10-12 metres into the ground," says Philip. "They alone cost £30,000. Then, when digging the hole, you have to support the piles with 'wailing': big steel girders like giant acroprops. Just hiring them cost £11,000."

All in all the new 'beach chalet house' was quite an undertaking. It took nine months to get planning permission, as everyone from the nearby golf club to the neighbours objected to the scale of the new house.

"But there were no real grounds for objection," says Philip. "Then it took another eight weeks to get Building Regulations approval and to tender out the work. We chose Kingston Building Contractors of Tiverton who estimated a 48-week programme, although in fact it took 54 weeks. This was because of various changes — mainly cosmetic such as resiting the swimming pool, as well as changing the window pattern."

The new house is T-shaped and is some eight feet longer than the original, giving it a 30 per cent larger footprint. It has two storeys (plus a basement level) and is constructed of concrete blocks, part-insulated cavity walls with weatherboarding outside and a roof of Delabole slate. Because they could not expand further they dug down and they now have an open plan basement with a games room, bar area, laundry room, sports storage area and cinema. The ground floor comprises the entrance hall, kitchen/diner and five bedrooms which all lead out onto the front terrace with its spectacular views towards the dunes and sea, and seven-mile-long beach. The first floor is given over to a study-cum-library and huge sitting room.

"IT TOOK A YEAR TO BUILD THE HOUSE AND GARAGE, WE'RE DELIGHTED WITH OUR NEW HOME AND BELIEVE THE PROCESS HAS BEEN WORTH IT — TERMITES AND ALL!"

There is also a double garage with another bedroom, playroom and bathroom above.

"The couple were very keen to use local craftsmen and local materials which were eco friendly and/or biodegradable wherever possible," says Philip. "Inside we have laid oak flooring from Exmoor on the upper two levels with underfloor heating by Nu-Heat, slate from Delabole in Cornwall for the kitchen worktops and local limestone for the bathroom backsplashes and basin surrounds."

The basement has reinforced concrete slab flooring with a pine floor above it. There's a working chimney serving a hearth on the first floor and an Aga flue on the ground floor. All the doors and window frames are of Douglas fir except for the front door of oak and there's a balcony on the first floor and a terrace which encircles the bedrooms on the ground floor.

As there is no mains gas, a 4,000-litre subterranean tank was installed to supply the house with LPG gas for the condensing boiler.

Outside, the couple's garden was designed and planted by Rupert Golby. They had all non-native trees and plants removed and replaced them with local species such as fuchsias, cotoneasters, lavenders, euphorbias, grasses, conifers and holm oak.

Jim Lawrie of Timber Landscapes built the decking, fencing and garden furniture. The decking is flush with the patio of reconstituted stone slabs, but best of all, according to Fiona, is the new retaining wall which is drystone and was made by a local craftsman.

The house cost just under £1 million to build. "It took a year to build the house and double garage," says Philip. "We're delighted with our new home and believe the process has been worth it — termites and all!" ∎

PROJECT NOTES

FACT FILE

Names: Ben and Fiona White
Area: North Devon
House type: Three storey, five bedroom self-built beach house
House size: 262m²
Build route: Architect and main contractor
Finance: Private
Construction: Concrete blocks, part-insulated cavity with weatherboarding
Build time: One year
Land Value: Already owned
Build cost: £1 million
Total cost: £1 million
Current value: £5 million
Cost/m²: £3,817

COST SAVING
80%

USEFUL CONTACTS

Architect Philip Domville-Musters: 01392 873846 **Termite expert** Robert Verkerk: 01344 623911 **Quantity surveyor** Phil Baker, Baker Ruff: 01823 251356 **Structural engineer** Mike J Ralph: 01237 424042 **Builders** Kingston Building Contractors: 01884 821820 **Site agent** Martin Willis: 01392 812101 **Electrical contractor** Martin Easterbrook of James Electrical Wiring: 01271 346652 **Plumber** AMS Ley: 01271 343710 **Joiner** Cottrel Joinery: 01884 257234 **Swimming pool** Swimwell: 01271 862952 **Bathroom cabinetry** David Copp of Pilton Cabinet Works: 01271 372341 **Garden designer** Rupert Golby of Banbury: 01295 810320 **Decking, fencing and garden furniture** Jim Lawrie of Timber Landscapes: 07721 773250 **Kitchen maker** GS Haydon & Sons: 01769 572134 **Kitchen designer** Gramlick Designs: 01608 664573 **Kohler Belfast sink** The Kitchen Sink Company: 01243 841332 **Lighting** Rodd's Electricals: 01271 372577; Amos Lighting: 01392 677030

MAKING THE MOST OF VIEWS

The house occupies three storeys, with the main living spaces and bedrooms all on the ground floor to ensure the layout makes the most of the stunning vista. The basement has a games room, utility, shower and storage space, while on the first floor a drawing room leads out onto a balcony.

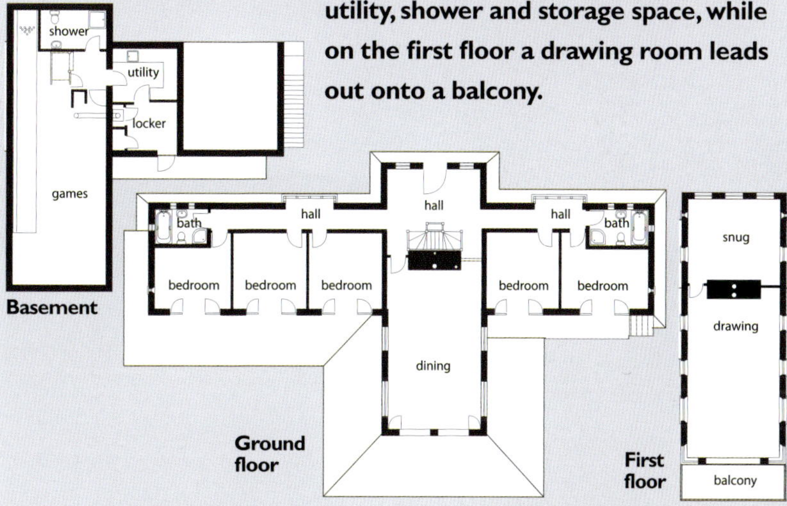

"THE FAMILY WANTED SOMETHING BUNGALOW-STYLE AND FRANK LLOYD WRIGHT WAS THE BEST INSPIRATION FOR THAT"

SENSIBLE & SUSTAINABLE

First-time self-builders Philip and Margaret Nierop have constructed their unique eco-friendly home on a particularly challenging site, nestled deep in the Devonshire countryside

Our two-acre plot came with many of the problems that H&R readers are often warned about," recalls Philip Nierop with a grin. "Difficult access, sloping ground, no mains services and as we soon discovered — bats!" Undeterred, Philip and his wife, Margaret, decided to continue with their self-build dream, encouraged by the elevated rural location of their secluded Devon site and the stunning far-reaching views it enjoys.

The couple had decided to relocate from Lancashire to the West Country once their children, Lionel and Katharine, left for university. After selling their home they moved south into rented accommodation while they hunted for a plot — which took just seven weeks.

"People were amazed that we found our land so easily, but we spent those weeks doing nothing but visiting estate agents, who made it clear that they thought we were wasting our time," says Philip. "We drove around the area looking for potential infills, checking out leads on Plotfinder.net, and spent our evenings trawling the web."

It was Margaret who first spotted the derelict 1930s bungalow, just four miles from the centre of Exeter, described on the internet as 'suitable for renovation/possible demolition'. The couple looked up the location on an Ordnance Survey map and almost dismissed the plot as being too close to the A30, until they realised that it was 700 feet higher than the busy trunk road.

Being the first people to view the property, the couple wasted no time in making their offer via a sealed bid. Their proposal was successful and in no time Philip and Margaret began to compile a detailed brief for a replacement dwelling on the site. "We'd already undertaken a huge amount of research and attended self-build shows, so by the time we began talking to architects we had very firm ideas of what we wanted," says Philip, who wrote a four-page brief which included optimum room sizes based on the family's previous homes.

In essence, the couple envisaged a light, open house designed for the 21st century —contemporary in style and ecologically sound but not overtly 'eco' in appearance. They wanted rooms which could connect to the garden and would lend themselves to entertaining — making the most of the views.

The couple scheduled a meeting with Paul Humphries

Architects, an award-winning practice specialising in contemporary and eco-friendly property designs. "We'd renovated several period houses, and loved the character of these old buildings, but we were tired of trying to heat them and fed up of having cold feet every winter," Philip explains, "so a new build really was a total change of direction and we wanted to include as many ecological elements as possible."

The resulting design was so carefully considered that Philip and Margaret's new home barely deviates from the practice's initial sketch proposal. "We loved it from the word go," says Margaret. "In fact, we were quite overwhelmed, and the planners were extremely supportive of the design."

The single-storey house is characterised by walls of full-length aluminium-framed windows and glass doors in many rooms, lined internally with timber, which give access to the garden and superb views of the surrounding countryside.

The property's timber-frame construction has been clad externally with a combination of pink-painted render and Siberian larch. A one-room-deep bedroom block effectively acts as a windbreak on the exposed site, curving to meet the living area which features glulam posts and beams.

Designed to remain below the ridge height of the previous bungalow, the house has been dug into the

Above left and middle: Steps lead up to the kitchen, which is fitted with cream cabinets and shiny black granite worktops
Above right: An L-shaped piece of reinforced glass directs water down from the flat roof into the rainwater-collection pond — an elegant alternative to guttering
Top right: The external walls of the timber-framed house have been clad in horizontal larch and painted render, with an unusual zinc roof. Solar panels are positioned above the front door
Below right: The bold combination of natural and manmade materials makes a dramatic design statement, creating a striking focal point here thanks to exposed glulam posts and beams

hillside and the floor levels are stepped to follow the contours of the sloping site.

The roof is predominantly clad in zinc, with a flat section of Roofkrete above the main living space on which the solar panels are sited, and an overhanging brise soleil shades the west façade where glazing maximises solar gain in the winter.

The building has been highly insulated — tiled floors in the kitchen and living room act as an efficient heat sink, and underfloor heating from a 2kW ground-source heat pump is operated during off-peak hours. Water from a newly sunk borehole is solar heated, and a seven metre-long rectangular rainwater-capture pond serves the garden.

Planning permission was easily achieved for the new house, but unforeseen problems arose when the discovery

"WE HAD TO DESIGN A SEPARATE GARDEN BUILDING TO RE-HOME THE BATS, WHICH USED UP MUCH OF OUR CONTINGENCY FUND"

of bat droppings in the disused bungalow postponed the build. "We had to pay for an expensive survey and were instructed to design a separate garden building to re-home the bats, which cost over £11,000 to build and used up much of our contingency fund," says Margaret.

One year later and the existing bungalow could finally be demolished, with strip foundations designed to the complicated shape of the new house.

Excavating the site to accommodate the ground-source heating pipes proved a more complex and expensive task than first anticipated, and further site-specific problems ensued. "We knew that access wasn't fantastic, but one delivery driver actually ended up in tears and refused to come back," recalls Philip.

The post-and-beam timber frame was constructed off site by a local company, and took eight weeks to erect.

Margaret took charge of ordering materials and chasing deliveries while Philip, who has a furniture-making qualification, worked on site on a daily basis. "We did a phenomenal amount of reading and planning, but nothing could have prepared us for the raw reality of a self-build project," Philip admits.

However, the finished house is a testament to the couple's determination. Tall, thin windows and low-level lighting illuminate the curving corridor of the bedroom block, from which steps lead up into the airy living room. Here a contemporary log-burner stands against a half-height wall, and porcelain floor tiles have been laid over the underfloor heating. Illuminated from above by a roof lantern, the living space is overlooked by the raised kitchen and its towering wall of feature glazing which overlooks woodland beyond.

"We could write a book about this build, it's been so eventful, and we've had a steady stream of people knocking on the door, wanting to see inside the house," says Philip. "After experiencing such a warm, environmentally friendly home we could never go back to living in a draughty older property, but we now realise just how demanding self-building can be — no matter how well prepared you think you are! ■

PROJECT NOTES

FACT FILE

Names: Philip and Margaret Nierop
Professions: Retired
Area: Devon
House type: Four bedroom single storey
House size: 252m²
Build route: Self-managed subcontractors and DIY
Finance: Private
Construction: Timber frame with zinc roof
Build time: May '06 – April '08
Land cost: £298,000
Build cost: £362,000
Total cost: £660,000
Value on completion: £800,000
Cost/m²: £1,436

COST SAVING
33%

COST BREAKDOWN

Preliminaries	£18,000
Professional services	£16,500
Groundworks	£39,000
Externals	£12,800
Timber frame	£49,500
Roofing	£38,500
Windows, rooflights and external doors	£39,000
Electrics	£13,100
Plumbing and sanitaryware	£30,600
Kitchen and utility	£13,600
Other – structural and internal	£90,600

MAKING THE MOST OF COUNTRYSIDE VIEWS

This four-bedroom single-storey house has open-plan living areas, with steps leading up from the main sitting room to the kitchen and dining room and down to the bedroom block, following the contours of the site.

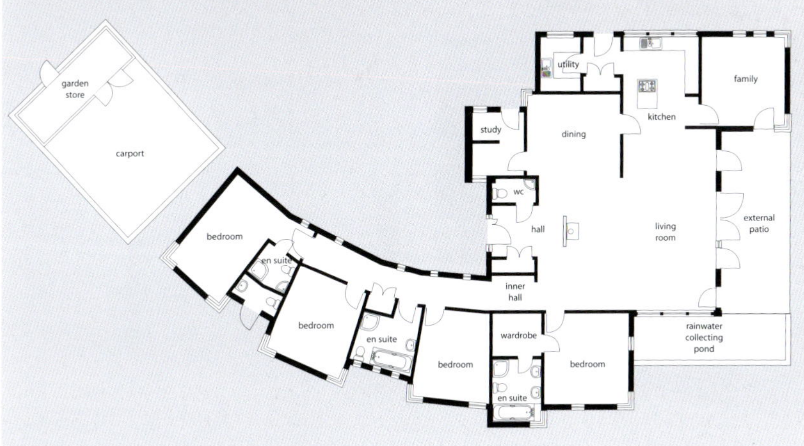

USEFUL CONTACTS

Design Paul Humphries Architects Ltd: 01395 276598 **Timber frame** Westructure Timber Frame Ltd: 01392 411211 **Warmcel cellulose insulation** Excel Industries Ltd: 01685 845200 **Floor insulation** Kingspan Insulation Ltd: 0870 850 8555 **Plasterboard** Fermacell UK: 0870 609 0306 **Flat roofing membrane** Roofkrete Ltd: 01647 277475 **Doors and windows** Velfac Ltd: 01223 897100 **Ground-source heat pump** Kensa Engineering Ltd: 01872 862140 **Kitchen** Alaris: 01463 227777 **Timber cladding** Vincent Timber: 0121 772 5511 **Electrics** Electrical and Security Solutions: 01392 203465 **Plumbing** DW Plumbing & Heating Engineers: 01392 681507 **Underfloor heating** Uponor: 01455 550355 **Sewerage system** Biodigester Ltd: 01278 786104 **Flooring** Devon Tiles: 01404 811209 **Zinc roof work** A&S Roofing: 01837 810287 **Bathrooms** Plumb Centre: 0870 1622 557

WHITE LIGHT

WORDS: HEATHER DIXON   PHOTOGRAPHY: DAVE BURTON

The kitchen, from
Plain & Simple
Kitchens, is divided
from the sitting
area by a half wall
that accentuates
light and space

Matthew Spurr had never built a house in his life, but that didn't stop him from creating one of the most ambitious self-build projects in East Yorkshire. Not only did he push the boundaries of local design with his white-rendered house, but he also succeeded against the odds to build a very individual property in the heart of a village of traditional houses in a Conservation Area.

"You can't build something like this without talking to lots of people first and getting them to understand what you want to achieve," asserts Matthew. "You have to put yourself in other people's shoes."

However, patience and perseverance paid off for

"YOU CAN'T BUILD SOMETHING LIKE THIS WITHOUT TALKING TO LOTS OF PEOPLE FIRST AND GETTING THEM TO UNDERSTAND WHAT YOU WANT TO ACHIEVE"

Matthew and his partner, Lisa Bebbington, who between them designed a striking 383m² four-bedroom property — complete with a two-storey glass and steel entrance hall — on a site once occupied by a traditional bungalow.

"It was a huge learning curve," says Matthew. "I set out to learn as much as possible, starting with planning issues. It was a minefield, but if you're going to do something, then it's worth doing it well."

Lisa and Matthew didn't originally set out to build their own home, but after months of looking around, they couldn't find anything they liked. "Every house we went to see needed renovation work so we thought it would be easier to design our own," says Matthew.

They bought the plot from a builder, who had razed an existing bungalow to the ground and then sold the land with detailed planning permission for a family house. "The house he had planning for was a conventional design and

The living room receives plenty of natural light through the expanses of floor-to-ceiling glazing. Although mainly open plan in its layout, the living room and kitchen are divided by a partial stud wall.

"WE BOTH LOVE ART AND ARCHITECTURE, SO WE DREW ON THE THINGS WE HAD SEEN TO CREATE OUR OWN HOME. THE DESIGN IS BASED AROUND A CENTRAL GLASS GALLERIED AREA AND SPACIOUS, OPEN LIVING AREAS"

we wanted something completely different — we liked the idea of having large, open spaces and plenty of glass to draw as much light as possible into the property," says Lisa. "We both love art and architecture, so we drew on the things we had seen to create our own home. The design is based around a central glass galleried area and spacious, open living areas.

"The aim was for the rooms to flow into each other, to create one large space divided into separate living areas." Lisa and Matthew sketched their ideas and took them to the architect, who put them into planning form.

However, before they could begin to achieve their dream, Lisa and Matthew had to prepare the site, which still contained the foundations of the bungalow and was completely waterlogged. They excavated the land and prepared it for the build while planning permission was passed. Lisa's father, who is a builder, then took on board the role of site manager to oversee the project, while Matthew visited the site three times a day.

The house is of standard brick and block construction on three metre-deep foundations, but it wasn't long before the build ground to a halt: "We were in London when we got a call from Lisa's father to say we would have to take part of the house down again," remembers

Above: The master bedroom has an en suite bathroom with limestone floors and walk-in shower
Right: A gym has been created on the top floor in the apex of the roof. Velux windows draw plenty of light into the room

Matthew. "The Building Regulations officer hadn't appreciated the size of the windows and wanted us to get detailed calculations from a structural engineer before we could press ahead."

The windows had to be encased in steel frames,

supported by girders, to take the weight of commercial-sized panes of glass. "We approached six different companies about the windows and none of them could achieve the finish we had in mind," says Matthew. "Only EYG Commercial could understand that we wanted the floors both inside and out to be completely flush with the glass between them. Technically, it was quite a challenge because the measurements had to be spot on. At one stage we had 15 men working on the windows to get them into place, slotting them into narrow channels in the ground." Even the cills were designed so rainwater would run round the tracking and escape through vents to prevent seepage into the house.

To maintain the contemporary edge, Lisa and Matthew chose concrete roof tiles over traditional red — but had to compromise over the exterior brick walls down the side of the house, which they would have liked in a more 'engineered' style. They also wanted to use silicone-based render but none of the contractors had worked with it before, so Matthew eventually agreed to standard render, which was painted white.

"One of the hardest tasks was getting people to understand exactly what we wanted, such as the floors being absolutely level all the way through the house, even though the floor materials were of different thicknesses," says Matthew. "You have to be absolutely determined to achieve the quality you want. I admit I'm a perfectionist, but sometimes it was like plaiting fog."

The build was beset with niggling problems, but Matthew and Lisa worked long, unrelenting hours to

"YOU HAVE TO BE ABSOLUTELY DETERMINED TO ACHIEVE THE QUALITY YOU WANT. I ADMIT I'M A PERFECTIONIST, BUT SOMETIMES IT WAS LIKE PLAITING FOG"

maintain the pressure and achieve exactly what they wanted, from bespoke floor-to-ceiling wardrobes and three beautifully finished bathrooms to the suntrap courtyard garden of white raised beds.

The house itself revolves around the main stairwell — a stunning structure of glass and steel. Designed by Lisa, the area is supported by steel girders bolted into extra-strength joists. The glass banisters were lowered into channels and secured into place with Rallithane, which allows a small degree of flexibility.

Additional specifications included a combi boiler and supporting pump, which were installed to create a three-bar high-pressure water system; 20 miles of cable that accommodates a fully integrated entertainment system; and a zoned water-based underfloor heating system that covers the whole of the ground floor.

The ground floor is largely open plan, the main living areas linked yet defined by different flooring or furniture. With its crisp, clean lines and vast expanses of glass, the house could have looked uninviting, but Matthew's pursuit of quality coupled with Lisa's artistic flair have resulted in a comfortable Modernist-influenced home.

The house is so well designed that every inch of space is used regularly and fits like a glove around their lifestyle. It has also been the catalyst of larger projects they have taken on since launching their business, New Life Developers, three years ago. "Our own house has been the ultimate learning curve," says Matthew.

But the self-build bug has become so addictive that Matthew and Lisa are selling their house and planning to build again to an even higher spec than before. "Once you become aware of the potential to create really innovative design, you find you are always ready to explore something new and create something different," says Lisa. "It's an ever-evolving story." ∎

PROJECT NOTES

FLOORPLAN

The ground floor is largely open plan, with kitchen, dining and living rooms divided by half walls or changes in floor covering. The double-height hallway has a striking staircase which leads to the four first floor bedrooms, two with en suites. The roof space is now a gym.

FACT FILE

Names: Lisa Bebbington and Matthew Spurr
Professions: Run property development company, New Life Developers
Area: Hull
House type: White-rendered Modernist self-build
House size: 383m²
Build route: Self-managed
Finance: Private
Construction: Brick and block; glass and steel entrance hall
Build time: February '02 – mid '03
Land cost: £200,000
Build cost: £400,000
Total cost: £600,000
Current value: £840,000
Cost/m²: £1,044

COST SAVING
29%

USEFUL CONTACTS

Developer New Life Developers: 01482 620784 www.newlifedevelopers.co.uk **Building supplies** Travis Perkins: www.travisperkins.co.uk **Aluminium windows** EYG Commercial: 0800 181888 **Balustrades and shower screens** McCollin Glass: 01482 329634 **Sanitaryware** Bathstore.com: 0800 023 2323 **Kitchen** Plain & Simple Kitchens: 0161 839 8983

CURVE APPEAL

Muswell House in Oxfordshire is the kind of confident and assertive architecture that people tend to either love or hate. The untreated cedar, handmade clay tiles and natural Cotswold stone which clad this brave and sustainable new house may be traditional, but its form is distinctly unconventional — with jutting oversized stainless-steel dormers and a massive curved roof dropping down like a tightly fitting skirt over the shapely outer walls.

For its proud owners, Nick and Sarah Paine, building such a unique and eye-catching home proved to be an incredibly uplifting and enjoyable experience, almost totally devoid of the traumas and tribulations often associated with such ambitious self-build projects.

"Of course there were problems, but overall they were pretty insignificant compared to the sheer pleasure of creating the house," says Nick. "After the builders had gone home I would wander around the site with a glass of beer, perusing the building and planning ahead for the following day. Many of the decisions were made as the house progressed, simply because everything was so unusual."

Once the couple had located their building plot — a small, awkwardly shaped piece of land in an Oxfordshire village, with existing planning consent for a three storey building — they approached award-winning architect Adrian James, who specialises in sustainable designs. His buildings stand out with their meaty modelling but are considerate in scale and the choice of materials: bold and uplifting on the outside, spacious and bright on the inside.

"We were determined not to stifle Adrian's creativity by giving him a detailed brief," says Nick. "To put restrictions on an architect of his calibre would have been pointless. We wanted a house of architectural significance — a true Adrian James design — not a watered-down version. We

"THE WHOLE HOUSE WORKS WELL FOR OUR FAMILY WITH PLENTY OF PRACTICAL AREAS"

A staircase with glass balustrades winds up from the basement to the four bedrooms above; four rooflights in the flat roof section provide natural light in the stairwell

"WE WERE DETERMINED NOT TO STIFLE ADRIAN'S CREATIVITY WITH A DETAILED BRIEF. TO PUT RESTRICTIONS ON AN ARCHITECT OF HIS CALIBRE WOULD HAVE BEEN POINTLESS"

Above: Twin basins and a walk-in shower make the master en suite wetroom extremely functional; clerestory glazing provides light from above

needed four bedrooms and an open plan living space and the rest we left to him."

The resulting three-storey house was designed to match its more conventional neighbours in its use of stone and tiles, but most definitely not in its form. The distinctive curved roof maximises the internal space, and the wall of glass to the open-plan living room capitalises on the splendid views to the south, while giant dormer windows incorporate glazed doors which open onto Juliet balconies with glass safety balustrades.

Constructed using a hybrid frame of timber and steel, the house is innovative both structurally and environmentally. A ground-source heat pump provides space heating for the massively insulated structure, and a heat recovery ventilation system uses stale exhaust air to warm incoming fresh air and retain a comfortable living environment throughout the changing seasons.

"I really enjoy finding out about the latest materials and building techniques, including eco-friendly options, so the house was always going to be stuffed with every kind of gadget!" laughs Nick. "Sarah wasn't convinced — particularly as the budget started to go out of the window as I got more carried away with sophisticated automated lighting and integrated music systems!

"She was concerned that there wouldn't be enough money left for finishes such as the walnut flooring, but I was having far too much fun to give up any of the boys' toys — which ended up swelling the budget quite a bit."

As an airline pilot, Nick — who had previously extended and remodelled several of the family's homes – was able to organise his flights around the build, ensuring that he could take on the demanding role of project manager, employing a hand-picked team of local tradesmen and specialist subcontractors for the task.

"The plot of land came with a small stone cottage, which we totally renovated while we were waiting the 18 months it took for revised planning permission to be approved," he explains. "It meant that we were able to sell our house and move into the cottage during the build — making me

ideally placed to oversee everything."

Nick's chosen team proved a young and enthusiastic crowd who brought a great sense of fun to the site. His 24 year-old foreman was keen to learn about the various methods and materials involved, and had a positive outlook about everything from sinking the ground-source heat pump to excavating a full-sized basement.

This lower ground floor level has been built into the slope of the site, and contains a playroom with a reinforced corner window to the north for seven-year-old Tom and his five-year-old sister, Georgia. There's a double garage, a laundry, a stylish cloakroom and a plant room as well as the self-contained studio space, with its own shower room and kitchenette, which Sarah uses for her business of importing jewellery.

"For me, it was vital that the basement should be massively over-constructed to prevent even the slightest possibility of damp," Nick states. "It was a real belt-and-braces affair, involving insulated concrete formwork (ICF), with drainage designed to divert moisture away from the building and an over-specified tanking system."

With the reinforced raft foundations, basement and concrete slab in place, the skeletal form of the imposing steel frame could be craned into position — a process which took mere days and which Nick found to be one of the highlights of the entire build. This was later infilled with a structural timber frame, and the result is a totally self-supporting form, offering maximum flexibility for the internal layout.

Windows were imported from Denmark and play a prominent role in the overall design, with the grey stainless-steel cheeks of the dormers protruding proudly from soft red clay tiles, which were used to clad the split roof — a complex task for the patient roofer. Between the two curving profiles, a flat-roofed 'spine' offers space to conceal unsightly services including the soil stack and satellite dish, and is inset with four self-cleaning roof windows allowing plenty of natural light onto the landing and two of the upstairs bathrooms.

At entrance level, the upper ground floor is predominantly dedicated to a large, open plan kitchen/ dining/living space, with a curving free-standing stud wall acting as a room divider — behind which Sarah has created a private adult refuge. A bank of full-height sliding windows ensures that the main living area is filled with light and enjoys uninterrupted views across fields and lush open countryside.

"We wanted to avoid wasted space, and felt that a separate dining room wouldn't be used, so an open plan room was the obvious choice," says Sarah. "Every day there are different birds and wildlife to watch through the glass, and when it's warm we can spill out through the doors onto the deck, which has its own built-in speakers for music just like the rest of the house."

Incredibly, the complex build took just ten months to complete and came in at a relatively modest £450,000.

"Adrian James' design is beyond anything we could ever have envisaged — it's absolutely extraordinary," says Nick. "He's made the whole house work for our family, with plenty of practical areas such as the large pantry which opens off the kitchen.

"This was an incredibly tight site, but building a basement has given us all the space we need. There's absolutely nothing that we would change — everyone paid phenomenal attention to detail and the finished house really is exactly what we'd both hoped for." ■

PROJECT NOTES

FACT FILE

Names: Nick and Sarah Paine
Professions: Pilot and jewellery importer
Area: Oxfordshire
House type: Three storey, four bedrooms
House size: 317m²
Build route: Self-managed subcontractors
Finance: Self-build mortgage
Construction: Steel and timber frame
Build time: Oct '06 – Aug '07
Land cost: £200,000
Build cost: £500,000
Total cost: £700,000
Value on completion: £1,000,000
Cost/m²: £1,577

COST SAVING
30%

USEFUL CONTACTS

Architect Adrian James Architects: 01865 203267 **Engineers** OMK Design: 01865 793000 **Kitchen** Crown Imperial: 01227 742424 **AV system** Stardraw: 020 7203 8395 **AV insulation** Cyber Homes: 0845 094 2718 **AV panels** The Multi-room Company: 01452 858260 **Lighting** Mode Lighting: 01920 462121 **Ventilation system** Allergy Plus: 01926 612690 **Stainless steel** Cotswold Metal Roofing: 01865 883787 **Canopy** LG Kimber: 01844 237890 **Windows/stairs** CAD Joinery: 01865 303077 **Groundwork** J&S Contractors: 07860 821929 **Liquid screeds** ALD Plastering: 0115 965 7940 **Underfloor heating** Continental Underfloor Heating: 0845 108 7001 **Insulated concrete framework** Quadlock: 0870 443 1901 Heat pump Ice Energy: 0808 145 2340 Easi Joists Wyckham Blackwell: 01675 442233 **Roofing** Aztec Roofing Supplies: 01869 323111 **Roofer** Steve Cherry: 07778 459965 **Plumber** Richard Curtis: 07816 831765 **Wetroom** DiyWetroom.com: 01629 815500 **Stone** Cotswold Natural Stone: 01993 867392 **Sanitaryware** and plumbers' merchants Nicholls: 01869 369880 **Aluminium windows** Milena Windows: 01993 831436 **Builders' merchants** Sidalls, Bicester: 01869 252780 **Electrical factors** Edmundsons: 01869 247157 **Cabling** VDC Ltd: 020 7700 2777

HOW THEY GOT THAT CURVED ROOF

The impressive curved roof was not, according to architect Adrian James, actually that difficult to create. "The essence of it is that you use small or non-rigid elements except for the primary structure which was constructed using curved steels — but those were the only bits that were curved; timber joists span between them.

"We used a flexible insulation packed between the joists, and then a batten with Tri-iso foil insulation laid over, followed by a batten and a counter batten, which together created a curve.

"A key design point was that at the top of the roof we didn't go for too shallow a pitch, so water can't penetrate, but we did install a breathable membrane, just in case.

"To finish the roof off we used clay tiles, which are small and have a camber already, meaning they're perfect for sweeping around a gentle curve like this. Slates would have been too big and flat."

CURVE APPEAL

The basement level contains a studio with its own shower room and kitchenette, a double garage, playroom and utility room. The ground floor is predominantly an open-plan kitchen/dining/living space, with a room divider creating an adult drawing room area and a separate study and pantry. Upstairs, the master bedroom has an en suite and dressing room; the two children's rooms share a family bathroom and the fourth en suite bedroom is for guests.

Basement

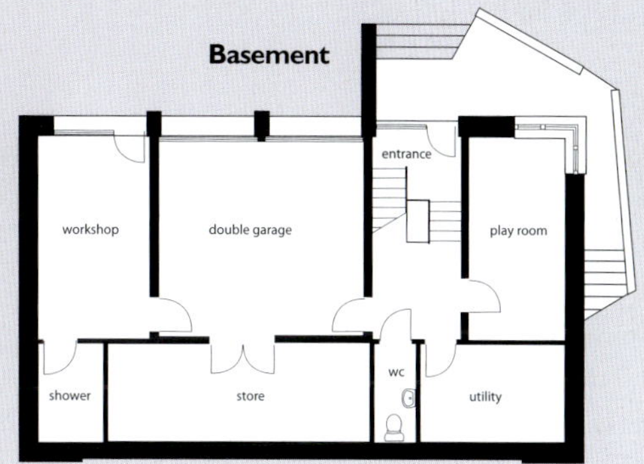

Ground floor

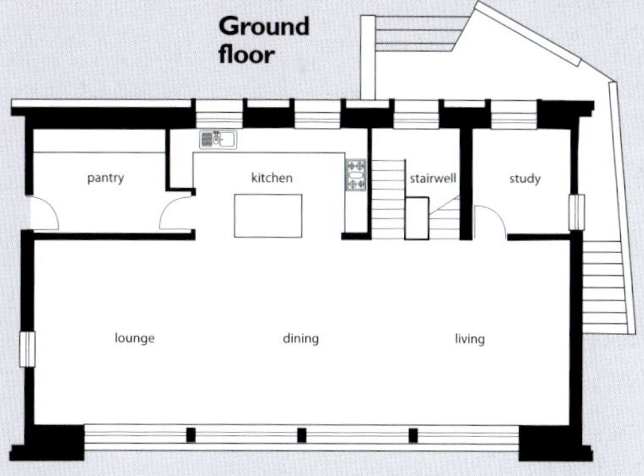

First floor

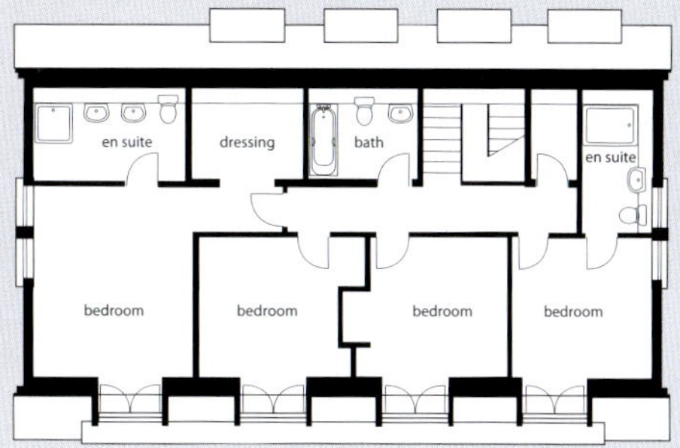

SMALL WONDER

There's a Zen-like quality to Geoff and Sarah MacCormack's newly built West London home which instantly engenders a feeling of calm. The front of the four-storey Glass House stretches a meagre three metres across, literally wedged into place between existing tall brick and stucco neighbours on this otherwise traditional Victorian street. And yet the tiny and ethereal-looking glass-fronted property still somehow manages to hold its own. "I knew that building anything on such an awkwardly shaped scrap of land was going to be difficult, particularly as we live in a Conservation Area," admits Geoff. He and Sarah had spent 18 years living next door to the site, which housed a long, single-storey garage — formerly stables — which belonged to the adjacent off-license.

The couple have two daughters — Iraina and Adriana — and had spent some time eying up the potential plot with a view to building a brand new family home there. Eventually they began negotiating to buy the freehold of the crumbling brick building, pending planning permission.

"We'd undertaken a great deal of work to our maisonette, but the one thing we didn't have was any outdoor space," Geoff continues. "Building a contemporary house next door would give us the chance to incorporate a small terrace area and increase our living space as well. It was too good an opportunity to miss."

Determined to try to get planning for something contemporary and bold, the MacCormacks engaged Boyarsky Murphy, a London-based practice of chartered architects with an international profile and a reputation for producing exciting solutions in glass: useful when attempting to bring natural light to such a small, hemmed-in plot.

"We were adamant that we didn't want to build a mock-Victorian house, and liked the fact that Nicholas Boyarsky and Nicola Murphy are a husband and wife team," Sarah explains. "It meant they were more likely to understand our needs as a family and come up with

The wedge-shaped basement kitchen-cum-TV den is the largest room in the house, fitted with Poggenpohl cabinets and simple glass splashbacks. Two thick panels of glass set into the roof terrace above help flood the space with light

a balanced design. Having scale models made of the new house really helped us to understand and visualise how it would all work."

The first design met with some opposition, and meant that the MacCormacks needed to lose the top floor of the house — which would probably have been used as a gym, but would also have obscured windows of the neighbouring property. They also made various other changes, including stepping the wedge-shaped house back from the road to create a useful York-stone driveway.

Aided by a specialist planning consultant, at last the design team managed to circumnavigate the minefield of planning constraints and conditions to produce a workable floorplan for a three-bedroom house over four levels. A basement was always on the cards, given the existing wine vaults on the site, and this has now become the hub of the home — a spacious kitchen-cum-TV den with comfortable seating and light dropped down from glass panels inset into the ceiling.

"Of course we worried about having a virtually windowless basement — especially as this is the largest room in the house," Geoff says. "We trusted Nicholas and

"LITTLE DID I KNOW WHEN I WAS FIRST LOOKING OUT AT THIS TINY SITE FROM OUR KITCHEN WINDOW NEXT DOOR THAT THIS AWKWARD SPACE COULD BECOME SUCH A LIGHT AND AIRY FAMILY HOME"

down concrete panels which are etched with a Buddha's face and surrounded by ivy growing up against the rear wall of the MacCormacks' terrace.

"The water feature came in four panels, precast in concrete and stabilised with steel rods," says Geoff. "They were so heavy that it took two men to drag each piece into place, and we needed a structural engineer to check it would be safe — particularly as we have the glass panels to either side of it, dropping light down into the kitchen."

Geoff was involved in landscaping the terrace, and the Buddha was also ultimately the inspiration for the rest of the Glass House's interior design. The couple have introduced a monochromatic Oriental theme, with black furniture, white walls and rectangular ceramic floor tiles that create a seamless flow between the indoor and outdoor living areas. "With space at a premium it made sense to keep everything as minimal and uncluttered as we could," says Sarah, "and it also gives the house a calming atmosphere."

Fortunately the MacCormacks found a willing buyer for their previous home, which enabled them to move into rented accommodation for the remainder of the build. Demolishing the existing single-storey stable building on the site and setting the new house back slightly has not only given the family a useful off-street parking space, but has once again revealed the decorative pillars of the neighbouring property which had previously been obscured from view.

"It was tricky building on such a narrow site, and there were a number of different party wall agreements involved," says Geoff, a musician and producer who has recently written a book chronicling his travels around the world during the 1970s with close friend David Bowie. "I considered using a builder friend of mine, but in the end

Nicola to solve any issues of light, though, and now we can stand in the kitchen and look up through the clear glass to the lights, ivy and reflected water in the living room above. It creates a really tranquil atmosphere and we spend most of our time down in the kitchen."

In complete contrast to the bright yet cave-like basement level, the art-strewn ground-floor living room opens directly onto an outdoor patio through a wall of folding glass doors — reminiscent of Moroccan riads which are designed and built around a central courtyard, often with a fountain. In this case, a sheet of water cascades

The obscure glass windows resemble Japanese rice paper screens, allowing light but affording privacy

it seemed safer to take the advice of our architects, who project managed the build and chose an experienced building contractor they knew."

The basement was excavated and constructed in reinforced concrete, while the upper floors of the building are lightweight, rendered, steel-framed boxes which appear to have been almost randomly stacked to form intricate angles, but which were meticulously designed like a 3D puzzle to maximise every potential scrap of living space.

Many people would baulk at the idea of a house with such limited views, but the obscure glass allows in plenty of light and is inset into the dark grey aluminium framework like Japanese rice paper screens — an image which is further enhanced by simple oak bedroom floors. Clever conceits include the dual-purpose door at the top of the house, which serves both the dressing area and master bathroom — easily pivoting across to offer privacy when required.

"Having the sheltered outdoor terrace really has made all the difference to the way we live," says Geoff. "When the doors are pushed back and the lights and waterfall switched on at night it's really very beautiful. In fact, the whole house has exceeded our expectations. Little did I know when I was first looking out at this tiny site from our kitchen window next door that this awkward space could become such a light and airy family home." ∎

PROJECT NOTES

FACT FILE

Names: Geoff and Sarah MacCormack

Professions: Musician/producer/writer and personal assistant to QC

Area: London

House type: Three bedroom terraced house

House size: 167m²

Build route: Building contractor

Finance: Private

Construction: Concrete basement, steel framing, rendered ply-sheathed stud walls, asphalt roof

Warranty: Zurich

Build time: Nov '05 – Sept '06

Land cost: Undisclosed

Build cost: £400,000

Current value: £1.5 million

Cost/m²: £2,395

"WITH SPACE AT A PREMIUM IT MADE SENSE TO KEEP EVERYTHING AS MINIMAL AND UNCLUTTERED AS WE COULD..."

FLOOR PLAN

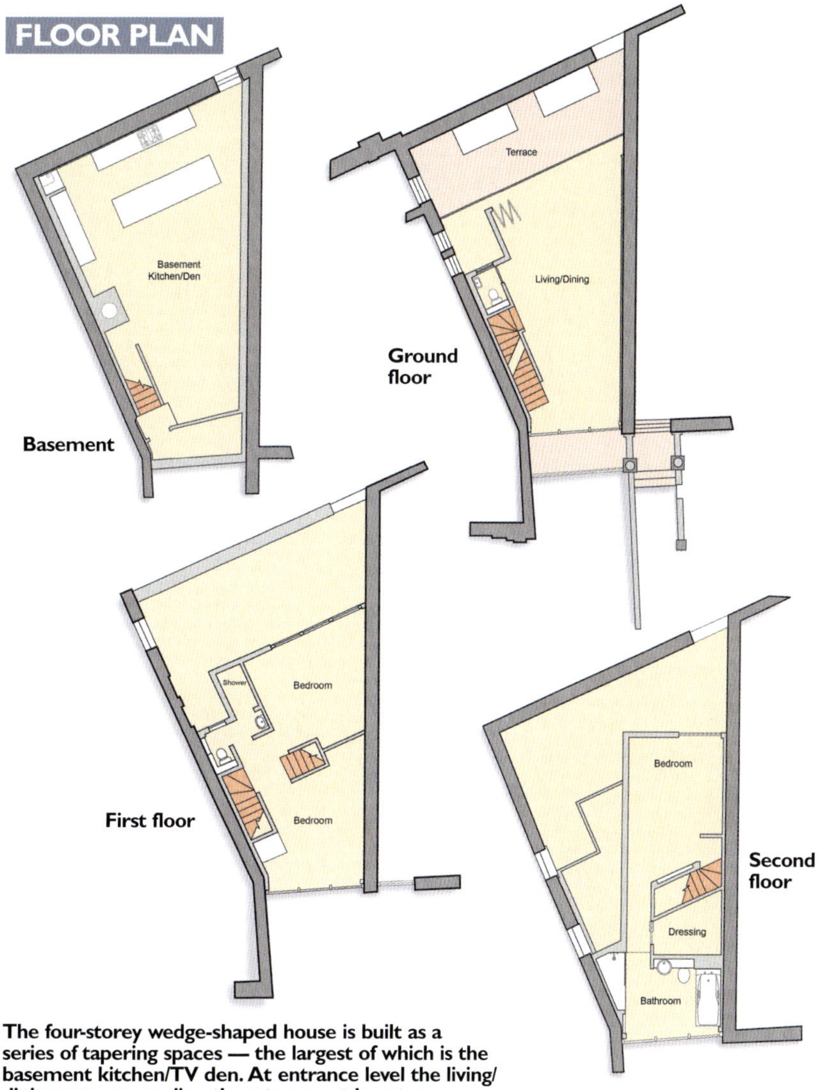

The four-storey wedge-shaped house is built as a series of tapering spaces — the largest of which is the basement kitchen/TV den. At entrance level the living/dining area opens directly onto an outdoor terrace, and the narrow staircase leads up to two bedrooms and a shower room on the first floor, with the master bedroom, dressing room and bathroom at the top.

USEFUL CONTACTS

Geoff MacCormack's limited edition book, From Station to Station: Travels with Bowie 1973 – 76, is on sale via Genesis Publications **Architect** Boyarsky Murphy Architects: 020 7388 3572 www.boyarskymurphy.com **Planning consultant** Washbourne Greenwood Development Planning: 01722 414 100 **Building contractor** Philiam Construction & Developments: 020 8905 7995 **Structural engineer** Michael Baigent Orla Kelly: 020 8568 4871 **M&E consultant** McDonnell Langley: 020 8763 0270 **Kitchen** Poggenpohl Group UK Ltd: 0800 298 1098 **Quantity surveyor** PT Projects: 020 8868 2123 **Aluminium and glass curtain walling** Technal: 01924 232323 **Sanitaryware** Ideal Standard: 01482 346461 **Barbican sink (ground floor WC)** Twyford Bathrooms: 01270 879777 **Slate flooring** Delabole Slate: 01840 212242 **Underfloor heating** Osma: 01392 444122 **Folding glass doors** Reynaers Ltd: 0121 421 1999

SEEING THE LIGHT

The tubular steel staircase has solid oak treads and glazed balustrades, and acts as the spine of the house. The modern building provides a simple setting for the family's antique furniture

We had been living in an Edwardian semi in South London and moved to Oxford in 2002 because of my job," explains Oliver Braddick. "Three of our four children have now left home, so we needed to find accommodation for ourselves and our 16 year-old daughter, Ione. Our son Hugo is an architect, and we liked the idea of working with him to design a modern house."

Oliver and his wife, Janette, are both university professors who wanted to live in the city, where building plots are extremely scarce. By chance they discovered a piece of land for sale in residential north Oxford which seemed ideal — although the purchase proved to be a tortuous process. The land was part of the back garden of a large Victorian house which belonged to an Oxford college that had used it for student graduate accommodation, and was occupied by derelict lock-up garages and an electricity substation. This needed to be relocated to a corner of the plot where it wouldn't obstruct access to the site, and negotiations took some time to complete. Additionally, the garage tenant demanded payment to quit the site which involved legal action.

"Even though our offer for the plot had been accepted we were unable to gain vacant possession for several months and ended up buying another house in Oxford where we lived throughout the build," says Oliver. He and Janette discussed their ideas for a new house with their son Hugo, who was a final-year student working in the Banbury office of Acanthus Clews Architects and came to live with them during the build. "We knew that Hugo would be sympathetic and that we could communicate with him well. He made sure that our existing furniture would fit by cutting out scale models of the piano, table and dresser and placing them onto the plan," says Oliver.

The Braddicks' brief was for a contemporary two-storey house which would be airy, energy efficient and receive copious amounts of sunlight. The site is a tight plot, surrounded by neighbouring gardens,

making space economy and privacy significant issues. "The front of the plot faces south," Oliver explains, "and we very much wanted to get the benefit of sunlight into the house and also the garden, so it didn't make sense to have a back garden which would have been in the shade of the house."

Hugo responded by positioning the house at the north end of the site, which maximises the southern aspect and usable garden area, but is far enough back from the boundary walls to allow ease of construction and servicing. Principal living spaces are arranged along the building's south side to benefit from good sunlight levels and a relationship with the garden, with secondary spaces such as the utility room and bathrooms to the north.

The external load-bearing brick and block walls have been constructed in yellow brick to provide continuity with the surrounding environment, and the walls, swimming pool, landscaping and planting combine to form an attractive courtyard which incorporates a variety of textures. "We would have preferred to use a more contemporary blue/grey engineering brick, but the

"ALL OF OUR PREVIOUS HOUSES HAVE BEEN PERIOD PROPERTIES WITH SEPARATE ROOMS... IT MEANT WE LIVED IN A COLLECTION OF BOXES"

planners insisted that the house should fit in with more traditional neighbouring buildings," Hugo, 29, explains. "It was the only element of the original design that they requested we change, and in retrospect it may have been a little harsh and austere for this landscape."

The main feature of the house is the curved front façade — a two-storey glazed, aluminium-framed screen, which provides views and access to the garden and presents a striking aspect to the street. Horizontal shading devices cut out high-angle sun and combine with internal blinds and electrically operated skylights to allow precise control of the natural light and ventilation the house receives.

"In some ways we are living in a goldfish bowl facing the street," says Oliver, "but the house is set back 20 metres from the road and has been enclosed by a yellow stock brick wall, in the style of a mews courtyard, which makes full use of the space and gives us privacy on the ground floor. The double-height atrium has been fitted with electrically operated blinds which we can lower in the evening to give privacy to the upper floor."

The building's other three sides are wrapped in a heavy, well-insulated wall, punctuated by smaller deep-set windows. This approach allows the house to benefit from passive solar gains in winter while avoiding overheating in summer, reducing overall energy consumption. These thermal and aesthetic strategies are complemented by the house's construction technology. A hybrid structure of load-bearing masonry and a steel frame provides thermal mass while allowing the open plan layout of the ground floor. Energy-efficient underfloor heating leaves spaces uncluttered, and low-emissivity double glazing in the south façade helps prevent heat loss in winter and excessive solar gain in summer.

The open plan living spaces on the ground floor work around a central staircase, and include the kitchen, lounge, breakfast and dining areas, all of which enjoy a direct connection with the garden. To the darker north side of the house are the utility room, WC and book-lined snug, with a store sandwiched between the house and rear garden wall. "It's nice to have a separate snug room for watching television and reading as an alternative to the main open plan part of the house," says Oliver.

The first floor is more cellular, with bedrooms and a study arranged along the south side of the plan and top-lit wet spaces to the north. The master bedroom suite is separated from Ione's bedroom, shower room and kitchenette by a double-height space over the living area, crossed by a bridge adjacent to the stairs. "There is a folding partition between Ione's bedroom and the

"IT'S NICE TO HAVE A SEPARATE SNUG FOR WATCHING TV AND READING, AS AN ALTERNATIVE TO THE MAIN OPEN PLAN PART OF THE HOUSE"

neighbouring guest room so that, when she's there on her own, she can open the partition and have one large space," Hugo explains.

Detailing throughout the house is restrained and simple, maximising the sense of space and providing a calm backdrop for feature elements and the family's collection of antique furniture, which sits well in such a contemporary setting. The staircase and bridge are high-profile, high-cost elements of the interior. Solid oak treads are cantilevered off a tubular steel spine and the light open nature of this structure is further emphasised by a glass and metal balustrade.

"All our previous houses were period properties with separate rooms, which meant that we lived in a collection of boxes. You find that you're spending most of your time in about 20% of the space, and some rooms are rarely used," says Oliver. "We don't sit around the big dining table any more than we did before, but it's now part of the environment instead of being behind a closed door. After experiencing this kind of home it would be very difficult to go back to the way we lived before." ■

PROJECT NOTES

WALLS OF GLASS

There is no better way to maximise the use of natural light and passive solar gain in a building than to incorporate large areas of glazing on the south-facing elevation. This can be achieved by combining several large-framed casement units, or by using frameless floor-to-ceiling double glazed units. To achieve a glazed area of more than 25% of the total area of a new dwelling and still meet the building regulations, it's necessary to specify low-E glass and to 'trade off' the extra glazing against energy savings elsewhere, using the Carbon Index method.

FACT FILE

Names: Oliver and Janette Braddick
Professions: Professor of experimental psychology and professor/medical researcher
Area: Oxford
House type: Four bedroom detached house
House size: 250m²
Build route: Building contractor
Construction: Masonry and steel frame
Warranty: Architect's certificate
Finance: Cambridge Building Society
Build time: Dec '02 – Oct '03
Land cost: £380,000
Build cost: £423,000
Total cost: £803,000
House value: £900,000 +
Cost/m²: £1,692

COST SAVING
11%

FLOORPLAN

The ground floor is primarily open plan, with a kitchen, dining, living and music areas, and separate utility, WC and snug to the rear of the plan. Upstairs, all bedrooms have en suite facilities; Ione's room has a small kitchenette.

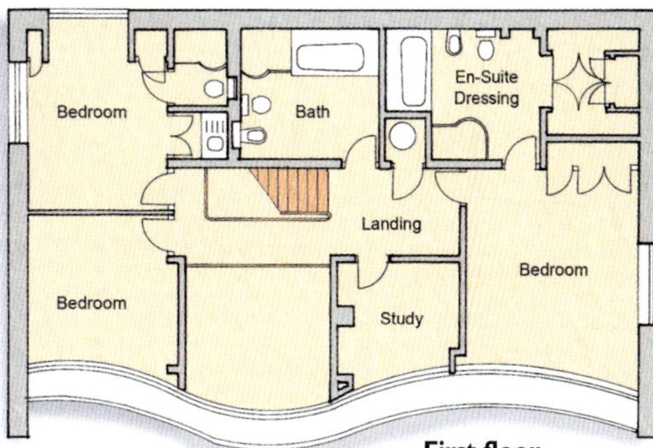

First floor

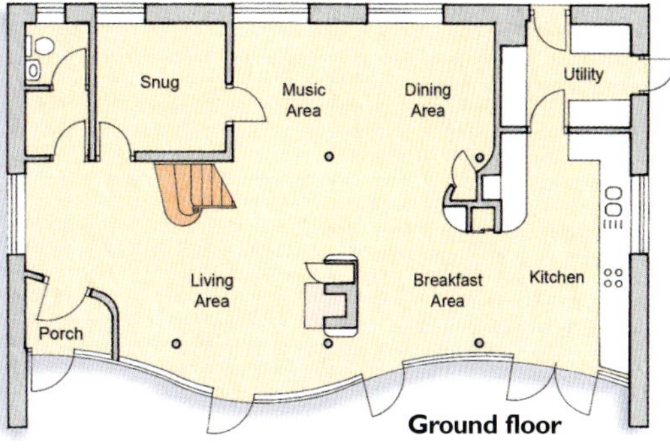

Ground floor

USEFUL CONTACTS

Architect Acanthus Clews: 01295 702600 **Builder** Knowles & Son: 01865 249681 **Electrical engineer** Bruce Butcher, Oxford: 01865 727058 **Plumbing** Uniheat: 01865 242708 **Curtain walling and windows** IPC Windows: 01635 239070 **Roofing membrane** Sarnafil Ltd: 01603 748985 **Globe lighting** The Conran Shop: 020 7289 6851 **Shower** Matki plc: 01454 322888 **Bricks** Ibstock Brick Ltd: 0870 903 4000

MAKING WAVES

Peter and Linda Swanson have built a sleek, contemporary coastal home with feature glazing to maximise the stunning views and flood the interiors with light

WORDS: CAROLINE EDNIE PHOTOGRAPHY: NIGEL RIGDEN

The house has been designed so all the living spaces have views out to sea. On the north-facing side, rooms look out over surrounding hills. The sloping nature of the site allows the design to incorporate steps down to a spa area

"We built Killearnan Lodge as a house to be lived in and enjoyed, as opposed to something to be looked at and to go 'ooh aah!' to," says Peter Swanson. Even so, he and wife Linda are delighted with the striking newbuild home they now share on the Black Isle in the Scottish Highlands.

For although Killearnan Lodge is undoubtedly the practical living and breathing family home that the couple envisaged in the first instance, it is also, nevertheless, charmingly unique in its looks, as well as impressive in terms of its sprawling size — all 410m² of it.

Above: The northern side of the lodge has been kept very traditional, with a large entrance porch
Top right: Sleek white units in the open-plan kitchen contrast with the traditional family room
Right: The drawing room leads off from the entrance hall, is sited to maximise the ocean views

"The brief was simple," explains Peter, a local businessman. "The house's main aspect was to be across the water, so to this side of the building we wanted a lot of glass so that all the public rooms had wonderful views out to the sea. In terms of style we wanted a New England-type feel to it. On the other — north-facing — side of the house that looks onto the surrounding hills, we were keen to create Highland lodge-style interiors, so on this side everything has been kept very traditional with stone-worked edging and a big porch."

Peter and Linda originally bought the land which now houses Killearnan Lodge as an investment around four or five years ago. "It's an area that we liked to go walking in — it's a place of particular scenic beauty," says Peter. "Then after we had bought the site, every time we came out to visit it to have a walk around the area, we kept saying that we must build a home here."

At the time the couple lived in a large Victorian villa in Inverness, which proved to be the main testing ground when it came to dipping their toe in the self-build and renovation water. "Our previous house — and the related outhouses — was a major project for us. We started renovating the main house from scratch: taking the roof off it, re-plumbing, rewiring, re-heating and taking it back to what it was — back to the original features. We'd done a couple of renovations before that too — I'd like to think all of them were sympathetic," says Peter.

Killearnan Lodge is the couple's first major new build and as a result it proved a different yet no less demanding challenge. Indeed, the house has been designed as a one-and-a-half-storey home. However, when the couple realised how large the footprint of the house was going to be on one level, they realised they had no use for the first floor. "It occurred to us that we might not need to go upstairs at all," explains Peter. And at 410m², and cleverly built into the sloping hillside, there is certainly no shortage of space inside the house.

Essentially, Killearnan Lodge comprises three en suite bedrooms, with an additional bedroom which currently features as a large office space, in the eastern wing of the house. The open-plan kitchen, dining and family room (as

well as utilities and bathroom) are situated in the western end of the house, as is the music room, containing Peter's impressive collection of guitars.

At the heart of the house is an expansive entrance area to the north with sliding doors that retreat into the wall so that the whole centre depth of the house can be opened up. This area culminates in a similarly expansive drawing room/lounge area, taking full advantage of the wonderful south-facing sea views.

"We have one bedroom above the garage and that's it as far as the upper level goes," says Peter. "When people go up into the roof space they go completely wild, as it's just this huge, huge space. It's the whole length of the house, so effectively it could accommodate an additional seven en suite bedrooms — maybe more. I've been tempted to make it into a huge games area but I've been warned off that idea by Linda!" laughs Peter.

The Swansons achieved their unique vision in collaboration with Billy Reynolds of young Dingwall-based practice, Reynolds Architecture. "I'd known of Billy through a builder friend and had a look at some of his work," explains Peter. "I then had a chat with Billy and he

Left: Large feature glazing in the family area allows spectacular views out to sea
Above: Peter's music room stores his large collection of guitars

had some good ideas in line with my wife's vision for the house. Linda wanted an architect that could share her vision and one that she could work with closely as part of a team. Billy's got great ideas and great vision, and he's also 'user friendly'! As a result the collaboration from day one was first class."

The actual building of Killearnan Lodge — which was constructed using a bespoke timber frame and blockwork with white harled finishes, atop of which is a slate pitched roof — took close to a year, rather than the anticipated 10-month time frame. By this time, as Peter explains, he and Linda were desperate to get into their new home. "Our previous house sold after three days on the market, and we had to move out three weeks later. For the duration of the build we were renting a small two-bedroom flat — for myself, Linda, daughter Emma and our dog. So we were keen to keep on schedule."

Peter describes the build project as "a bit like an S curve". The site itself was a challenging one due to the steepness of the site, therefore a builder with a strong civil engineering background was chosen to tackle it. "The site is on a hill — a cut and fill site — so we had to cut into the hill and there had to be a lot of piling installed underneath to make sure the house didn't flex. This part of the build — namely the engineering and groundworks — was important," says Peter. The couple were on site every day to check progress. Indeed, Linda in particular was extremely hands-on with certain aspects of the build.

In terms of the interiors, Linda sourced most of the finishes and materials herself, and as a result has enhanced the light-filled spaces by means of a simple white and neutral backdrop and blonde ceramic flooring combined with the richer tones of the merbau timber floors.

In addition, Linda was also responsible for elements of the build such as landscaping of the sloping site — which also features a spa area with hot tubs and changing area. Linda is also currently busy extending outbuildings such as the stables and tool house.

"One of our friends has said that Linda is never happier when there's cement and sand lying around

"WE WANTED A HOUSE WITH OODLES OF LIGHT, AND WE'RE HIT BY IT ON EVERY ASPECT"

the front of the house," laughs Peter. "Killearnan Lodge may be finished but we've got five builders here at the moment working on various ongoing projects."

On a practical, energy-efficient level the house out-performs the Swansons' previous much smaller house. "We have underfloor heating that works very well, and although we have huge amounts of glass, which one would expect to account for some heat loss, it actually has the opposite effect. It only takes about two minutes of sun, even in the winter months, and the place is roasting. Our bills are much smaller than our previous house. It's a very efficient house for its size."

Indeed, there is little that Peter doesn't like about the new house. "We wanted a home with oodles of light, and we're hit by it on every aspect. The house picks up the light in the morning right through to the evening, and the view out from the front of the lodge is spectacular — you see ducks, otters and seals — it's like having our

Top: The minimalist main en suite bathroom features a frameless glass shower enclosure and discreet corner bath from Thistle Bathroom Studio
Above: The master bedroom opens onto a gallery with large French doors to make the most of the views towards the sea. A dressing room and en suite also lead off

very own menagerie!"

Peter has certainly put down roots in his new seaside home. "I think that we've achieved everything that we wanted to; in fact, we see this not only as our long-term home but also as our spiritual home." ◼

PROJECT NOTES

FACT FILE

Names: Peter and Linda Swanson
Professions: Businessman and homemaker
Area: Black Isle, Ross-shire
House type: Single-storey villa
House size: 410m²
Build route: Main contractor
Finance: Private
Construction: Timber frame and blockwork with suspended concrete floor
Warranty: NHBC
Build time: Ten months
Land cost: Undisclosed
Build cost: £800,000
Current value: £1,000,000
Cost/m²: £1,900

COST BREAKDOWN

Materials, frame, external walls, joinery, windows, blinds, doors, internal walls

	£320,000
Roof	£30,000
Flooring	£14,000
Plumbing	£30,000
Electrics	£42,000
Kitchen/built-in fittings	£24,000
Sanitaryware	£20,000
Landscaping/external works	£107,000

ONE-LEVEL LIVING

All the living spaces are on one floor, incorporating four bedrooms – three with en suites – an open-plan kitchen/dining/family room, a music room, garage and a large entrance hall which leads onto the drawing room. The large roof space area is currently unused. A hot tub area with changing rooms is situated on a lower level.

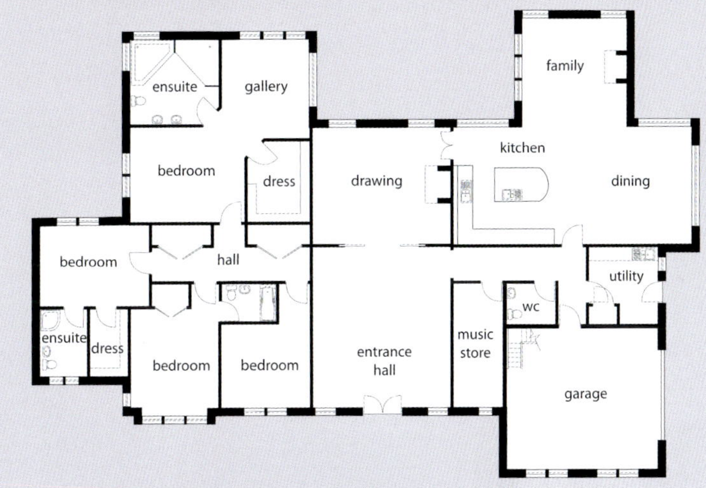

EUROPEAN UNION

Stuart and Trevor gave their architect a brief for a large, two-storey villa with an open plan feel and flexible living space

When Stuart Matheson and Trevor Blackman decided to undertake their first self-build project, they approached the task in hand with more zeal than zen. In fact, their quest to source every aspect of the build, from the construction method to the light switches, took them on something of a homebuilding pilgrimage of Europe. As a result of this methodical and meticulous approach, Stuart and Trevor are now in possession of a perfectly customised bespoke home set in a quarter of an acre of one of Edinburgh's most venerable enclaves.

The fact that Stuart and Trevor managed to secure the location was a miracle in itself, since sites in this exclusive suburb of Edinburgh rarely come on the market. "Originally, we were looking to buy a property closer to Edinburgh, as we were living on the outskirts in a 1930s villa," explains Stuart who, like Trevor, works in the city's legal and financial district. "But none of the properties we saw compared to our own house, which we'd spent more than seven years doing up. Then I saw this piece of land advertised in the local newspaper and realised we could actually build our own bespoke house — so we purchased it in May 2002. The land came with planning permission but we didn't like the house that had been designed, so we started again from scratch."

Since this was to be Stuart and Trevor's long-term home, a half-hearted approach just wasn't an option.

"ROD WAS SUCH A CONTRAST TO THE BIG COSTLY FIRMS. AND DESIGN-WISE IT WAS A VERY GOOD COLLABORATION BECAUSE HE'S VERY CLIENT-FOCUSED"

"We interviewed a number of architects — nine in total — and I then narrowed it down to three," Stuart continues. "The first one we chose we later parted company with, because the design was beyond our budget — twice our budget in fact. Unfortunately, by taking them on board we lost £10,000 and had to start again from scratch." Eventually, word of mouth led to locally-based Rod Malloch of RMA Architects. "Rod was such a contrast to the big costly firms. And design-wise it was a very good collaboration because he's very client-focused."

The brief that Stuart and Trevor presented to Rod was essentially for a large two-storey villa, with the first level embracing an open plan feel with lots of flexible living space, and a first floor featuring four bedrooms and three bathrooms. And this is duly what Rod designed spatially. Furthermore, Rod has orientated the extensively glazed main living spaces – dining, lounge and study – and master bedroom (with impressive balcony area) towards the south-facing secluded garden, which is also something of a suntrap.

The zinc monopitch roof is designed to increase the height and elevation of the south side and bring more light in, as the ceiling heights get higher and higher in the south-facing bedrooms. The design incorporates larch timber cladding as well as render. "The house is in a Conservation Area so we had to use natural materials," explains Rod. The result is a truly unique modern house incorporating traditional timber finishes. "Originally we were unsure about the timber on the top part of the house, but I think it actually makes the house," says Stuart.

"THE BLINDS ARE ATTACHED TO A WEATHER STATION AT THE SIDE OF THE HOUSE SO IF THE HOUSE GETS TOO WARM IN SUMMER, THE BLINDS AUTOMATICALLY COME DOWN"

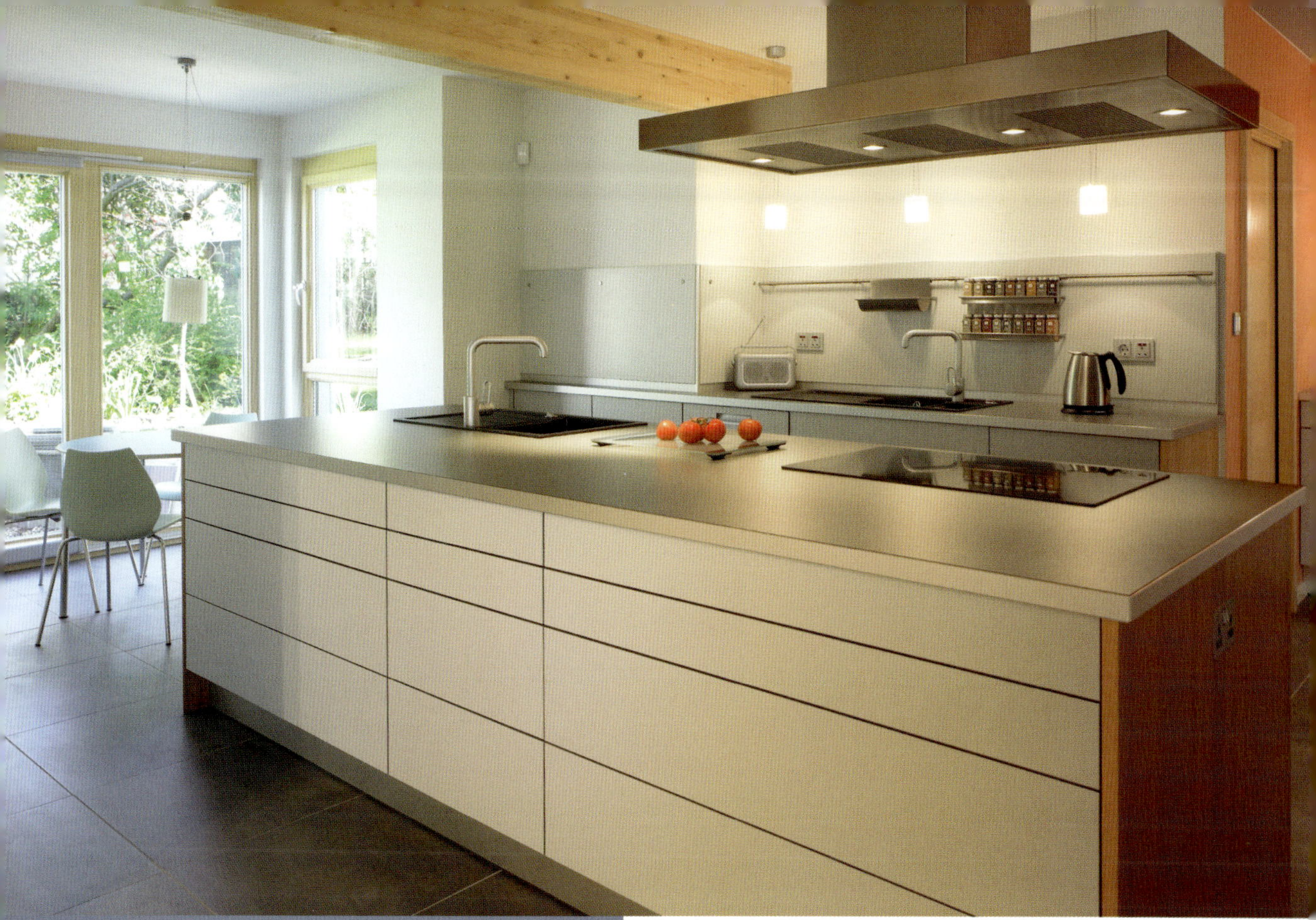

Above: Like so many of the fittings in the house, the kitchen was sourced from the Continent
Right: The south-facing bedrooms are light and airy
Below: The balcony area is perfectly positioned to make the most of the suntrap garden

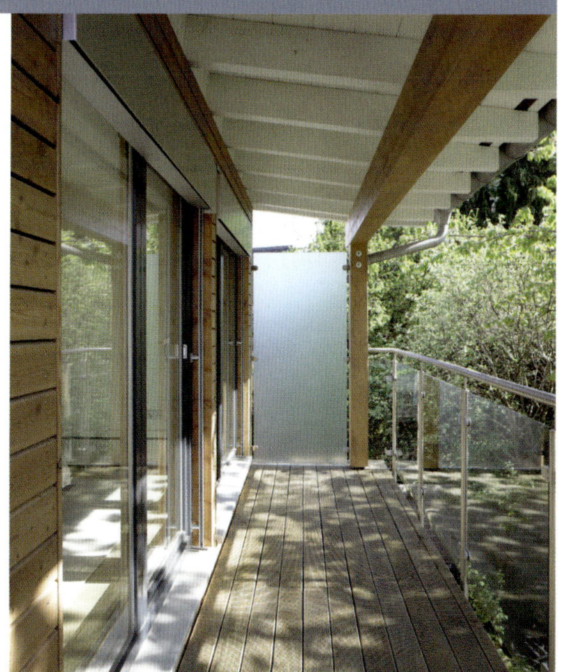

A contemporary house in a venerable Conservation Area is generally not regarded as the stuff of pain-free planning, and Stuart admits that the three-and-a-bit-year building process did have its moments. "Planning was painless enough but once we got to the Building Control stage it was trickier as they hadn't seen this type of house before, so it took a while to get the building warrant." The main reason for this was the Griffner construction.

"We were concerned about the way things are built in Britain and the length of time projects take, so we went in search of a different construction method," explains Stuart. "In Germany and Austria most of the houses are factory built — off the shelf or bespoke. We liked the feel of Griffner houses (an Austrian company that has been in business for around 10 years). The result is, I think, the first house that the company has built in the UK."

Essentially, the whole house was constructed in the Griffner factory. The components – which arrived in six trucks – feature built-in insulation and render on the outside with plasterboard on the inside. The advantage of the factory-built conditions meant that the build was not at the mercy of the elements, and the construction kit went up in five days. Prior to this, the foundations, slab and drainage were installed by a local contractor.

The design uses larch timber cladding, combined with render, and has a zinc monopitch roof

"THE REASON WE WERE SIX MONTHS LATE WAS THAT ALL THE TIMBER CEILINGS AND BEAMS HAD TO BE FIRE TREATED IN ORDER TO MEET BUILDING CONTROL RULES"

The internal fitting out was completed by the Irish branch of Griffner Coillte and includes many systems sourced by Stuart and Trevor on their European reconnaissance trips. These include the cutting-edge double-glazed windows by Austrian company Hrachowina Bauelemente Produktions, and the heating and electrical systems – including an EIB European Instabus electronic home system – by F&F Haustechnik. "The electronic home system controls the lighting, heating, and the blinds," explains Stuart. "The blinds are also attached to a weather station at the side of the house so if the house gets too warm in summer, the blinds automatically come down."

Stuart admits that although he and Trevor are delighted with the results, there are a few aspects of the build that they might have done differently: "While the construction process took place we rented three different flats. It took much longer than we anticipated, and if we did it again I think we probably would have kept our house and sold it when we moved," he admits.

"The reason that we were six months late was that all the timber ceilings and beams had to be fire treated in order to meet the UK Building Control rules, and this hadn't been anticipated. When the untreated timber went up it was lovely and light, but when it was treated it became oppressive, so we got our German contractor to wallboard the ceilings," Stuart explains.

"Also, at the outset Griffner Coillte made it clear that they would have done everything for us, but we decided to appoint a separate tradesman for the tiling and ask the kitchen manufacturer to take care of the installation. As it transpired these were the two least successful elements of the process.

"But if we forget about the time frame and how stressful it was during the build period," continues Stuart, who oversaw the whole build, "then I am really happy with the end result." In fact, such is Stuart's satisfaction that he's already thinking about doing it again. I think the whole thing would be much easier the second time around!" ■

PROJECT NOTES

FACT FILE

Names: Stuart Matheson and Trevor Blackman

Professions: Legal and financial professionals

Area: Edinburgh

House type: Detached five bedroom house

House size: 266m²

Build route: Factory built. Underbuilding and slab on separate contract

Finance: Private

Construction: Timber frame

Warranty: 10 Year Premier Guarantee

Build time: Nov '04 – Sep '05

Land cost: £340,000

Build cost: £560,000

Total cost: £900,000

Current Value: est. £1m

Cost/m2: £2,105

COST SAVING
10%

FLOORPLAN

The ground floor has a large living space with an extra guest bedroom if required. The master bedroom has a large balcony and dressing space plus dressing room.

USEFUL CONTACTS

Architect Rod Malloch, RMA Architects: 0131 346 0263 **Structural engineers** Malcolm Jacob: +353 (0)1462 6701; Andrew Brown: 0131 229 5553 **Main contractor** Griffner Coillte: +353 (0)443 7800 **Plumbing, heating, electrical, Instabus electronic home system** F&F Haustechnik: +43 (0)4224 82178-0 **Windows** Hrachowina Bauelemente: +43 (0)1258 3611-0 **Sanitaryware** Duravit: www.duravit. co.uk; Grohe: 0871 200 3414; Cesana (shower enclosures): www.cesana.it **Kitchen** Bulthaup: 020 7495 3663 **Kitchen appliances** De Dietrich: 0870 060 3230 **Fridges and freezer** Liebherr: www.liebherr.com **Insulation** Homatherm: +49 (0)346 514 1661 **Ceilings** Fermacell: www.fermacell.co.uk

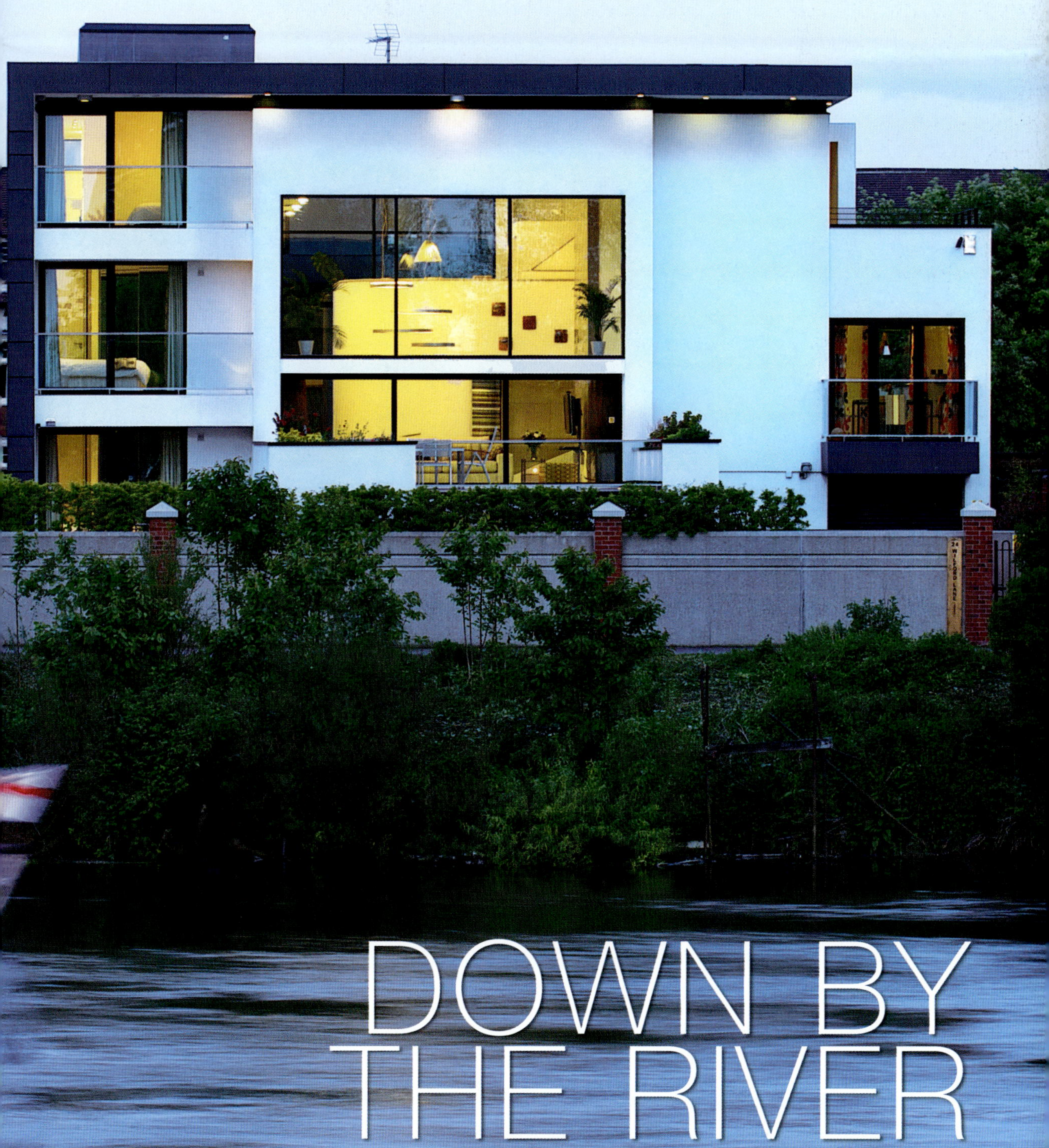

DOWN BY THE RIVER

Roger and Jane Paulson's first self-build is an extraordinary contemporary-style riverside home built for a very ordinary £1,000/m²

WORDS: JASON ORME PHOTOGRAPHY: JEREMY PHILLIPS

So it's a sunny day when H&R visit Roger and Jane Paulson at their little piece of California on the River Trent in Nottingham, and we're sat outside on one of their several terraces eating a lovely lunch watching the passing entertainment that the river brings. We're listening to the cheers rising from a game of 20/20 cricket nearby (you can see the floodlights from the terrace). H&R is having a much better time than usual on a typical Monday lunchtime and thinking that surely there has to be some catch to all of this?

Roger and Jane's story, in a nutshell, goes like this: charming, down-to-earth people who have never built a house before but manage to pull off an audacious contemporary home, with none of the downsides that other contemporary homes seem to have, in the best location their home town has to offer, and all for around £1,000/m² — a ridiculously low price for something of this quality, and around half the price of many projects H&R has seen that have the same feel but none of the quality of design.

It's not as though Roger and Jane approached this project in an entirely conventional or risk-free way either — indeed, it sometimes feels as if they kind of ended up here through a mixture of circumstance and good fortune rather than the usual cold calculation. "We had been living in our 1930s house — the house our children grew up in — for 20 years," says Jane. "Once the children left, and we thought about extending and remodelling it for the fourth time, we began to think perhaps we needed a change. We wanted to give ourselves a bit of shock treatment to do something, well, a bit different."

Different for Roger and Jane meant purchasing an interesting rectangular riverside development site in

The new home sits
next to the river,
with no less than six
terraces to make the
most of the views.
The main terrace
is structurally
independent of the
house in case of
flooding

Left: The main living space is big on style and impact. The light fitting helps to create a sense of cosiness in the huge atrium space. Sliding glass doors from Allied Glazing are the only barrier — even the floor finish is the same inside and out

the local neighbourhood just a few minutes' walk from Nottingham city centre. It was home to two rather run-down buildings — a 1960s dormer bungalow (which was next to the river, at the back of the plot) and a coach house to the roadside front. "In truth, it was a brave decision," says Roger. "It's not like the road is full of million-pound houses, and the dormer bungalow at the rear was derelict — a home for squatters and local drug users."

There followed much discussion about what to do with their new life-changing property, and the decision fell to build a house for themselves in place of the dormer bungalow, replacing the coach house at the front of the site with a block of apartments that would help, in time, to finance the whole venture. "It was something new and exciting for us, and we were obviously wary but just excited to have a project to work on," says Jane.

The couple then made the first of their key decisions — to take up a contact made through friends and meet with local designer Andy Roberts, who was keen to get into

"THE ROAD IS NOT FULL OF MILLION-POUND HOUSES, AND THE DORMER BUNGALOW AT THE REAR WAS DERELICT — A HOME FOR SQUATTERS AND LOCAL DRUG USERS"

bespoke contemporary homes in addition to his day job in a practice devoted to more commercial projects. They all hit it off right away, Roger and Jane liked what Andy had to say on house design (more of which later) and Andy got to work on making the most of the site layout.

"The site posed several constraints," says Andy, "all of which influenced the design in some way." First, Andy needed to work out a plan for the apartment block that would maximise the amount of apartments in the space — along with their requisite car-parking spaces, turning areas and so on — but would also allow the house that effectively sits behind it, and facing it, to have privacy and singularity. Cue much work with the local planning department, which Andy knew pretty well anyway, to convince them of their plans.

Second, the river obviously posed a flood risk so any new development would have to design out any potential flooding. Third, the rear of the house faced north, so the design would have to take this into account not just from an outside living perspective but also in a thermal context, particularly pertinent considering the amount of glazing within most contemporary designs.

With these parameters in mind, Andy began an intensive briefing process with Jane and Roger, which Jane in particular took up with enthusiasm. "I asked her to initially go through around 300 images I'd got, and she'd collected, from magazines, and not just put them into piles of 'like', 'don't like' and 'don't know' but tell me, for each one, what it was that she liked about them," says Andy. "I could then begin to interpret why and perhaps see the reasons behind her decisions that might not have been obvious to her. For example, I noted that she liked contemporary spaces that focused on the doorways, and it was only when I put four or five of these images together that I noticed a common theme, which in this instance was full-height doors."

This intensive programme was highly enjoyable for the

"SO MANY HOMES ARE BUILT REALLY WITHOUT THE OWNERS IN MIND, RESULTING IN WASTED SPACES AND AN UNEASY FIT"

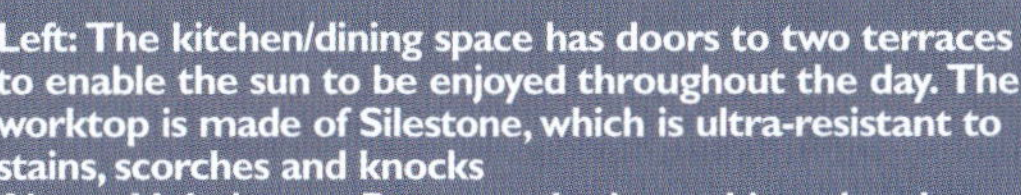
Left: The kitchen/dining space has doors to two terraces to enable the sun to be enjoyed throughout the day. The worktop is made of Silestone, which is ultra-resistant to stains, scorches and knocks
Above: Upholsterer Roger made the cushioned pads on the wall (and the built-in handrail) that soften the contemporary lines. There's a hidden door leading to a stairwell that serves the bedrooms

couple. "It was just so refreshing for us to really think about houses in such a way," says Jane.

Andy continues: "So many homes are built really without the owners in mind, resulting in wasted spaces and an uneasy fit. We worked tirelessly on this theme, so that there was a mix of open and cosy spaces, of drama and intimacy, and most importantly places for all parts of their lives. So the result is that they have the perfect spot for Sunday afternoon barbecues [including a simple sheltered outdoors space — how simple but brilliant], Saturday evening dinner parties, watching the tennis on the telly, sitting out on a Sunday morning enjoying the river, and so on. Every place has its time, and every time its place."

Armed with a full brief, Andy then hit upon a way of working that would be key to the whole process.

"I wanted two things out of the project in essence. Firstly, to show that we could build high-quality contemporary spaces to a modest budget and at a guaranteed price; and secondly, that I wanted Roger and Jane to concentrate their thoughts on the things that mattered to them — the decisions about key interiors.

"I call it decision overload," Andy continues. "Self-builders in my experience seem to spend so much energy on every detail of the project that they are completely exhausted when it comes to thinking about the things that really matter. They're also pressured into making detailed decisions before any of the space has been created; it's very difficult to visualise. When a self-builder is busy worrying about other things, like plumbers turning up late or materials delivery or a tiny construction detail, they miss out on the key decisions, and the fun of it all.

"I also wanted to take away a lot of the budget worry for Roger and Jane. The budget we approached in the same way as a commercial venture; namely, we guaranteed a price for the weathertight shell, and when it came to the fitting out, allotted PC (prime cost) sums that Roger and Jane could then elect to go over if they desired. I said to them that the

shell itself would cost £780/m² (a fixed price of £265,000) and the interiors around £220/m². This was partly going from experience but also because I knew contractors and the prices they would charge, but also we did an awful lot of creative 'value engineering'."

This other commercial-sounding term — value engineering — would prove to be the key to Roger and Jane achieving a well-beyond-average look on an average budget. "I wanted things to look great but realised that, with a bit of creativity, Roger and Jane could achieve them in a relatively good-value way. So, for example, on the side of the apartment block that Roger and Jane face, rather than building a simple wall we opted for plywood boxes that were then given different polished finishes. It cost a couple of thousand pounds more but was well worth it. With the front door we wanted to mimic the look of the brilliant garage door but couldn't afford to, so the joiner

made it up for us and we saved £1,000s.

"Likewise, we were efficient with the guys on site. For a start, in the first hour on site we walked them around individually, showed them the plans and really sold how different it was to them. They really bought into it, and we had zero problems even though some of the detailing was quite different to what they were used to. There was a lot of craftsmanship in evidence, and I think people responded to that."

This is a deeply thoughtful and sophisticated approach to self-build. Roger and Jane have enjoyed a very pleasant middle ground — somewhere between the hands-on, up-to-wellies-in-the-mud self-build battle, and the hands-off, traditional architect/client approach. They also benefitted from an exceptional site foreman — Andy calls him "a datum of exceptional quality", and it's difficult to disagree; the number-one reason contemporary homes fail is poor on-site practice.

"We'd be tempted to move and do it all again," says Roger, sitting back and looking out over the river. "But I doubt we'd get a better home than this, or a better location than this in the whole city." ■

PROJECT NOTES

FACT FILE

Names: Roger and Jane Paulson
Professions: Upholsterer and Medical Researcher
Area: Nottingham
House type: Contemporary-style three bedroom, three storey
House size: 450m²
Build route: Architect designed and managed
Finance: NatWest
Construction: Blockwork and steel
Build time: June '06 – Aug '07
Land cost: £250,000
Build cost: £465,000
Total cost: £715,000
Value on completion: Unknown
Cost/m²: £1,033

AN INTERNAL BALCONY

The house's main living spaces are sited predominately on the first floor, to make the most of the fabulous views from a higher outlook. The house has six terraces in total, with the main terrace structurally independent. On plan it's easy to see the modular approach to the layout, with a distinct bedroom block on the side, housing three bedrooms sharing their own stairwell, each with an outside space; the middle block for living, and the left hand block for utility.

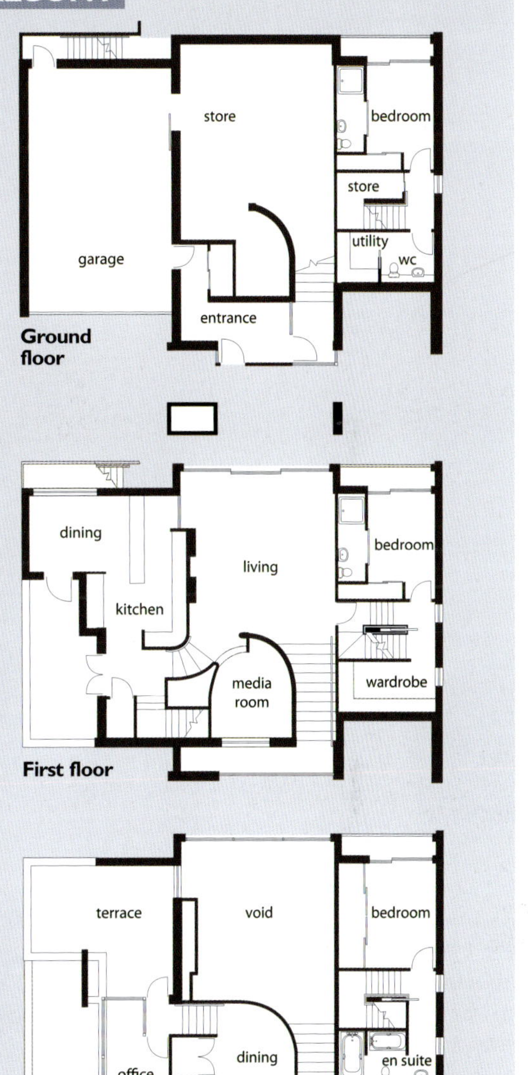

SITE SPECIFIC

A small, awkward urban site inspired a particularly creative design solution for green self-builders Jackie Strube and Alan Stone

WORDS: JASON ORME   IMAGES: NIGEL RIGDEN

Vision is a much over-used word in self-build circles — as in, 'We're glad we had the vision to appoint such a brilliant architect,' or perhaps, 'We had the vision to imagine this three-acre greenfield site as the setting for our new dream home.' But no one could argue the fact that real 'vision' is just what Jackie Strube and Alan Stone had when they took on what must surely have been one of the most unattractive plots in Britain — and went on to create a sleek, sustainable new house for themselves.

The couple, who had lived in a terrace in Brighton for 13 years, set out with the aim of building something as energy efficient as possible but couldn't face giving up living within close reach of the seafront and town centre. After months of searching for something that they began to suspect wasn't there, they stumbled upon a rather unusual bit of land coming up at auction — and it looked a million miles away from what they expected a self-build plot to look like. "It was very small," begins Jackie, "and wedged in between two rows of terraces — it had been used for years as a builders' yard. It had access from the street down a sloping driveway and when you got there, it was small and almost triangular-shaped. It was covered in debris and a plentiful supply of discarded mattresses as well as a rusting car."

Not a terribly appealing proposition then, one would think — but it gets a lot worse. The 150m² site was completely overlooked on three sides by the backs of the

"THE HOUSE WAS BUILT IN TIMBER FRAME TO ENJOY LOW U-VALUES ON THE THINNEST WALL DEPTH"

terraces next to it and came with planning permission for a disabled-use bungalow — the site only getting consent for development strictly on the basis that it had a limited ridge height no higher than a single storey with flat roof, not exceeding the height of the neighbours' fences.

Not entirely surprising, then, that the couple were able to purchase the plot for £86,000. They then set about working out what to do with it.

"We knew we wanted something that would have a minimal impact on the environment, in terms of energy use but also in terms of the immediate vicinity. In a way, the plot being in such a bad state helped us to gain local support for our plans, because anything would have been an improvement on what was there," explains Jackie.

Ollie Blair from local practice DRP Architects was called in to help come up with a design that met the environmental requirements but also satisfied Jackie and Alan's needs for viable and comfortable living accommodation in the best way possible — for this was to be a family home. "It was a small area to work with and we knew that we had to make the most of any space that we could create," explains Ollie, who goes on to describe the two key difficulties in the design as a lack of "space and light".

The resulting house is certainly one of the most enterprising solutions to a difficult site we've ever seen. Hidden behind large wooden gates and based on a broadly T-shaped design, life in the house revolves around the open

Left: The main living space, with its polished concrete floor, combines eating, living and cooking functions. Above: The interiors are surprisingly light and tranquil using natural light brought in from above

plan space which contains a kitchen, dining area and living space. Two bedrooms and a bathroom are situated in the other section of the house. Every space is used — a corridor doubles as a library, a small recess behind the front door is host to the utility cupboard.

The house was built in timber frame, which the couple opted for not just because of the perfectly valid sustainability argument but also because it could enjoy low U-values on the thinnest possible wall depth. For a house this tiny — the total floor area is just 80m² — there is no sense of tightness or clutter. While this is helped by the fact that the couple bought lots of new furniture and cleared out their collectibles before moving in — much of the retro-chic new furniture was bought on eBay — it's also down to the mastery of a really clever layout.

This is a scheme that really squeezes out every last dash of space from the limited amount available on the site. A lot of the build cost went into site preparation, in particular digging down as much as possible to enable extra volume without breaching the ridge height restrictions; secondly, the exterior walls of the house were built right up to the boundary, to ensure the most efficient use of space. Yet at the same time, although the house doesn't have much of a garden, there is a surprisingly pleasant courtyard-style space accessible through the double doors of the main bedroom. It all feels unbelievably tranquil.

"It's very quiet. We can't overhear anyone's music,"

Top: The house consists of many green features, including a sedum roof, which helps to reduce water run-off and, it is argued, improve the thermal efficiency of the roof structure
Above: Narrow windows help to bring in incidental light wherever possible
Right: Collected rainwater is recycled using galvanized steel guttering from Lindab. Lime-based render allows walls to breathe

says Jackie. You'd also think that a house of this size and in this overlooked position would feel dim, but thanks to a series of strategically placed roof lanterns, vertical light — the most consistent of all lights — streams in, infused throughout with the help of neutral interior themes.

In addition to the incredible use of space and light, it's the eco features that make the house all the more impressive. Fed up with paying soaring fuel bills in a cold and damp terrace, the couple determined to make their new home as cosy and manageable as possible. First of all, despite its many problems, the site was south facing, so Jackie and Alan made the decision to make all south-facing rooms have sliding doors to make the most of the available light, also maximising solar gain. The floors are all polished concrete (ie concrete poured in situ and sealed) which not only looks great and enables the underfloor heating to work incredibly well, but also acts as an impressive heat store for all that passive solar gain and for the underfloor heating too.

Along similar lines, a sedum roof not only reduces the physical impact of the house on those overlooking it – from the back bedrooms of those neighbouring terraces it must just look like a nice bit of garden – but it also helps to collect rainwater (although the thermal performance of grass roofs is a point for debate). Outside, the paving is made up of shredded recycled tyres that feel rather bouncy to walk on, while the rainwater is collected in old barrels. Inside, low-voltage lighting works alongside sheep's wool insulation to reduce energy consumption. Even the interiors have a green theme — the remarkable orange worktop is made from recycled glass.

"It has been quite a gamble," says Jackie, "but it has worked." It most certainly has — the house is a masterclass in the joys of small living and is testament to the belief that only in the constraints of a plot such as this and eco objectives such as Jackie and Alan's, can such a pleasing and innovative solution be reached. ■

PROJECT NOTES

FACT FILE

Names: Jackie Strube and Alan Stone
Professions: Work in local government
Area: Brighton
House type: Two bedroom single storey
House size: 80m²
Build route: Main contractor
Finance: Private
Construction: Timber frame
Build time: Aug '06 – May '07
Land cost: £86,000
Build cost: £200,000
Total cost: £286,000
Current value: £300,000
Cost/m²: £2,500

COST SAVING
5%

PERMEABLE DRIVEWAYS

October 2008 saw the introduction of the 'Future Water' legislation by the Government. This states that homeowners who want to pave over their driveway with a non-permeable surface, such as tarmac or concrete, will be required to obtain planning permission first. The aim is to encourage the use of permeable hardscapes that will allow rain water to soak away and avoid flooding. Hardscape surfaces such as gravel are a neat solution that won't require planning permission, but there is a permeable paving option too — Aquaflow from Hanson Formpave. This has a SUDS system that allows rainwater to filter down the sides of the block pavers, through a layer that cleans it (making the rainwater PH neutral), and into a sub-base under the driveway. This cleaned water is then stored and released at a controlled rate back into water courses to avoid flooding, or a pump can be fitted allowing homeowners to harvest the rainwater and reuse it for non-potable purposes.

USEFUL CONTACTS

Architect DRP Architects:01273 888080 **Windows** Rationel:01869 248181 **Galvanized steel gutter system** Lindab:0121 585 2780 **Underfloor heating** Uponor:01455 550355 **Condensing boiler** Vaillant:01634 292300 **Rooflights/ lanterns** Glazing Vision: 01842 815581 **Green roof** Bauder:01473 257671 **Green driveway/paving** Hanson Formpave:01594 836999

AN UNUSUAL SITE DEMANDS A CREATIVE FLOORPLAN

The angled T-shaped design is based around a main living/eating/cooking space, with two bedrooms fed off a corridor hallway. Plenty of French and folding sliding doors help to give the impression of more space, as well as create more light, in this 80m² scheme.

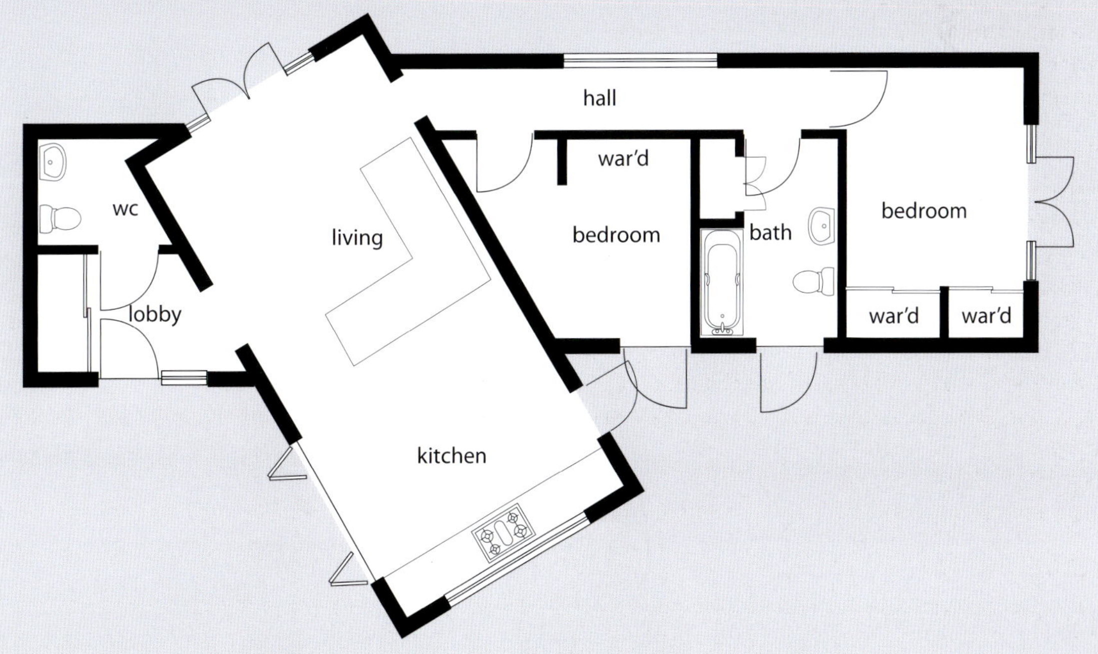

A NEW ANGLE

Adie and Lana Harkin's extraordinary new eco home juxtaposes soft curves with sharp angles to dramatic effect

WORDS: DEBBIE JEFFERY   PHOTOGRAPHY: JEREMY PHILLIPS

When Adie and Lana Harkin first saw the design for their new family home, they were completely blown away. Tired of the traditional house they'd lived in for the past 14 years, they'd become restless and planned to move on, until they realised that replacing their old home with an exciting new model solved all their problems in one hit.

"Our stone-clad 1940s house came with four acres of land," says Adie. "We were delighted when we first bought it and went on to build a large annexe with a basement swimming pool and games room on the site, but as time moved on we became more and more unhappy with the main house, which was dark, old-fashioned and not particularly well built."

The couple viewed numerous properties to buy but nothing suited, and as Adie had always harboured an ambition to build his own home, they approached local architect Julian Marsh, who is well known for designing contemporary and environmentally friendly buildings — several of which the Harkins had read about and admired.

When the planning officer first saw Julian's proposal for a replacement dwelling in the green belt he simply sat and smiled. "We were concerned that he felt we were crazy to take on such an ambitious project, but he actually loved the whole idea and it sailed through planning," Adie recalls.

The three-storey house is carefully arranged in relation to the outdoor space, partially embedded into the sloping ground to meet height restrictions, and literally growing up out of the hillside. This low-energy design incorporates solar panels on the south-facing roof, a rainwater-recovery system for watering plants and flushing WCs, and passive stack ventilation.

A double-height hallway joins two distinct vertical elements — the main living spaces and an informal kitchen-cum-dining room, which all lead onto outdoor terraces that make the most of the orientation.

"By digging down into the site we were able to place two of the four en suite bedrooms on the lower level for our sons Sean and Adrian," says Lana. "Our eldest son, Kevin, is away in the army and stays in the separate annexe when he comes home, and we felt that the other

boys would also prefer their own private area where they can make as much noise as they like."

The couple's 12 year-old daughter, Christina, has her own enviable room and en suite up on the first floor, positioned to the other side of a bridge-style landing from the master suite, and both bedrooms open onto balconies. So unusual and complex is the design of the house that none of the rooms form traditional boxes, but instead employ curves, voids and angles to create exciting shapes and spaces.

"When I tried to sketch out a room layout I kept coming up with a square house, so it was amazing to see Julian's design on paper — and even more incredible to watch it growing out of the ground," says Adie. "Our brief was very basic. I didn't want huge, unwelcoming rooms and Lana simply asked for a kitchen sink facing to the front of the house. Other than that we left it to Julian

to work his magic and we certainly weren't disappointed!"

Not everyone was so enamoured with the couple's plan, however, and their daughter was initially anxious about seeing their old home demolished while the family moved into nearby rented accommodation for nine months. Later, they returned to live on site in the existing annexe complex next to the new house, with Adie acting as site foreman, project manager, labourer and tea boy, working long hours every day throughout the build.

"I was more used to wearing a suit than lugging hundreds of concrete blocks, but I have to say that I thoroughly enjoyed the whole process," he explains. "I was happy to organise the various tradesmen because I knew exactly the standard of finish I wanted. I would follow everyone around with a spirit level — which they

"I KNEW THE EXACT STANDARD OF FINISH I WANTED AND WOULD FOLLOW EVERYONE AROUND WITH A SPIRIT LEVEL!"

obviously hated! In the end, though, not one floor tile was laid squint and the workmanship is truly superb."

Once the previous two-storey house had been demolished, excavation work began to create the lower ground floor bedrooms and bathrooms, and Adie found he was in his element. He also took on the role of interior designer, ordering materials and choosing all the fixtures and fittings for every room in the house.

"I don't particularly enjoy shopping, but absolutely nothing came with us from the old house – it all looked too dated – so we started from scratch and selected minimal, contemporary designs and bold colours which would complement the shapes of Julian's building," Adie says.

Despite enjoying the daily challenges of constructing such a large and ambitious house, first-time self-builder Adie still admits to the odd moment of self-doubt. The property is massively insulated, and the external insulation and render required dry weather conditions before it could be applied to the blockwork walls. Weeks of endless rain held up the whole project and left Adie worrying that his family were suffering needlessly.

"I did briefly wonder whether we should have just bought a modern house, but now that it's finished and everyone is so pleased, I know that we did the right thing," he says. "Not only is it bright and open, which is a real contrast to our previous house, but it also feels healthier to live in, and whenever we're away we can't wait to return home."

With no hard and fast budget set for the project, Adie admits that costs spiralled out of control almost as much as the shape of the house, due to the high level of specification he and Lana chose as the work progressed. The final build cost came in at around £950,000. Determined not to scrimp, the Harkins have incorporated

The home cinema features an impressive wide screen, theatre seats, spotlighting and black-out blinds

"I'M NO ECO WARRIOR, BUT I KNEW IT MADE FINANCIAL SENSE TO INCLUDE THINGS LIKE RAINWATER HARVESTING"

state-of-the-art music, lighting and security systems in addition to the many environmentally friendly features throughout the house. Even all of the new furniture had to be custom-made in order to fit the unusual angles of the house, with joiner Steve Adcock crafting everything from bespoke cupboards to wardrobes.

"I'm no eco warrior, but I knew it made sound financial sense to include things like rainwater harvesting — both for ourselves and for future owners of the house," says Adie. "It would seem awful to have this opportunity and not consider the bigger picture, and Julian Marsh excels at this kind of design."

Within two years of their old home being unceremoniously flattened, the family were happily ensconced in their contemporary new abode. The boys love having their own space and also occupy the main sitting room in the evenings, which was specifically designed with a wall-mounted plasma screen and concealed cabling for gaming. Adie, however, heads for the neighbouring snug, with its curved red wall, comfortable sofas and stylish woodburning stove, which is the ideal place to relax and read the papers.

"We all have our own favourite rooms, and I tend to spend a lot of time in the kitchen," says Lana. "It's a large house but every inch of space is well used, and in the summer we really enjoy throwing open the glass doors onto the various balconies and terraces. Light was what we craved, and we're certainly enjoying plenty of it now. In fact, we've gone from one extreme to the other, and living in such a bright, open space lifts everyone's mood." ■

PROJECT NOTES

FACT FILE

Names: Adie and Lana Harkin
Professions: Businessman/ entrepreneur and homemaker/mother
Area: Nottingham
House type: Three-storey, four-bedroom detached house
House size: 335m²
Build route: Self-managed subcontractors
Finance: Private
Construction: Insulated blockwork, stainless steel-clad roof
Build time: Nov '05 – July '07
Land cost: £850,000
Build cost: £950,000
Total cost: £1,800,000
Current value: £2,300,000
Cost/m²: £2,836

COST SAVING
22%

USEFUL CONTACTS

Architect Marsh Grochowski Architects: 0115 941 1761 **Insulated render** Sto: 01505 324262 **Slate tiles** Porcelanosa: 0800 915 4000 **Kitchen** Wentworth Kitchens, Nottingham: 0115 982 0007 **Control system for lighting etc** AMX UK Ltd: 01904 343100 **Interior joinery** Steve Adcock Interiors: 0115 950 2055 **Glass staircase** Mitchell Architectural Ltd: 0115 987 6565 **Security** Mercury Fire & Security: 0115 931 2324 **Engineer** Ward Cole: 0115 950 4645 **Environmental consultants** Furness Green Partnership: 0115 948 2612 **Electrical contractors** Ian Smith Electrical: 01949 843253 **Plumbing contractors** Howvale: 0115 945 5050 **Windows** Ideal Combi: 01582 860 940 **Roofing** JTC Roofing: 07740 279030 **Underfloor heating** Sensible Heat: 01273 475834 **Interior glass doors** Moda Interiors: 01332 554995 **Woodburner** Robeys: 01773 820940

FITTING INTO UNUSUAL SPACES

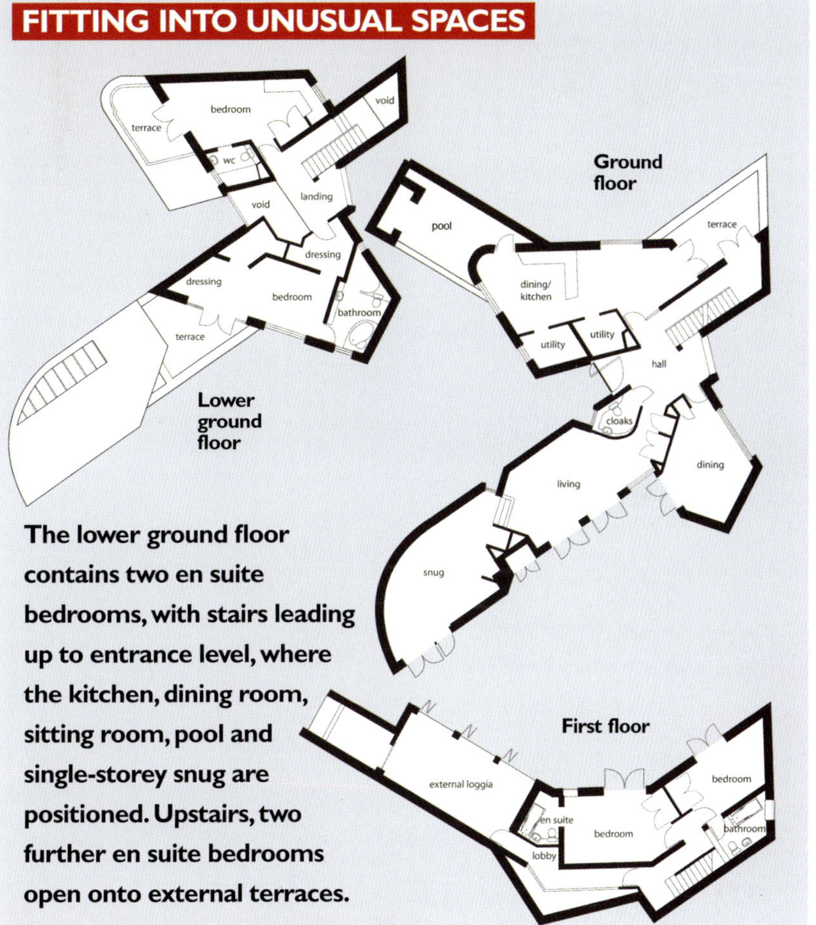

The lower ground floor contains two en suite bedrooms, with stairs leading up to entrance level, where the kitchen, dining room, sitting room, pool and single-storey snug are positioned. Upstairs, two further en suite bedrooms open onto external terraces.

CREATING CURVED WALLS

Adie and Lana Harkin's house is full of unusual angles but it is the curves which require the closest attention to detail, in order to get a surface that is smooth and evenly bowed. Externally, there are a number of ways to achieve the look, including drawing out the desired curve on plywood or using a steel framing product such as Flex-Ability, but producing a rendered smooth finish is a bit trickier. Combining external insulation and a thick coat of render from a specialist manufacturer such as Sto is probably your best bet.

Internally, curves are notoriously hard to get right — most plasterboards can be curved when wetted but it's not an exact science. The best option is to specify a curved plasterboard, such as Lafarge's GTEC Contour Board (lafargeplasterboard. co.uk) which is a lightweight, high-strength 6mm-thick plasterboard which enables the creation of curved features in wall linings, partitions and ceilings. It's suitable for direct decoration or gypsum skim-coat plastering.

Gyproc's Glasroc MultiBoard is another option (british-gypsum. com). It's made using glass-fibre reinforcement, and so can be easily bent.

PREFORMED CHARACTER

Paul Gyseman's new riverside home combines cutting-edge design with the latest in prefabricated building systems

WORDS: CLIVE FEWINS   PHOTOGRAPHY: JEREMY PHILLIPS

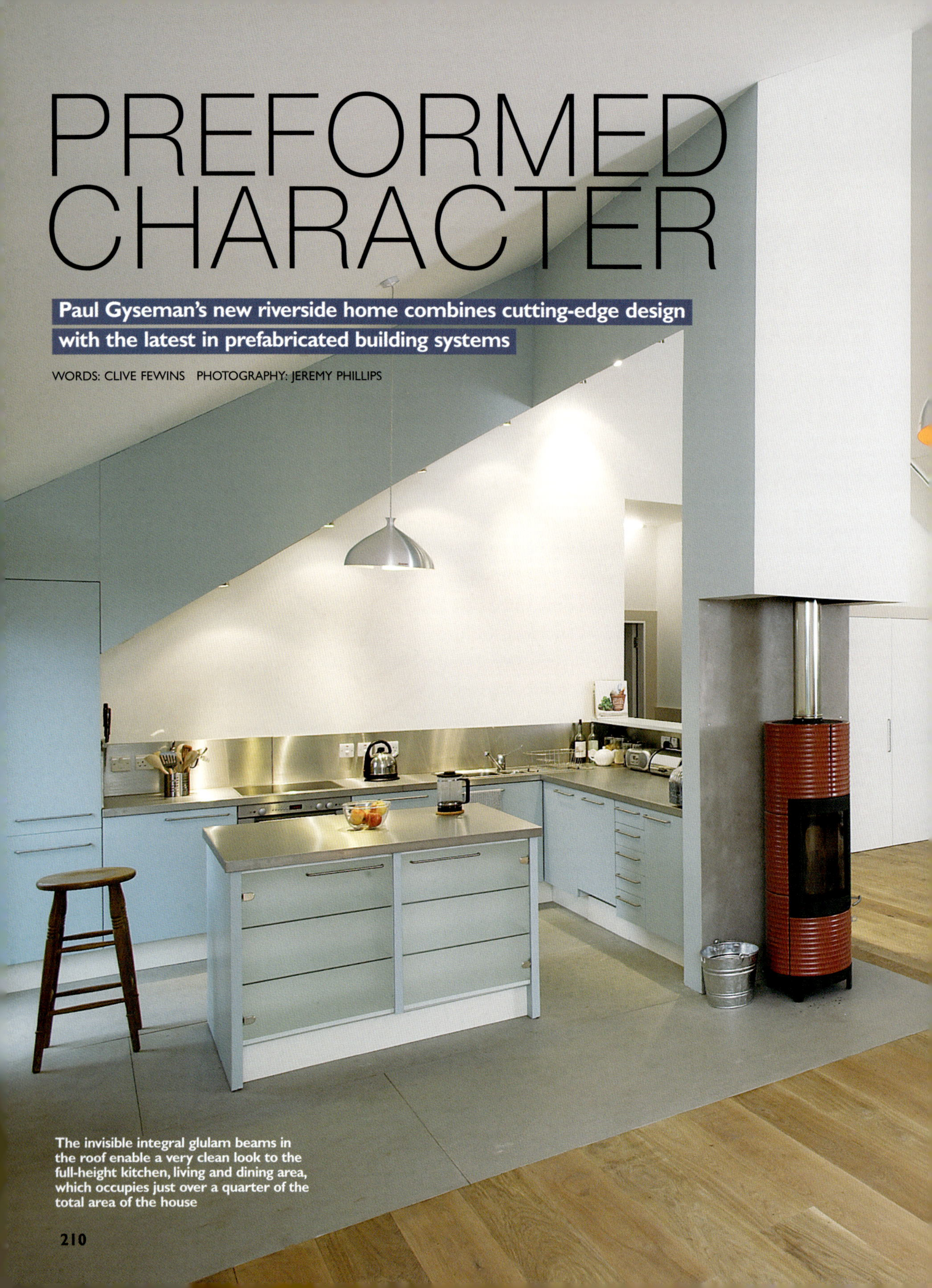

The invisible integral glulam beams in the roof enable a very clean look to the full-height kitchen, living and dining area, which occupies just over a quarter of the total area of the house

Paul Gyseman is looking forward to the day when he will be able to walk to the end of his raised decking and lower his fishing rod into the infant river Wensum. That time is still a month or two away as he has just moved into his new house in rural Norfolk and there is a lot of work in store designing the garden surrounding the 214m² building, which was built using an engineered system constructed off site.

However, the river is only six metres away from the single-storey house, so there's plenty of incentive to learn to fish — particularly because gaining permission to place the house in that position proved quite a stressful task.

The original permission – which came with the plot – was for a house to replace the long rectangular single-storey brick building that had started life as a chicken shed and later housed an engineering workshop. Through the friends who had originally found the plot for him – structural engineer Alan Conisbee and his wife Marie – Paul secured the services of award-winning architect Anthony Hudson and decided to apply for permission to place the new house nearer the river.

"We realised that to get what we wanted it would be wise to stick to the long, low shape that had been approved," Paul says. "In other words, the footprint had not changed, but the house, if we were to succeed, would move about 12 metres."

The planners at Breckland District Council had no objection, but the permission depended upon whether the Environment Agency, who are responsible for the river, would approve, and this hinged on whether the site was liable to flooding. Through commissioning a detailed report, Paul was able to satisfy the criteria that the risk of a flood was likely to occur no more frequently than once in 100 years, so the permission went ahead.

All this took most of 2003, but Paul was in no hurry as he was living in a flat in London that he intended to keep, for the foreseeable future, after moving into the new Norfolk house. Besides, he already had permission to build, so this was his fallback position.

A condition of the approval was that the floor level of the house should be raised one metre above the ground and that all the electrics should be positioned one metre

above the floor. There are also some elements in the build — for example the MDF wall linings — that are deliberately designed to be sacrificial in the unlikely event of a flood.

In addition to this, orientation proved quite a problem and led to long discussions with Anthony and the project architect, Dieter Kleiner.

"The problem was how best to position the house so that it performed to its maximum (we already had a panelled building using off-site construction techniques in mind) and at the same time make the most of the rural location," Paul says.

Eventually Anthony, Dieter and Paul decided to position the long low building with its double-pitched roof end-on to the river, which is to the north of the site. This means that the large window in the north-east corner that wraps around the building affords a view of the river. It brings in morning light in the dining area, while the afternoon light comes through a seven metre-long bank of windows to the north of the entrance that both slide and fold back.

The sophisticated nature of the window — it passes unsupported round the corner of the building — has been possible because of the nature of the construction system they chose: a panelled system that's made-to-measure in 'cassettes', or complete insulated panels of sandwiched material, that interlock together on site. The manufacturer is Framework Construction Design and Management.

The invisible integral glulam beams in the roof panel system enable a very clean look to the full-height kitchen, living and dining area, which occupies just over a quarter of the total area of the house. Paul says. "They also gave a very good price — just under £240,000 — and were keen to do the job."

"We'd been doing schools and other local authority buildings but we're keen to get into the bespoke self-build market," says Martin Peat, contracts director of Framework. "Every one of our structures is bespoke — we don't have standard panel sizes — and for self-builders we can also do frame-only packages.

"The key to our system is the ring beam — an arrangement of glulam beams invisible from the inside," he says. "This surrounds the building at plate level, and, together with the engineering of the roof, enables windows such as the wraparound one with frameless glazing at the north-

"I LIKE THE CONTRAST BETWEEN THE SMOOTH MATERIALS USED IN THE INTERIOR AND THE ROUGHNESS OF THE OUTSIDE"

east corner to be 'hung' from the structure. In theory we could have included more windows like this in the house and they could have been somewhat wider if desired.

"The roof panel system with its invisible integral glulam beams also allows for the absence of visible roof trusses on the inside of the roof on a single storey house like Paul's."

Dieter has a keen eye for angles and has made this space especially interesting by creating a 'frame' feature of the boxed-in main flue to the log burner and flue from the kitchen extractor system.

"These are two unavoidable necessities, and could look very ugly as they have to vent directly through the steeply pitched roof," says Paul. "Dieter has got round this cleverly by making a unified feature of them that also contains the kitchen lighting.

"I like the contrast between the materials used in the house, and also between the smoothness of the interior and the roughness of the outside," says Paul.

"The exterior cedar shingles are the key here. I think they give the house an organic look that suits the wooded surroundings perfectly. This is because in different lights they have a patchwork effect that I call an 'autumn leaf look' when the light shines on them. I think the house looks just right in its setting.

"To me, it's a house that is visually very attractive from the outside, mainly because there's no break where you would expect to see gutters," Paul says. "There is a soakaway beneath but that's all. Using a construction system like Framework has proved an ideal way of building this house and made it exceptionally warm and well insulated — heating is by the a log burning stove and a handful of electric wall-mounted heaters that are on a very low setting. The other thing I like about it is that it's really built to last and it suits my lifestyle." ■

PROJECT NOTES

FLOORPLAN

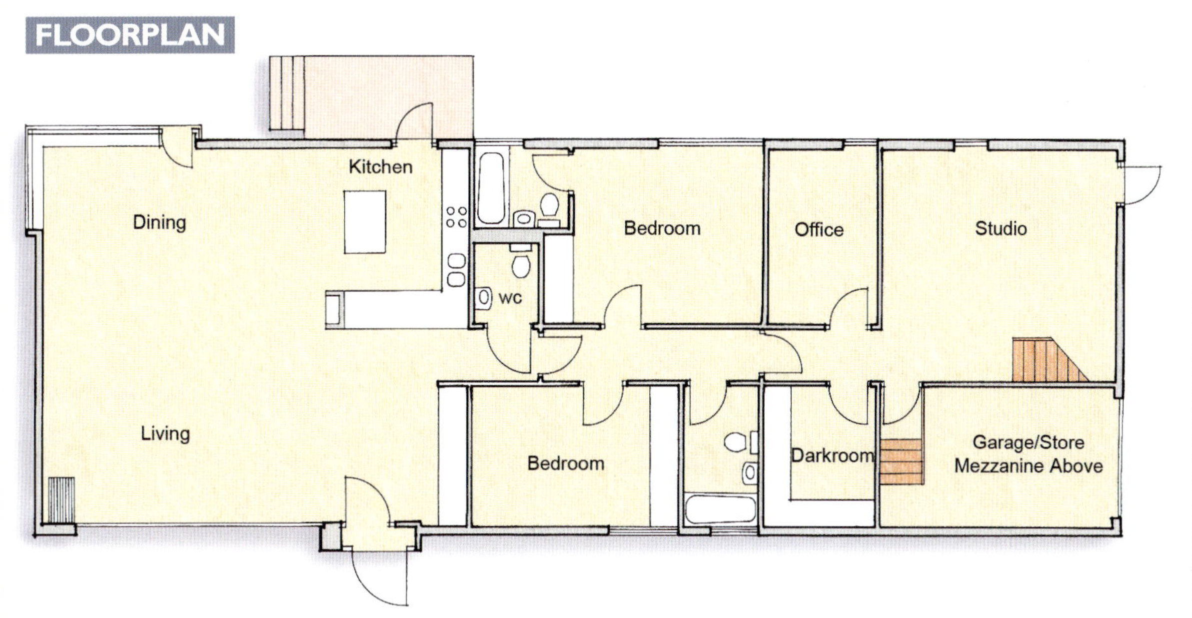

The open-plan living space dominates the single-storey dwelling, with the bedrooms situated in the more private area. A small mezzanine space which can be used as a third bedroom is situated above the garage.

FACT FILE

Names: Paul Gyseman
Professions: Retired trademark agent
Area: Norfolk
House type: Two bed detached
House size: 214m²
Build route: Main contractor
Construction: Off-site pre-engineered panel system
Warranty: Framework
Sap rating: 102
Finance: Private
Build time: May – November '04
Land cost: £125,000
Build cost: £287,000
Total cost: £412,000
House value: £400,000
Cost/m²: £1,341

COST BREAKDOWN

Framework contract	£250,000
Fees: Architect and QS	£37,000
TOTAL	**£287,000**

STRUCTURAL INSULATED PANEL SYSTEMS

Pre-fabricated 'sandwich' panels consisting of two layers of building board – usually OSB – wrapped around a core of insulation, are becoming established as an airtight and energy-efficient alternative to mainstream building systems. Known as Structural Insulated Panels or SIPs, they're pre-assembled off-site, can be cut to shape — and assembled back up on site within a matter of days.

USEFUL CONTACTS

Architect Hudson Architects: 020 7490 3411 **Structural engineer** Alan Conisbee Associates: 020 7700 6666 **Construction** Framework CDM: 01234 744720 www.frameworkcdm.com **QS** Roger Rawlinson: 020 7354 8286 **Windows** AM Profiles: 01246 856000; **External sliding doors** Folding Sliding Door Co: 0845 644 6630 **Log burning stove** Anglia Fireplaces: 01223 234713 **Shingles** Coyle Timber: 01225 427409 **Front Door frame and surround** BE Wilde: 01603 400341 **Windows** AM Profiles: 01246 856000 **Sanitaryware** Abacus: 020 7281 4136; **Kitchen** Richardson and Peat: 01234 741400; **Asbestos removal** Quick Strip: 01953 604399; **Sewage plant** Binder Ltd: 01473 830582

THE TREE HOUSE

The overall winner of this year's Daily Telegraph Homebuilding & Renovating Awards is a new family home on a dream site in Somerset that sets a new standard in sensitive contemporary home design

WORDS: JASON ORME   PHOTOGRAPHY: JEREMY PHILLIPS

t took us years to find the right site for our dream home," says Jim Dyer, "but when we first set eyes on 'The Trees' we instantly knew it had been worth the long wait." But for Jim and his wife Becky — both architects — finding the perfect location was just the start of their self build journey. There were plenty more challenges ahead.

"When we initially came across the site, it was occupied by a 1960s Modernist timber-frame bunga- low which had been designed by a local architect. It was actually very well designed and we initially thought to adapt it, but the more we investigated it, the more unviable this became," explains Jim.

The bungalow was set down a quiet lane in a small village in the Chew Valley, one of a couple set back from the building line as backland development — handily, closer to the spectacular views. Both Jim and Becky were in no doubt that redevelopment would be controversial. To add to the difficulty, the site was

located in a Conservation Area and an Area of Outstanding Natural Beauty.

Becky explains: "We wanted to build an open plan contemporary house that would take inspiration from the site, harmonise with the mature landscape and capture the wonderful views."

Prior to purchasing the site, Becky and Jim moved into rented accommodation nearby and began smoothing the path for the impending planning application by approaching neighbours and talking over their own concerns about the redevelopment. "One of our earliest design decisions was to try and reflect and enhance the character of the site, that is, to continue the views below the tree canopy by visually raising the house 'off the ground'. To achieve this we needed to create an open plan area throughout the ground floor and remove the visual barriers between internal and external space through the use of full-height wrap-around glazing. The cellular sleeping accommodation could then be located within the tree canopy and wrapped in natural timber cladding, topped by a low monopitch copper roof," explains Becky.

"We were keen to continue the idea of living in the tree canopy through the use of open-joint natural timber cladding and the layering of windows and timber screens on the upper level, to allow light and shade and visually soften the elevation, rather than create a solid flat box," says Jim.

"The initial reaction of the planning office was very encouraging," continues Jim. "Our case officer gave us a positive response and indicated that she would support our scheme, and so we continued on, making plans ready to start, occasionally keeping in contact with the planning office. However, to our horror, on the day we were about to submit our planning application, the planning office did a U-turn and advised that they would only accept a traditional two-storey house on the site. We were devastated, particularly as we were so far down

the line. We believed this decision was at odds with planning policy and prepared to go to appeal, but thankfully we managed to have the application taken to the planning committee after appealing to our wonderful local ward councillor. We lobbied hard and, thankfully, got committee approval despite planning office objections. It was a huge emotional roller coaster!'' recalls Jim.

Planning finally negotiated, Jim and Becky completed the purchase of the site and put the drawings out to tender, to local main contractors. Unfortunately –

perhaps owing to the unusual nature of the design and the volume of construction details issued (thinks Jim) – the quotes came back catastrophically high. ''At that stage we had to take a deep breath,'' explains Becky.

''We could still have pulled out of the whole thing and sold the bungalow on with planning permission for redevelopment, but we had fought long and hard and were determined that we wanted this to be our family home. We decided that the only way we could get this thing built was to take over the project management

Clean lines and minimalist furnishings offer an unhampered flow between rooms. The floating staircase was made locally by Phil Clarke

"WE WANTED TO FOLLOW THROUGH THE CONCEPT OF SOMETHING THAT WAS EFFECTIVELY TRANSPARENT AT EYE LEVEL WHICH THEN FILLED OUT FURTHER UP, EXACTLY LIKE A TREE"

each trade directly and buying all the materials ourselves rather than through a main contractor certainly made the whole process more stressful, but financially we couldn't have done it any other way," explains Becky.

The works were at first fix stage when Jim returned to full-time work and Becky then took over the day-to-day project-management duties. "It was particularly difficult to come home from work each day and have to go up to the house and work into the night," recalls Jim.

Three months on from completion, it's difficult to imagine this immensely tranquil home being the scene of any possible disruption. It would have been very easy to build a statement house here — something that tries to show itself off rather than make the most of its beautiful location. Becky and Jim's decision to clad the upper storey of the house in western red cedar rather than the more obvious Modernist's choice of a stark white render is a masterstroke. Materially and aesthetically cedar is perfectly suited to the natural spirit of this glorious home. The first floor windows benefit from sliding screens which are designed to both help keep the sun out but also to let the cedar motif continue uninterrupted.

As much as the house is designed to complement the setting, it also exploits it. The wall-to-wall glazing at ground floor level by Prism Architectural Glazing would not have been possible on a site that wasn't so well secluded by trees and in such a favourable position away from neighbouring windows.

Inside, the clean lines and minimalist furnishings fit perfectly with the simple exterior. There's a clear flow between rooms and despite being open plan, a sense that the rooms do not totally overwhelm the young family that lives here. A beautiful floating staircase of solid

duties and do most of the low-skill trades ourselves." This was all the more difficult as Jim was now between jobs and Becky had just given birth to their second child, Tom.

"Acting as main contractors had its moments," says Jim, "but it did enable us to keep a close eye on day-to-day developments on site which, in a project of this sort which requires high-quality finishing in the details, was critical. We found that the most difficult thing was dealing with subcontractors, several of whom seemed to operate to their own rules and time frames. Dealing with

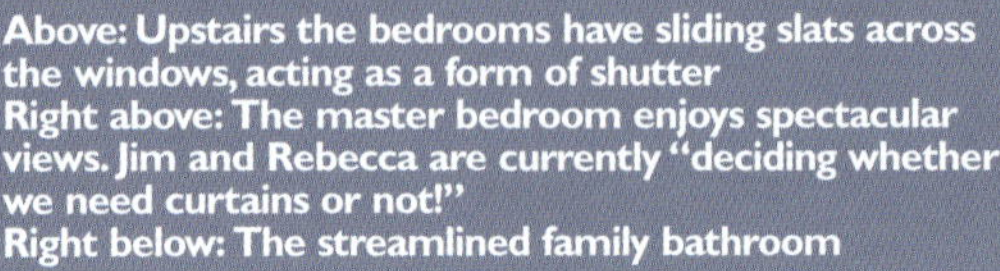

oak has been created by a talented local carpenter called
Phil Clarke – who also made the louvred screens on the
exterior – and leads up to the first floor landing where
a clever long, thin window follows the corridor at eye
level to the bedrooms and office, meaning that light can
enter this more exposed, northerly side of the house but
minimising heat loss and privacy issues.

One of the most impressive elements of this project is
not just the way that Jim and Becky have overcome the
many hurdles in their path, or that they have achieved
their dream of a contemporary house that's so sensitive
to the natural beauty of its secluded site — but that
they've kept the budget so low. Their total outlay of less
than £270,000 works out at £1,200/m² – pretty much
bang on the money. Considering the amount of specialist
work that went into this stylish modern home, and the

"ACTING AS THE MAIN CONTRACTOR MADE IT MORE STRESSFUL, BUT FINANCIALLY WE COULDN'T HAVE DONE IT ANY OTHER WAY"

truly unique nature of the interior scheme, that's quite an
impressive achievement.

The Trees is something special because it sets a new
standard for contemporary homes. It's not, for a start,
slavish in its adherence to rigid design guidelines set out as
standard fits — this is a truly unique, bespoke, and most
importantly, thoughtful solution to a unique and charming
site. It's a busy family home with all the paraphernalia
that entails — but it's also immensely stylish. Most of all,
though, it's everything that the average contemporary
house isn't — it's natural, soft, sensitive and understated;
it's good value; it's respectful and earthy. And that's why
it's our best new home of the year. ■

PROJECT NOTES

FACT FILE

Names: Jim and Rebecca Dyer
Professions: Architects
Area: Somerset
House type: Four-bed contemporary home
House size: 227m²
Build route: Self-managed
Finance: Private
Construction: Steel and timber frame
Build time: Sept '06 – July '07
Land cost: £310,000
Build cost: £266,498
Total cost: £576,498
Current value: £750,000
cost/m²: £1,174

COST SAVING
23%

USEFUL CONTACTS

Groundworks Midas Construction: 01275 463026 **Flooring** Junckers: 01376 534700 **Steel frame** MJ Patch & Co: 01275 472279 **Glazing** Prism Architectural Ltd: 01638 510091 **Glass** Pilkington Optitherm: 01745 536500 **Kitchen** MFI **Built-in cooker** Bosch: www.boschappliances.co.uk **Staircase/ kitchen/external timber screens** Phil Clarke Joinery: 07740 429294 **Sanitaryware** Duravit: 0870 730 7787 Joinery C & S Carpentry Ltd: 01934 514306 **Dry-lining and plastering** Lee Evans: 07725 635633 **Heating engineer/plumber** Mendip Heating & Plumbing Services Ltd: 01761 241453 **Copper roofing** JE Gibbings: 01454 776622 **Fireplace** Mendip Fireplaces Somerset Ltd: 01749 344015 **Painting and decoration** Dave J Watts: 01275 871109 **Dining table and chairs** www.macandmacinteriors.com

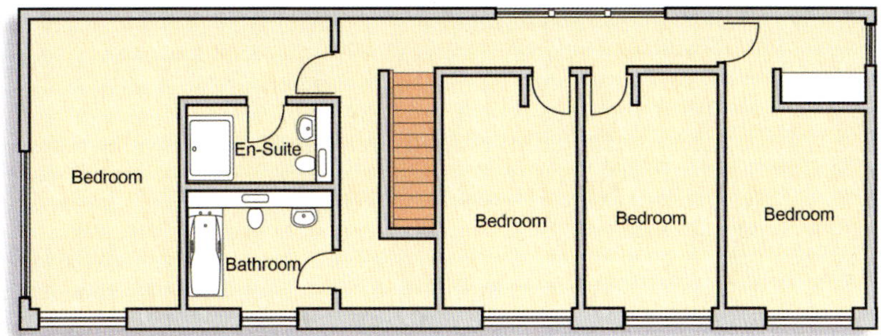

First floor

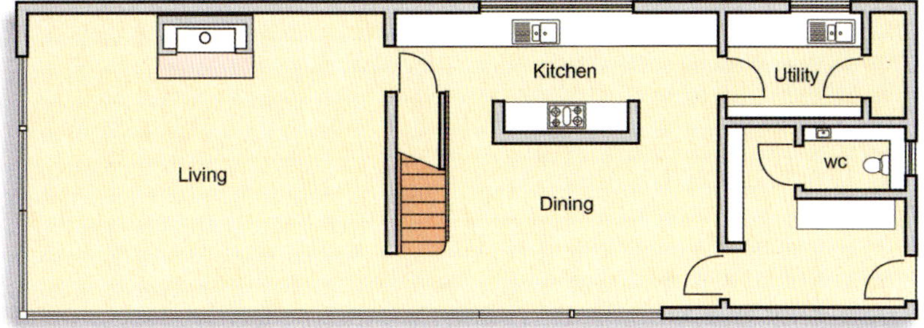

Ground floor

FLOORPLAN

The main living areas are to the west of the floorplan to make the most of the views. The ground floor has a very defined walkthrough, with the entrance shown top right, making the kitchen/dining area the hub of the house.

MODERNIST APPEAL

Neil Hemingway and Jonathan Wood have overcome a long planning battle to build a striking modernist home

WORDS: HEATHER DIXON
PHOTOGRAPHY: DAVE BURTON

In planning terms, it should have been a straight-forward build. The house was to be tucked into a sunken triangle of land at the bottom of a private garden, surrounded by mature trees — the white-painted concrete and steel property would be barely visible from the road and finished to the highest standard.

But Neil Hemingway and his partner, Jonathan Wood, were forced to spend £12,500 fighting for their right to build something radically different, when Kirklees planning councillors drew up a list of objections based on its size, colour and design. "We had to employ a planning solicitor and go to appeal," says Neil. "We managed to get every objection overturned, but it cost us a huge amount of time and money. The whole thing was a nightmare."

Although the plot had planning permission for a conventional detached house, Neil and Jonathan wanted to push the boundaries of design with their first self-

build home. "We wanted a stylish modernist house with high rooms and a very solid feel," says Neil. "We don't like compartmentalised properties. Why build a house with five or six bedrooms when you only need three or four? We wanted to create a house in which every bit of it would be used on a daily basis." As a kitchen designer with clients all over the country, Neil knew exactly how to combine art and architecture with a domestic twist. The property would include an open-plan ground floor with adjoining swimming pool and a personal mezzanine-style gymnasium, contained within a beautifully proportioned L-shaped building with floor-to-ceiling windows stretching the full length of the property.

The focus of the 550m² house would be a state-of-the-art German kitchen where Neil would cook for family, friends and house guests who shared his appreciation for creative design. But not everyone saw the property in the same light. When Neil and Jonathan applied for permission

to change the outline plans and build a radically different, much larger, house on the plot, they met with a wall of opposition from the planning committee.

"Until then everyone had been very supportive and helpful," says Neil. "The local planning officers were very much in favour of our design and the building regulations officer was equally supportive — but then we hit a brick wall when the planning committee overruled everything we were trying to achieve. By this time we had started the build. We had to go to full appeal and it cost us a fortune, but we won on every single point."

One of the council's main objections was the size of the proposed house, but Neil and Jonathan convinced them that the property would be built at such a low level and surrounded by so many mature trees that it wouldn't affect the local landscape.

There were strong objections to the house being painted white, even though there were 43 other white

houses within a third of a mile radius of their home. Another major criticism was that some of the windows overlooked a neighbouring property — even though they would be too high to see out of and designed purely to allow extra light into the house.

"We argued every point and won hands down," says Neil. By this time Neil and Jonathan had taken the risk to press ahead regardless and had almost completed the property.

From the outset, it was never going to be a conventional build. The steeply sloping land had to be excavated to create a low, flat level for the house, which measures 100ft x 50ft. More than 500 cubes of concrete were then used to create 22 two-metre-square pillars which would form the foundations for the main steel structure of the house.

"The concrete plant we sourced it from was shut down to everyone but us for a whole weekend just so they could supply us with enough concrete," says Neil. Massive steel columns, weighing 50 tons in total, were then lowered in by crane to create the main L-shape of the house, with steel girders forming the outline of the floors. The ground floor is beam and block with screed, while the first floor and roof are made from galvanised tin and poured concrete.

"It went up like an office block," says Neil. "Everything was industrial-sized because the proportions of the house are so big." Window frames were brought in from Europe to accommodate the largest domestic window panes they could find at 2.9 metres, which flood the house with light across the entire north-facing wall. To compensate for the potential extremes of temperature, Neil and Jonathan had an underfloor heating and cooling system installed throughout the house. There's a mini plant room containing a back-up boiler, gas water heater, the pool filtration system and the heart of the underfloor heating system. The house is also equipped with an air management system which brings fresh air in and circulates

"IT WENT UP LIKE AN OFFICE BLOCK, EVERYTHING WAS INDUSTRIAL SIZED BECAUSE THE PROPORTIONS OF THE HOUSE ARE SO BIG"

it round the house.

"It's very cheap to run," says Neil. "We also went well over spec with insulation. It's insulated to death." This, and the fact that the property sits so low in the hollow, adds to its extraordinary sense of tranquillity. "You can't hear a thing down here," says Jonathan. "It's like a retreat. We're only five minutes from the M62 yet we could be in the middle of the countryside."

The flooring throughout is 60cm² natural limestone tiles, which are so dense that they had to be water cut with drills. The limestone extends outdoors to minimise the divide between house and garden, and onto the balcony which overlooks the garden. This is cleverly designed in three terraces with decking and Astro Turf for all-year-round easy maintenance. Only the gymnasium and office contain engineered oak boarding for visual contrast. Once the house was built, the exterior was covered with a German system of rendering, which is one of Neil and Jonathan's only regrets.

"Although it's not supposed to, it stains like mad and is very difficult to clean," says Neil. "If I did it again I would use cement render and have it painted. Other than that, we wouldn't change a thing."

Neil and Jonathan have addressed the interior fittings with as much attention to detail as the exterior, including full-height Italian doors in all rooms, a metal framed staircase which was slowly heat-curved over a period of two weeks, and state-of-the-art sound and lighting systems.

The house has become such a talking point in the area that it was recently nominated for the Civic Society House of the Year Award — a welcome accolade after such a long planning battle. However, Neil and Jonathan have now caught the self-build bug. Although they planned the house as their ultimate, long-term living space, they've been offered another building opportunity close by which is "too exciting to resist!

"It will be a wrench to leave because we've put so much into this house, thinking we would be staying here long term," says Neil. "But we don't get sentimental about things — when you're offered another opportunity which is potentially even more exciting than this one, you don't hesitate for too long." ∎

PROJECT NOTES

THE APPEALS PROCESS

If the local planning authority decides to turn down your planning application, going to appeal is an obvious reaction. If you do decide to appeal – it should always be a last resort – you must do so within six months of the initial decision. Appeals should be directed to the Planning Inspectorate, which is part of the newly formed DCLG; decisions are almost always made by a Planning Inspector, who will inform you of the process. In less than two per cent of cases the Secretary of State will be involved in the case, but this is usually reserved for larger, controversial schemes. The decision is made on the basis of local planning policies and all other relevant facts. The appeals process itself is free — however, the expenses involved in using solicitors and experts can be excessive (and costs can only be recovered if planning authorities have been deemed to have acted 'unreasonably', which is very rare). About one third of the cases that are taken to appeal are allowed.

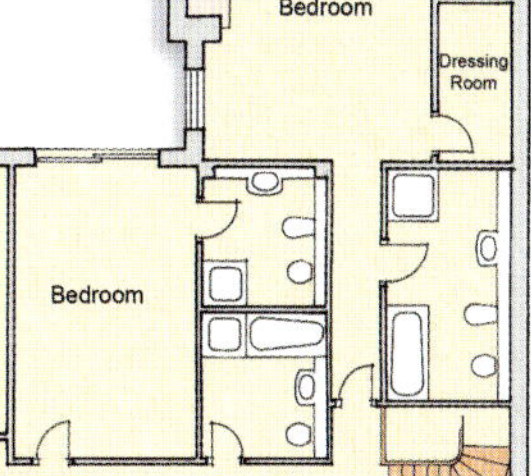

First floor

FACT FILE

Names: Neil Hemingway and Jonathan Wood
Professions: Neil runs the kitchen design company, Neil Hemingway Design
Area: Huddersfield
House type: Four bed, four bath concrete-and-steel detached new build
House size: 557m²
Build route: Self-managed
Construction: Steel frame
Finance: Private
Build time: March '03 – Sept '04
Land cost: Undisclosed; Our estimate £350,000
Build cost: £850,000
Total cost: £1,200,000
House value: £1,500,000
Cost/m²: £1,526

COST SAVING
20%

FLOORPLAN

The two storey home contains four large bedrooms with plenty of balcony space. The ground floor has an open-plan arrangement, with a pool taking up much of the floor area.

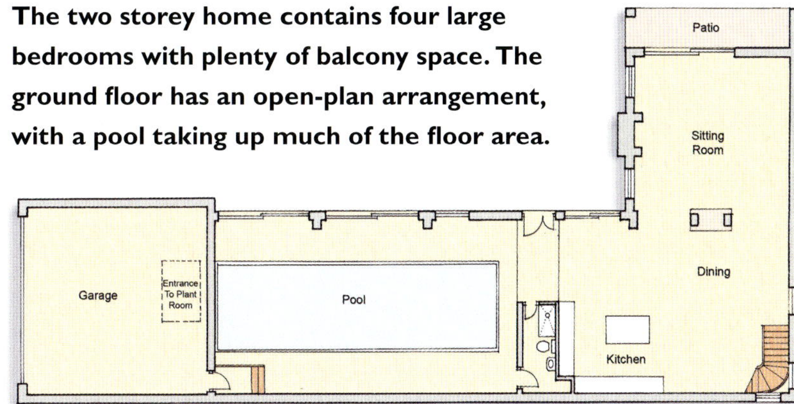

Ground floor

USEFUL CONTACTS

Beckermann kitchen, Italian doors, furniture, flooring Neil Hemingway Design: 01484 659995 **Underfloor heating** Velta: 01484 860811 **Ventilation** ADM: 01756 701051 **Glass** Wakefield Glass: 01924 375338 **Builder** Nigel Clay: 0034 6378 75783 **Pool with heat-retaining cover** Executive Leisure: 01924 479717 **Roof** Kirklees Roofing: 01924 495948 **Stairs** Walker Metalwork: 01422 310011 **Gates** Yorkshire Electric Gates: 01937 558251 **Bathrooms** Atlas Bathrooms: 01484 547110 **Steel frame** Allott Steelworks: 0114 276 6882 **Exterior stone** Johnson Wellfield Quarries: 01484 652311

LOW LEVEL LIVING

Grant Duncan has built a truly spectacular light-filled modern villa full of interesting curves and angles

WORDS: CAROLINE EDNIE PHOTOGRAPHY: ANDREW LEE

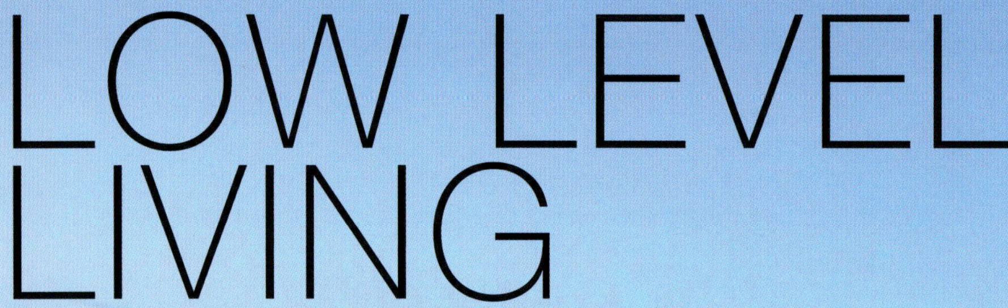

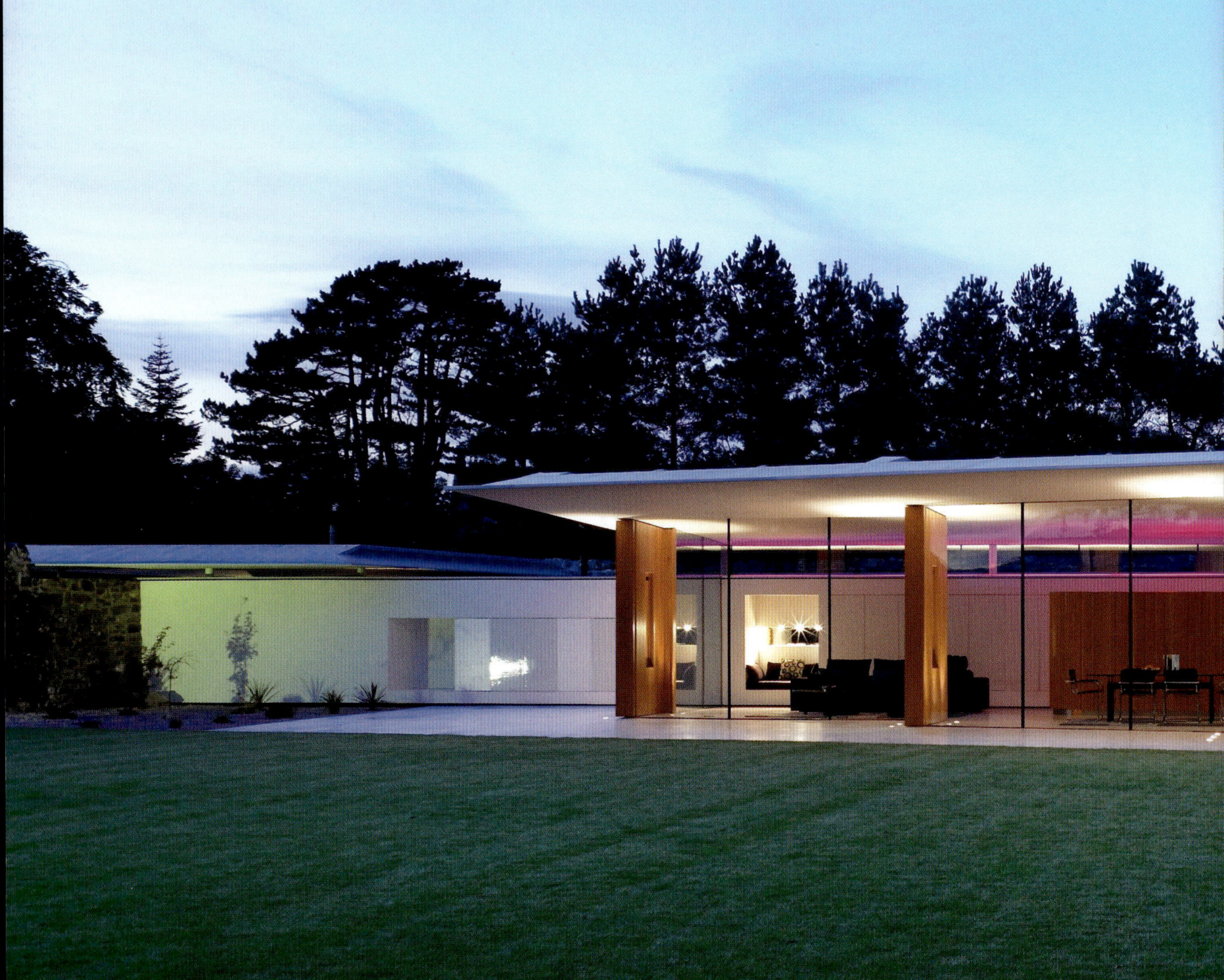

The starting point for Grant Duncan's stunning modern villa, set into a secluded former walled fruit garden in Fife, didn't just involve the usual design brief. Instead, Grant prepared a picture board containing everything that inspired him — "that made [him] tick" – from David Mellor cutlery to a classic Ferrari model and Mies van der Rohe's Barcelona Pavilion. Presenting this to the architects, Grant's picture-board design vision was then distilled into Duncan House, which is without exaggeration one of the finest contemporary homes in Scotland — and an enjoyable and user-friendly one to boot.

Duncan House first took shape around ten years ago when Grant was visiting a friend in rural Fife and noticed a piece of land nearby that was for sale. "The site sits within a walled garden on the site of the former Kinloch Mansion House (a traditional residence remodelled in 1869 in the Scots Baronial revival style). There were two gardens back to back — our site was the fruit garden and the garden next door, the vegetable garden. We bought the site when it first came to my attention but sat on it for a little while until we decided what to do," explains Grant.

"THE ROOF HAS AN AMAZING OVERHANG, LIKE AN AEROPLANE WING. IT LOOKS LIKE IT'S FLOATING"

The catalyst to move forward arrived in the form of architect Gareth Hoskins and his team of Liam McCafferty and Kathy Li. "We wanted something contemporary and decided to interview around seven or eight well-known Scottish architects," Grant explains. "At that time Gareth was just emerging and we chose him as we felt that we could really work with him. And the rest is history!"

Grant admits that there was one aspect of the final design that really swayed his decision. "The thing that attracted me to the design that we chose was the roof. It's an amazing overhang, like an aeroplane wing. It's so thin it just looks like it's floating."

Elsewhere, the design reflected Grant's desire for a minimalist home with white walls and lots of glass. "We also wanted a house where we were utilising all the space in the property. We had previously lived in a seven bedroom traditional stone mansion house that was twice the size of this place, but we didn't use a lot of the space in the old house, whereas there is very little of this house that isn't used."

As a result of Grant's very open brief and a 'not-for-profit' approach to the budget, Duncan House is impressive, to say the least, in terms of its ambition.

The single-storey house uses the traditional language of thick Scottish harled walls with niches – a bit like old Scottish castle walls – set against the stone boundary walls of the garden. The main white render walls of the house form an L-shape. The first cuts through the garden wall to lead visitors into an entrance garden whilst screening them from the main spaces of the house. The second wall runs perpendicular to the first on the axis of the original central path through the garden. This wall screens the bedrooms and bathroom that look east onto a private orchard. The

Floor-to-ceiling glazing
makes for lots of passive
solar gain; three doors
in the lounge connect
indoors and out

The main living area is open plan and the curved 'wooden croissant'-shaped kitchen has been designed in such a way that it doesn't hide the chef away from the rest of the house

living spaces sit within the angle of the two walls, facing south towards the main garden.

The south and west edges of the living area are defined by three giant glazed planes featuring "the biggest sheets of double glazing we could get," says Grant. The living area features a small formal living area, a dining space and 'wooden croissant'-shaped kitchen area, then the main informal family room. Since neighbours aren't an issue, the three bedrooms in the eastern wing are fully glazed with separation walls between each also functioning as built-in storage units.

"The connection with the garden works very well," says Grant. "Every bedroom has a door that leads out to the garden, and the living room has three large doors that also open out, so in summer the house almost becomes one with the garden. There's a lot of solar gain, and the way that the overhanging roof has been designed means that the temperature is constant — the high summer sun doesn't get caught full on, yet at the same time the low winter sun gets in."

The remarkable 'floating' roof is square in plan (where one half of the triangle covers the living area and the other overhangs outside) and cantilevers around five and a half metres. It's only a few inches thick, and this impressive feat of engineering has been achieved via a steel structure,

Above and right: None of the bedrooms is overlooked, allowing for extensive glazing and solar gain. All bedrooms lead onto a private orchard

wooden joists, insulation then finally a Sarnafil waterproof membrane. "We looked at lead and zinc but they wouldn't have been as sharp — they would have been boxier," explains Grant. "It's one of the few materials that would have suited the house in order to achieve the tight crisp lines. It's like a modern-day felt — it's very malleable, light-weight and durable."

"There are some amazing details in the house," says Grant. "The drum room is a beautiful space — and the most expensive room of the house relative to its square footage. It's a timber frame (white wood) structure, two sheets of ply and then plasterboard and plaster to the interior with air-dried oak cladding. The room is oval but the roof is round with a glass atrium which lets the light in from above. It's an incredibly complex but amazing feature. I use it as a music room — and my children play instruments so when they are in it they bash the drums or keyboards. It has wonderful acoustics — music seems to reverberate around it."

The main structure of the house has been constructed via a steel frame and blockwork. The whole house took

"EVERY BEDROOM HAS A DOOR
THAT LEADS OUT TO THE
GARDEN… IN THE SUMMER THE
HOUSE ALMOST BECOMES
ONE WITH THE GARDEN"

The house is set
against the stone
boundary walls
of the old garden,
while the main walls
of the house form
an L-shape. Visitors
are led into this
enclosed entrance
garden, screened
from the main
spaces of the house
so the building
reveals itself slowly

"I HADN'T DONE A SELF-BUILD BEFORE AND ALTHOUGH IT WAS STRESSFUL I'M GLAD I DID IT AS THE QUALITY IS THERE"

the best part of two years to complete: one year for the construction and around a year for the finishes. All elements of the build were supervised by Grant. "I lived nearby and supervised daily, but my approach was hands-off — I was just overseeing it, making sure that the quality of the workmanship was up to a certain standard and organising men and materials. I hadn't done a self-build before and although it was stressful I'm glad I did it as the quality is there, and I might not have achieved this high standard by employing a company to oversee the project. We used hand-picked tradesmen and the finishes in the house are very, very high quality. My friend Max MaCance, who did a lot of the timber details, has created finishes that are more like furniture in terms of the standard of craftsmanship."

Elsewhere, Grant's minimalist ethos presents itself in a series of pristine white walls, oak and limestone floor finishes, much of which he sourced himself. "But I ran everything by the architects before I committed to the materials," he explains. "There were certain things that the architects had to persuade me to keep, such as the box window at the front door which I didn't really want as I wanted a straight white crisp wall. But they convinced me that the window offered a sneak preview that was important to the design idea — which was a house that revealed itself slowly. I'm pleased I went along with this idea as it actually works really well."

Another area that works really well is the energy performance of the house. "I don't have any heating on from May to October. The efficiency is excellent and is all worked from a wireless thermostat so that the temperature in each room is controllable. The only downside is that kerosene powers the underfloor heating and hot water and since I moved in the price of fossil fuels have doubled.

"I wouldn't change any elements of the house," concludes Grant. "There are so many aspects of it that are amazing: as well as the 'Drum' music room and the roof, there's the various angles of the glass in the living area which creates a spectacular effect; the kitchen design which doesn't cut you off while you're cooking; and the open plan living space. It all works so well." ■

PROJECT NOTES

ONE LEVEL LIVING

The main living spaces are open plan, with the kitchen separated off by a curved partition. The three bedrooms and bathrooms are protected from public view, facing the orchard. To the left of the main entrance is the oval study, which Grant uses as a music room

FACT FILE

Name: Grant Duncan
Profession: Company director
Area: Fife
House type: Single-storey contemporary villa
House size: 260m²
Build route: Architect and main contractor
Finance: Private
Construction: Steel frame; blockwork
Warranty: Architect's certificate
Build time: Two years
Land cost: £90,000
Build cost: £500,000
Total cost: £590,000
Current value: £1,000,000+
Cost/m²: £1,900

COST SAVING
41%

'The Drum' music room is Grant's favourite room

USEFUL CONTACTS

Architect Gareth Hoskins Architects: 0141 221 0600 **Structural engineer** David Narro Associates: 0131 229 5553 **Quantity surveyor** Morham & Brotchie Partnership: 0131 556 2556 **Main contractor** R Lindsay & Co: 01592 260154 **Exterior finishes** Mackie-Robertson Building Services: 01592 653377 **Roofing** Samafil from AIM Developments: 01738 494949 **Windows** Solar glass, Leuchars Glazing: 01334 838815 **Specialist fittings** Sterling Homes: 01592 652875 **Joinery** Greg Myles Joinery: 01337 831321

COOL CROFT

John Cameron has built a new home on a sensitive site in the style of a traditional long house

WORDS: CAROLINE EDNIE   PHOTOGRAPHY: ANDREW LEE

The framed view that dominates the south wall of John Cameron's dining room could rival anything found on the walls of a national gallery. Yet this spectacular scene, featuring a sweep of Strathspey meadow culminating in the snow-capped peaks of the Cairngorm Mountains, is a living and breathing real-time landscape — and it's just one of the many bespoke and site-specific details that set John's contemporary rural self-built croft apart from so many of the generic kit houses that have become such a familiar sight in the current Highland landscape.

Yet Cameron Croft does not attempt to set itself apart as an all-singing, all-dancing addition to the dramatic landscape. Instead, the simple one-and-a-half-storey timber-frame structure respectfully follows the low-slung, landscape-hugging form of the traditional rural long house, and includes familiar details such as a slate pitch roof and white render finish. But it also provides a clever contemporary twist by featuring extensive glazing – around two thirds of the south elevation is glass – and materials and finishes that are technologically top-notch and maintenance-free. But ironically, although the touches are bespoke and the

materials first rate, Cameron Croft was built within budget parameters of £200,000 — comparable to the cost of a standard kit house.

The croft occupies part of a nine-acre site that John purchased from a local farmer around five years ago. John, who is originally from the area, admits that if it weren't for his family connection with the Caingorms, securing the site would have been very difficult. Fortunately the deal suited all parties involved, as the farmer would still be allowed to graze his livestock on John's land, while John himself would have an ideal site on which to build his new home.

Normally, planning consent would have been denied in such a sensitive rural location. However, an enlightened local councillor gave support to a limited number of planning applications in order to allow farmers to realise some capital. The purchase proved a timely one: in 2003, just as Cameron Croft was nearing completion, the house and site were assimilated into the newly designated Cairngorms National Park — a safeguarded area of great natural beauty, which would fall under the jurisdiction of a new Park Authority.

John initially bought the land without planning consent — taking a huge risk. Luckily for him consent was eventually given on the basis that the new home should follow a traditional style. "There was some initial planning resistance to our proposals because the house was so modern," admits the project's architect, Philip Flockhart of Edinburgh-based Morris & Steedman Associates. "But when I met the chief planner on site with a model, he thought it was fantastic. After resistance they showed great support."

Little wonder, since the house addresses the site beautifully. "There were no parameters to exactly where the house should be located," continues Philip, "but we decided to position it at the back of the site so that you can see the expanse of the field opening up towards the landscape. Harnessing the view east towards the nearby river also determined the site."

In order to maximise the views, the windows are arrayed in a long south-facing strip to capture the sun and scenery. Contrastingly, the north wall remains unbroken by openings. This blank wall is echoed in the garage wall which extends the appearance of the building as a long white strip in the landscape. "It's a simple and obvious solution, putting the rooms to the south and the circulation to the

back, on the north side. This makes the most of the great views and passive solar gain to the south and minimal heat loss to the north. It all makes practical and economic sense," explains Philip.

Many of the structural components and material finishes make sound practical and economic sense too. These include low-maintenance elements such as a white STO self-finish render. The gutter is also unusually positioned on the roof slope, allowing an uncluttered clean line between wall and roof to ensure that snow loading doesn't dislodge it. The natural slate roof structure, which is essentially timber trusses suspended off steel beams and spanning between the cross walls, is trimmed with maintenance-free powder-coated aluminium, as are the windows externally (with wood internally) which will require little in the way of painting.

Normally, the kind of glazed façade that characterises the house would relate to an entirely open plan interior, but John was keen to pursue a more traditional self-contained room layout. "I wanted separate rooms rather than an open plan arrangement, for cosiness. The kitchen and dining area is more of an open plan space as this is used as a gathering place. It's a very social area." As a result of this interior arrangement, the windows are positioned to correspond to the cross walls which divide up the rooms.

In terms of the internal arrangement, the croft comprises two entrance porches at either end of the north wall spine, with the main entrance located at the east of the building. The straight linking corridor along the length of the house is cleverly lit from above via a series of NorDan roof windows. John admits that this roof glazing is also instrumental in allowing air to circulate throughout the house, which is a must on a hot Highland summer day. Spine walls separate the south-facing accommodation, which includes the sitting room to the

"GREAT VIEWS AND PASSIVE SOLAR GAIN TO THE SOUTH AND MINIMAL HEAT LOSS TO THE NORTH MAKES PRACTICAL AND ECONOMIC SENSE"

"DULY A MAN CAME WITH BIRCH TWIGS AND INDICATED WHERE HE BELIEVED WE SHOULD DRILL, AND SURE ENOUGH THERE WAS THE WATER!"

west, the kitchen and dining area in the heart of the house, and an en suite bedroom to the east.

Directly above the dining area and ground floor bedroom are two additional bedrooms — one open plan, the other a self-contained en suite arrangement. Above the sitting room, a storage attic has been created. "Most houses of this type don't have any storage," says Philip. "But what we did was sacrifice the entire roof area over the sitting room to provide attic space for storage. However, we also raised the roof ties, which has resulted in a nice high ceiling in the sitting room: it's 10 foot high, which makes it a tall room."

The interior colour and material palette echoes the crisp minimalist finishes of the building's exterior. These include a Caithness slate fireplace, containing an easy-to-maintain Baxi log fire, designed by Philip. "The open log fire was priority number one," says John, who is also able to burn peat which he digs himself from the nearby moss. Caithness slate features extensively on the floor finishes, as does cherry wood. Continuing the timber theme, locally produced untreated larch is used in the decking, porch, screen and garage, and is already silvery with weathering. The timber finishes form a soft, natural adjunct to the house's direct, monochromatic palette.

The 12-month construction process was "remarkably painless", according to Philip. "The contractors, AW Laing of Grantown-on-Spey, were fantastic. In fact, when they had the frame up, they then neatly pasted up all of our drawings on the walls, which they methodically followed — I'd never seen this approach before. They were terrific contractors and did a great job. This is probably the best contract I've been involved with."

There were, however, a few added complications to the build due to the remoteness of the site. All the services had to be brought in: "The only public service I get is collection of the bins!" says John. Sewerage is

A straight corridor runs the length of the house, lit from above via a series of skylight windows

achieved via a septic tank and the rainwater that comes off the roof goes straight into a soakaway system. "Mains water is too far away so we had to find our own supply," he continues. "Duly a man came with birch twigs and indicated where he believed we should drill. Sure enough there was the water!" The water supply, essentially a pressurised pump, has to go through a treatment system located in an insulated, thermostatically controlled cupboard in the new larch-clad double garage. This cost around £10,000 to install — though John maintains that it is money well spent.

John admits this is probably the first as well as last self-build project he's ever likely to take on, however he also concedes that it was worth the wait. More so, it would appear, since Cameron Croft was assimilated into the Cairngorms National Park — its protected status has inevitably led to soaring land prices. "Although this is a small one-off house, it was a great opportunity to test ideas and create something a little bit different in the countryside," concludes Philip. "I think we have also ended up with a very valuable asset." ■

PROJECT NOTES

Architect: Philip Flockhart

FLOOR PLAN

The accommodation splits three bedrooms over two storeys, with a north-facing entrance corridor serving the main living space on the ground floor.

FACT FILE

Name: John Cameron
Profession: Business adviser and investor
Area: Strathspey
House type: One-and-a-half-storey detached property in nine-acre site
House size: 152m²
Build route: Main contractor
Finance: Private
Construction: Timber frame
Build time: One year
Land cost: Undisclosed (est. £100,000)
Build cost: £200,000
Total cost: £300,000 (est.)
current value: £375,000 (est.)
Cost/m²: £1,316

**COST SAVING
20%**

USEFUL CONTACTS

Architect Philip Flockhart: 0131 226 6563 **Main contractor** AW Laing: 01479 872818 **Quantity surveyor** John Mackenzie: 0131 243 2566 **Main contractor** William M Crowe: 01383 860721 **Exterior finishes** STO external render system, John Collings: 01505 324262 **Flashings** Ian Gray: 0141 427 1264 **Plumbing and heating** Graham McIntosh: 01479 831332 **Windows** NorDan UK: 01698 383364 **Sanitaryware** Scope Bathrooms: 0141 882 4545 **Kitchen** Crown Keswick Units, Allied Manufacturing Co: 020 8205 8844 **Insulation** A Proctor Group: 01250 872261 **Stone flooring and fireplace** Inverness Fireplace & Marble Centre: 01463 234844 **Cherry wood floor** Uniclic Quick Step: +32 (0)56 675211 **Doors** Timbmet steamed beech doors, M&V: 01623 420664 **Electrics** AL Brown Electrical: 01479 873328

VISION OF THE FUTURE

Richard and Sian Liwicki have built a contemporary, low-energy farmhouse in the walled garden of their Oxfordshire vineyard

When Richard and Sian Liwicki sit down to savour a well-earned glass of wine, they have the added satisfaction of knowing that the tipple they're drinking is all their own — produced from vines visible from the windows of their newly constructed farmhouse.

Bothy Vineyard continues an ancient tradition of wine making in the Vale of the White Horse, Oxfordshire, where the warm sandy soil and mature vines help to produce some award-winning wines; but, surprisingly, the Liwickis are relative newcomers to running their own vineyard.

"Richard's a keen wine buff, and enjoyed volunteering at our local vineyard as a way to unwind in the fresh air after work," recalls Sian. "When the owners mentioned that they were retiring, Richard jumped at the chance to buy Bothy Vineyard. He negotiated a reduction in his hours at Oxford University in order to make the change, and I gave up work to help run our new business.

"We're both scientists and have a great love of plants, as well as wine, so it seemed like the ideal choice — although it was also a challenge. Grape growing in

England is a very labour-intensive activity, but we're lucky enough to have a faithful band of friends and volunteers who help and support us."

The couple have two daughters – Sasha, six, and Zoë, four – and recognised that the vineyard would be an idyllic place to raise a family, located as it is in a peaceful rural hamlet. Planning permission had previously been granted for a traditional-style house with an agricultural tie to be constructed on the green belt site, and the Liwickis approached Richard's old school friend, architect David Wylie, to talk over their ideas for building a new family home.

They wanted a more contemporary design which would remain sympathetic to its setting, and would offer the privacy they needed as a family while remaining connected to the vineyard itself. David responded by ensuring that the

"WE LEARNT A GREAT DEAL FROM OUR PREVIOUS HOMES, AND WERE KEEN TO AVOID WASTED CORRIDOR SPACE"

new house would effectively become part of an existing walled garden on the edge of the vineyard, and arranged the property as a series of private spaces facing into the garden. The planning officer was enthusiastic about the sensitive proposal and, as no objections were received, the design was approved under delegated powers.

"We'd been living in a barn conversion about seven miles from the vineyard, which we sold before renting during the build," Richard recalls. "We learnt a great deal from our previous homes, and were keen to avoid wasted corridor space. We also wanted to build a low-energy house that would be visually exciting and would make the most of the wonderful views. David came up with a design which links the house to the garden wall and an old stone bothy on the site, and it seemed like the perfect solution to all our needs."

The Edwardian bothy – previously used for wine making – was in poor structural condition and needed to be

rebuilt. It was given a new first floor and now acts as the vineyard shop and office, connected to the two- storey house via a single-storey flat-roofed link tucked down behind the garden wall.

This lower section of the building contains the kitchen and dining room, which overlook the garden through a wall of glass. In the two-storey section of the house, the dining and living areas combine to form an L-shaped room beside a double-height conservatory, which faces south to make the most of the light and warmth from the sun.

"Even before you start using new technologies like solar panels it's important to site a house correctly, insulate it fully and plan everything as sensibly as possible," says Sian. "Our house has been designed to trap heat from the low sun during spring, winter and autumn days, with shading above the glass to reduce the glare of the high summer sun. We also have a massive curved blockwork wall in the conservatory which is rendered in clay and acts like a radiator, absorbing heat and releasing it slowly."

The building is highly insulated and draught-proofed, and benefits from a natural ventilation system, which was especially designed by David Wylie to provide cooling during summer days. Solar panels on the slate roof warm the family's water, PV cells generate electricity from the sun, and a weather station has been installed to monitor and measure changes in the internal and external environment.

The north and east elevations of the house are timber framed, and have been clad in a distinctive rain screen of untreated cedar, with stone from the site facing the remaining cavity blockwork elements. "It was actually more expensive to recycle our own stone than to buy it in from a local quarry, because of the labour involved in cutting and preparing the different-sized blocks," explains Richard, "but we had a fantastic stonemason and the weathered finish was worth the extra effort."

With David Wylie based in London, an Oxford architectural practice was appointed to project manage the 14-month build, which was completed by a small but enthusiastic local building team, keen to learn about the eco-friendly building principles and materials involved.

Above: The master bedroom bridges the house and features a round window overlooking the private garden and a projecting oriel window with views to the vineyard
Right: The best elements of contemporary design are in the details, such as the floor-to-ceiling glass shower screen and the shadow gaps in place of skirting boards

"To a certain extent we were all learning together, but our builders constantly talked to us and paid close attention to detail," says Sian. "The biggest problem was a delay caused by the German supplier of the glass curtain walling we needed, which held everything up and cost us additional rent.

"We did try to buy locally whenever possible, and chose renewable materials such as bamboo and linoleum flooring, but sometimes it was impossible to find what we wanted in the UK."

Richard and Sian spent a great deal of time working with David Wylie on the design, in particular discussing the way they like to live. They have reproduced certain features which they admire in other houses, such as the round windows, conservatory and double-height spaces, and the result is a practical and unusual family home.

Slit windows in the master bedroom overlook a void above the sitting room – enabling the couple to keep a watchful eye on the children from upstairs – and window seats offer inviting places from which to admire the views of the garden and the vineyard to the north-west.

The integral double-height conservatory is a dramatic multi-purpose space which is ideal for relaxing, drying clothes and growing plants. "It opens directly into the sitting room, which makes this whole area feel much larger," Sian explains. "Our converted barn had an open-plan kitchen and living area, but I'm from south-east Asia and often cook extremely spicy and pungent food, so this time we decided to isolate the kitchen and introduce a restaurant-style swing door."

Sian is at pains to explain that although their new home looks gorgeous, this is no idle showhome. "This is a working farmhouse, and at harvest time I prepare meals for large numbers of people, so it was important to have a hard-wearing kitchen and a practical utility with sinks and storage as well as a north-facing pantry," continues Sian. "The utility area has been built to the rear of the bothy shop, and connects directly into the kitchen, so I can walk through the house to serve in the shop and then return to domestic life.

"The entire house was devised so that we can run a business and retain our privacy at the same time. It's a concept which works extremely well and has made living here an absolute pleasure." ■

PROJECT NOTES

Ground floor

VINEYARD LIVING

On the ground floor, the kitchen and dining room sit in the single-storey section of the house overlooking the garden through a glass wall. In the two-storey section, the open living and dining spaces lead into the double-height conservatory, with two bedrooms to the rear. Upstairs are two more bedrooms with en suites. The office lies at the opposite end of the first floor accessed by a staircase from the utility.

First floor

FACT FILE

Names: Sian and Richard Liwicki
Professions: Vineyard owners and assistant registrar at Oxford University
Area: Oxford
House type: Four bedroom detached
House size: 300m²
Build route: Building contractor
Finance: Private
Construction: Stone-clad blockwork, timber frame, cedar cladding, slate roof
Warranty: Architect's certificate
Build time: Jan '05 – March '06

COST SAVING
33%

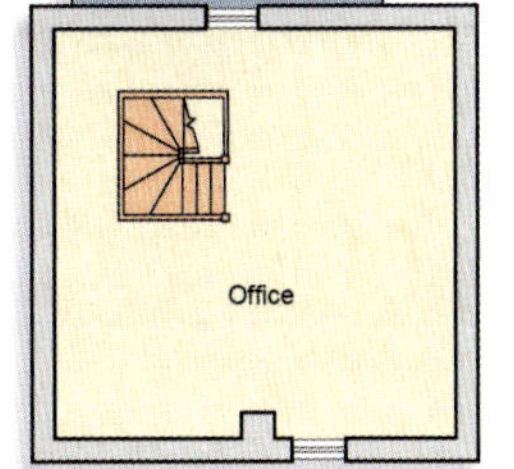

USEFUL CONTACTS

Bothy Vineyard: 01865 390067 www.bothyvineyard. co.uk **Concept architect** Wylie Associates: 020 8265 7620 www.davidwylieassociates.com **Project architect** Oxford Architects LLP: 01865 329100 **Builders** WG Carter Ltd: 01865 864626 **Staircase** Spiral Staircase Systems: 01273 858341 **Bamboo and linoleum flooring** Classic Flooring Ltd: 01865 773535 **Round windows** 3D Aluminium Plas: 01865 881403 **Oak doors (bothy)** OJ Joinery: 01559 371571 **Ventilation louvres** Bovema (UK) Ltd: 01244 400401 **Cedar cladding** D Smith Joinery: 01865 821095

The restored bothy now contains the vineyard shop and connects to the two-storey part of the house via a single-storey glazed link

CRAFTING LANDSCAPE

When Marina Dennis decided to build a new Highland home within the 40 acres of Strathspey crofting land that has been in her family for nearly 200 years, she was in little doubt about its look and location. Inchdryne Lodge would be built in a secluded birch wood and would be "unusual and innovative" in terms of design — and above all it would be a timber-frame house. "When my ancestors came here in 1809 the first house they built was wooden. So I always wanted to build a timber house as I felt that it was a very appropriate type of building to have on the edge of the ancient Abernethy forest," explains crofter Marina.

Following a design and build process that involved a 40-page grant application and a couple of planning hitches, as well as a few gale forces blowing the build schedule off-course, a wooden house did emerge — and a hugely impressive one at that. Essentially, Inchdryne Lodge is a timber-frame and timber-clad two-storey house with a single-storey bedroom wing located to the rear. The main body of the house features an impressive double-height living room with an adjoining open plan, single-height dining and kitchen area. Directly above is the master en suite bedroom which leads to an additional living area on the mezzanine level. The two remaining bedrooms (one en suite) and main bathroom are located in an L-shaped wing that's accessed from the main circulation corridor which runs parallel to the living space.

Inchdryne Lodge was partly financed by a grant from the Agricultural Business Diversification Scheme (ABDS) which is designed to support crofters and farmers, and their immediate families. This involved the challenging

The Douglas fir main frame and staircase are complemented by oak-lined ceilings and oak floors on the mezzanine level. Kahrs Maple Genua UV Oiled floors conceal underfloor heating on the ground floor. Tall windows, a rooflight and internal glazing keep the interiors flooded with light

Left: The house is designed to exploit the stunning views. The timber windows – predominantly positioned on the southern elevation – are from Treecraft, with glazed screens from Moray Glass. The house is also clad in timber, painted green, with a contrasting black steel Plastisol roof. Large supporting timber posts are left natural, and drainpipes are cleverly incorporated into the design

Above: The large airy living areas echo the woodland setting and are filled with light

> **"ONE OF THE MOST IMPORTANT THINGS WAS FOR THE HOUSE TO BE IN HARMONY WITH THE LANDSCAPE AND I THINK WE HAVE ACHIEVED THIS"**

afore-mentioned 40-page application as well as a business and diversification plan. "They had to make sure that we were up for the challenge," explains Marina.

"The condition of the grant was such that we had 18 months to build the house." But the project didn't quite hit the ground running when it was initiated in 2003, as the newly created Cairngorms National Park Authority called in the plans – as is their statutory right – and this delayed the build for six months. Further scrutiny by the local council planners meant that the construction team only had 12 months to complete the Lodge. "Thankfully, though, the main contractors, AW Laing, were wonderful," says Marina. This is the third home that I have built with their help. They didn't do the usual thing of disappearing to other jobs. They were on site the whole time and were very conscientious and honest."

The distinctive form of Inchdryne Lodge originated from a scribbled design by Marina's son Roddy, a squadron leader in the Royal Air Force. The final design was entrusted to Marina's friend Bernard Planterose of Ullapool-based North Woods Construction in collaboration with Chris Morgan of Edinburgh-based Locate Architects — a specialist in sustainable development and ecological design. Although Inchdryne was built via timber frame construction, there was no element of prefabrication involved. It was built plank by plank, using Highland-sourced Douglas fir for the main frame. The same timber was also used for the cladding and interior frame work.

"We wanted an unusual but contemporary house made of wood with lots of light and space, and taking advantage of the stunning views," says Marina. As a result the design includes extensive glazing, again locally sourced with timber frame windows from Treecraft in Dornoch, and glazed screens from Moray Glass. These feature prominently on the south-facing elevation. "We

"WE POSITIONED THE HOUSE FACING DUE SOUTH. IT'S IMPORTANT IN THE HIGHLANDS TO TRY TO HARNESS AS MUCH SUNLIGHT AS POSSIBLE"

positioned the house facing due south. It's important in the Highlands to try and harness as much sunlight as possible, because we have long winters here," says Marina. A black steel Plastisol roof completes the picture in terms of exterior finishes and this provides a fine visual counterpoint to the natural green hue of the external cladding.

The total build cost for this impressive venture was around £250,000, including the substantial decking and two car ports. In order to meet the strict budgetary parameters, Marina explains: "We had to ditch some ideas for cost reasons. When I was initially thinking about the design I was keen on solar panels but the cost was just so prohibitive." But Marina did manage to save some costs by having a ready-made gravel supply for the extensive groundworks. "I was very lucky in that I had a huge hillock in one of my other fields which produced the most fantastic gravel. We took thousands of tonnes and did the roads and foundations. The builders said that I should stop farming and sell gravel as I'd make a fortune!

"One of the most important things was for the house to be in harmony with the landscape and I think we have achieved this. I can honestly say that there is nothing I would change about the house. It has so many lovely touches. The south-facing dining area which extends into the garden is perfect for summer evenings. This area also faces the Granny Pine, a Caledonian pine tree that's over 300 years-old — it's an ancient monument. It's backlit and on wintry nights the light shines through — the whole effect is magical." ■

PROJECT NOTES

Marina Dennis' timber frame house is positioned within Cairngorms National Park on a secluded 40-acre plot, surrounded by woodland. Its position means that it is sited off-mains, which involved significant extra costs to provide services

FACT FILE

Name: Marina Dennis
Profession: Crofter
Area: Nr Nethy Bridge, Abernethy Forest
House type: Two-storey contemporary self-build
House size: 204m²
Build route: Architect and builder
Finance: Private
Construction: Timber frame, steel roof
Build time: Jun '05 – Mar '06
Land cost: Already owned
Build cost: £250,000
Total cost: £250,000
Current value: £375,000+
Cost/m²: £1,225

COST SAVING
33%

COST BREAKDOWN

Flooring	£9,000
Frame/materials	£45,000
External walls/joinery	£35,000
Windows, blinds and doors	£36,000
Roof	£20,000
Plumbing and heating	£14,000
Electrics	£8,000
Kitchen/built-in fittings	£15,000
Landscaping/external works	£8,000
Labour	£40,000
Misc	£20,000

AN INTERNAL BALCONY

The house is based around the central double-height living space, which leads onto a bedroom wing at the rear of the building, including an en suite and main bathroom. The living room also adjoins the kitchen/dining area which has a single-height ceiling to define the space. Upstairs, a large balcony provides seating space and leads onto the third bedroom with en suite.

Ground floor

First floor

WELL AND TRULY OFF-MAINS

Inchdryne Lodge's beautifully secluded setting did create complications – and unanticipated costs – in that it is off-mains: "There are no public services whatsoever, so we have a septic tank and a private water supply. We had to bring it 310 metres across the field and dig a trench to put in the water, electricity and telephone," explains Marina. "When I applied for an electricity supply I was informed that the transformer in the area didn't have sufficient capacity so I had to pay for a new high-voltage line. This was hugely expensive — £9,600 for the electricity supply. But the transformer now has an overcapacity of 50% so if it gets used by new houses being built in the area then I will get some of this money back."

USEFUL CONTACTS

Design team Bernard Planterose (North Woods Construction Ltd): 01854 613040; Chris Morgan (Locate Architects): 0131 620 0530 **Structural engineer** John Sinclair, Allen, Gordon & Co, Perth: 01738 639881 **Main contractor and kitchen** AW Laing Ltd, Grantown-on-Spey: 01479 872818 **Douglas fir and oak flooring** Cromartie Timber: 01997 412013 Black Plastisol Planwell: 01542 832170 **Plumbing and heating and sanitaryware** G MacIntosh Ltd: 01479 831332 **Electrician** MacPherson Electrical Ltd: 01479 831355 **Painting and decoration** Iain Michie: 01479 851343 **Windows – timber framed** Treecraft: 01862 810021 **Glazed screens** Moray Glass: 01343 541023 **Insulation** Out of Nowhere (Warmcell): 01309 692012 **Oak linings** Russwood: 01540 673648 **Chablis honed and filled floor tiles** HSBS: 01463 712666 **Maple Genua UV Oiled flooring** Kahrs: 01243 778747 **Barbas unilux 75 Cuatro Tunnel insert fire** Bonk & Co Ltd: 01463 233968 **Range oven** Aga: 01952 642000

CLIFFHANGER

Our Home of Year is more than just a spectacular design — Glyn and Jane
Martin's contemporary, eco-friendly new house is entirely at one with the
landscape, and was a true family affair, with everyone pitching in to lend a hand

For Annie Martin and her younger brothers, Will and Joe, Seacombe will always hold fond memories of childhood holidays and long, hot summers spent playing on the nearby beach. Back then, however, their parents' seaside holiday home in East Portlemouth, Devon, was little more than a timber shack with a corrugated tin roof and absolutely no mod cons — a far cry from its newly built successor.

Glyn and Jane Martin were initially attracted to the property's totally secluded setting and the incredible sea views which may be enjoyed from its elevated 1.5-acre site. Accessed by an unassuming stone track off the lane between East Prawle and East Portlemouth it stands above sandy Seacombe beach in an Area of Outstanding Natural Beauty, with spectacular coastal scenery spreading out below.

"We loved spending time at the house, despite the fact that it was literally falling down, with just a generator for electricity, gas lighting, no phone and rotten floors," Annie,

now 31, recalls. "My parents originally bought it at auction more than 20 years ago, and over time we extended the 1930s chalet and did it up on a DIY basis."

Years passed, and when Annie qualified as an architect the family began to consider the possibility of replacing their old single-storey holiday home with a new, more comfortable dwelling, specifically designed to take full advantage of the south-facing panoramic views.

"WE WANTED TO REFERENCE THE ORIGINAL BUILDING, FOR INSTANCE WITH THE TIMBER BOARDING"

Left: The Kitchen is made to a bespoke design from solid fumed oak, with black African granite work surfaces, the open plan kitchen benefits from a walk-in larder
Above: Bespoke oak, steel and glass folded staircase leads down into the open plan dining space, casting rainbows onto the white walls as the sun tracks around the house

"With no near neighbours we hoped the planners would allow us to build something contemporary," explains Jane, "but we're surrounded by National Trust land and there was a covenant which restricted the height of the property, so there were numerous hurdles to overcome before our plans were finally approved after about a year of negotiations."

In order to reduce the impact of the new two storey building it has been positioned further back on the site and the ground floor was excavated into an existing steep bank. The garage is constructed so that its planted roof is a continuation of the boundary bank — ensuring that the house only comes into view from the track near the entrance gate.

From the north and west it appears to be a modest bungalow, accessed from the driveway by crossing a timber bridge to the cedar-clad entrance. Walk inside, however, and the true nature of the house reveals itself, with huge windows and glazed balconies offering stunning views right out to sea.

Three bedrooms are located on the first floor with two en suites and a family bathroom, which take full advantage of the elevated view. The two main bedrooms both have recessed balconies, which provide sheltered external areas as well as helping to reduce the apparent weight of the first floor by cutting away the corners.

An oak staircase leads downstairs from the main entrance to the spacious living area and a large private walled garden beyond. Finishes are luxurious, with oak and limestone floors, underfloor heating and an air purification system. There's wi-fi throughout, a bespoke kitchen and a state-of-the-art cinema concealed behind a wheeled 'bookcase' door.

"WE LIKED THE IDEA OF BUILDING A CINEMA WITHIN A SECRET ROOM WHICH COULD BE ACCESSED THROUGH A DOORWAY HIDDEN INSIDE A CUPBOARD"

Above and top right: The cinema room is concealed behind a secret door in the main living space (above right) – its handle inset into a fake book with an appropriate title! The cinema is furnished with comfy chairs, a 106in screen with surround sound and a high-definition projector

"My brothers insisted on a cinema as part of the brief, and we liked the idea of building it within a secret room because the old bungalow had a bedroom extension which could be accessed through a doorway hidden inside a cupboard," says Annie. "We wanted to keep some references to the original building, for instance the external timber boarding, and to choose materials which would be in sympathy with the site."

The ground floor of the new building is embedded into the bank and has been constructed in solid rendered masonry, with the first floor structure in steel and timber, clad with untreated horizontal cedar boarding. Large areas of glazing are restricted to the south façade and durable zinc was chosen for the monopitch roof which will weather to an inconspicuous matt grey.

"My partner, Mark, is a carpenter who worked full-time on site during the build, so we decided to move into the old timber bungalow and lived there for 18 months while the new house was completed," recalls Annie. "It wasn't too bad during the summer, but in the winter it became really cold and damp, and we were glad to move out in the end."

Annie's parents Jane and Glyn purchased a caravan so they too could stay on site and be involved in the build process, with Jane taking a year out from her job teaching in a further education college. Building was largely completed on a DIY basis with subcontractors used to excavate the site, erect the steel frame and clad the roof with zinc. A glazier, electrician and plumber were also employed as required.

"As children we'd helped to do up the old bungalow, painting windows and getting involved, and here we were all working together again on its replacement," says Annie. "In summer it was fantastic to be outdoors in such a beautiful setting, but winter was a very different story

"IN SUMMER IT WAS FANTASTIC TO BE OUTDOORS IN SUCH A BEAUTIFUL SETTING, BUT WINTER WAS A VERY DIFFERENT STORY IN SUCH AN EXPOSED LOCATION"

The double bed in the master bedroom was custom made and offers panoramic sunrise views through full-height glazing which opens onto a sheltered balcony

in such an exposed location, and the weather could be quite wild."

Access onto the site was also problematic, and at one stage it was left to Annie to drag a stranded Jewson lorry out of the muddy field using a tractor.

Progress was slower than expected, which encouraged Glyn, with help from the rest of the family, to tackle even more of the work — including installing the ground-source heating, tanking the blockwork, plasterboarding, cladding the retaining perimeter walls with stone, landscaping and much more.

Mark undertook the carpentry work while Jane helped out with insulating, applying anti-corrosion agents to the steel, decorating and replanting the garden.

Stone excavated from the site has been recycled and used for garden and garage walling, a ground-source heat pump from Kensa is employed for the underfloor heating and a ventilation heat exchange provides clean, warm air throughout the heavily insulated house.

"I'm particularly pleased with how well the overhanging roof shades the glass in summer, and yet still allows the lower winter sun to warm the rooms," says Annie. "The ground floor is largely underground, so this also helps to keep the space at a fairly constant temperature throughout the year."

It was Glyn who ordered many of the materials, negotiating hard for the best possible prices, while Annie obtained quotes from various subcontractors and Jane kept detailed financial records. "There was no designated project manager, we all worked well together," says Glyn, an artist.

"Annie worked on site on Mondays, and her detailed plans were consulted to solve every issue. We were initially nervous about working with our daughter on a professional level, but we've been highly impressed with her abilities and, if anything, this project has strengthened our relationship."

With the new Seacombe completed, the old timber bungalow could finally be demolished in accordance with planning conditions. At last the Martins are able to enjoy the beautiful coastal setting all year round, retreating to the

Above: Natural local materials were sourced for the garage. The building nestles into the hillside so that it blends in with the scenery discreetly

sheltered balconies and first floor landing 'lookout' during particularly inclement weather.

Annie has recently given birth to her and Mark's first baby, Leah, and can already envisage history repeating itself. "It's lovely to think that Leah will enjoy the same kind of seaside holidays that we did as children, and we will look forward to spending time at Seacombe with the family," she says.

"Building the house has certainly brought us all closer, and it's been rewarding to think just how much of the work we managed to complete ourselves." ■

PROJECT NOTES

LINKING TO THE LANDSCAPE

Glyn Martin

On the ground floor, a striking contemporary staircase with a glass wall leads down to the open plan kitchen/dining room and neighbouring living room, where a bookcase door reveals the secret cinema.

Doors from the kitchen/dining room open into a larder, WC and store to the rear of the house. A bridge leads to the first floor entrance, where three bedrooms, two en suites and a family bathroom are located. The spacious landing area acts as a suntrap conservatory leading out onto a terrace, with steps down to the garden, and two of the bedrooms have their own covered balconies.

Ground floor

First floor

FACT FILE

Names: Glyn and Jane Martin
Professions: Artist and teacher
Area: Devon
House type: Three bedroom contemporary house
House size: 200m²
Build route: DIY and subcontractors
Finance: Private and mortgage
Construction: Blockwork ground floor; timber and steel framed first floor; zinc roof
Build time: May '06 – Sept '08
Land value: £300,000
Build cost: £350,000
Total cost: £650,000
Current value: £1,200,000
Cost/m²: £1,750

COST SAVING
46%

HOW THEY DID IT

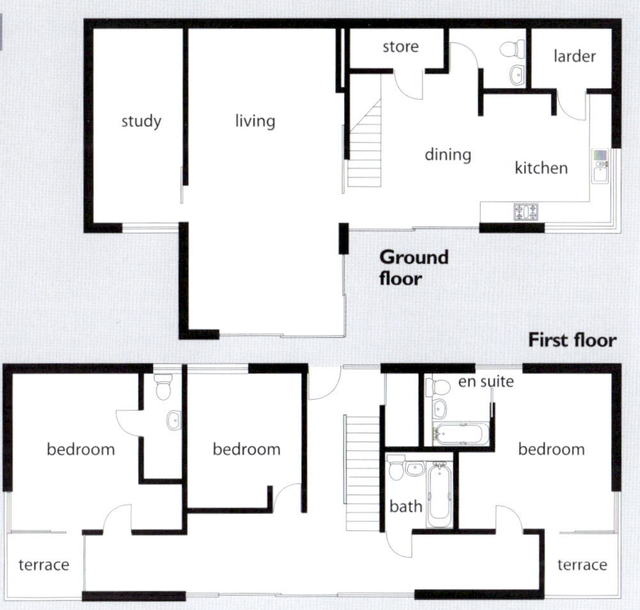

1. The steel frame structure is erected on the foundations.
2. The roof structure takes shape, with timber beams providing support.
3. Glyn and Jane spent the best part of two years on site, handling much of the labour themselves.
4. The new house begins to overshadow the existing bungalow.
5. The existing bungalow is then knocked down and the space is used for the extensive patio.
6. Glyn laid the stone wall himself, following it round to the garage.

USEFUL CONTACTS

Architect Annie Martin: 01626 773813 **Steel frame** Torr View Forge: 01548 521445 **Carpentry** MY Carpenter: 01626 773813 **Olsen sliding glazed door system** SWS: 01777 871847 **Zinc roof supply** Rheinzink: 01276 686725 **Roofing contractor** A&S Roofing System: 07976 417245 **Ground-source heat pump (supply only)** Kensa Engineering Ltd: 01326 377627 **Underfloor heating (supply only)** Radiant Heating Solutions: 01400 250572 **Kitchen, windows, front door** New British Design: 01363 777004 **Ironmongery** South Western Supplies: 01626 333900 **Glass** Paignton Glass Works: 01803 558096 **Heat exchange ventilation system** Vent-Axia: 0844 856 0590 **Structural engineer** Nicholls Basker Partners: 01626 776121 **Sanitaryware** Ideal Standard: 01482 346461
Seacombe is available for holiday rental: www.seacombe-devon.co.uk

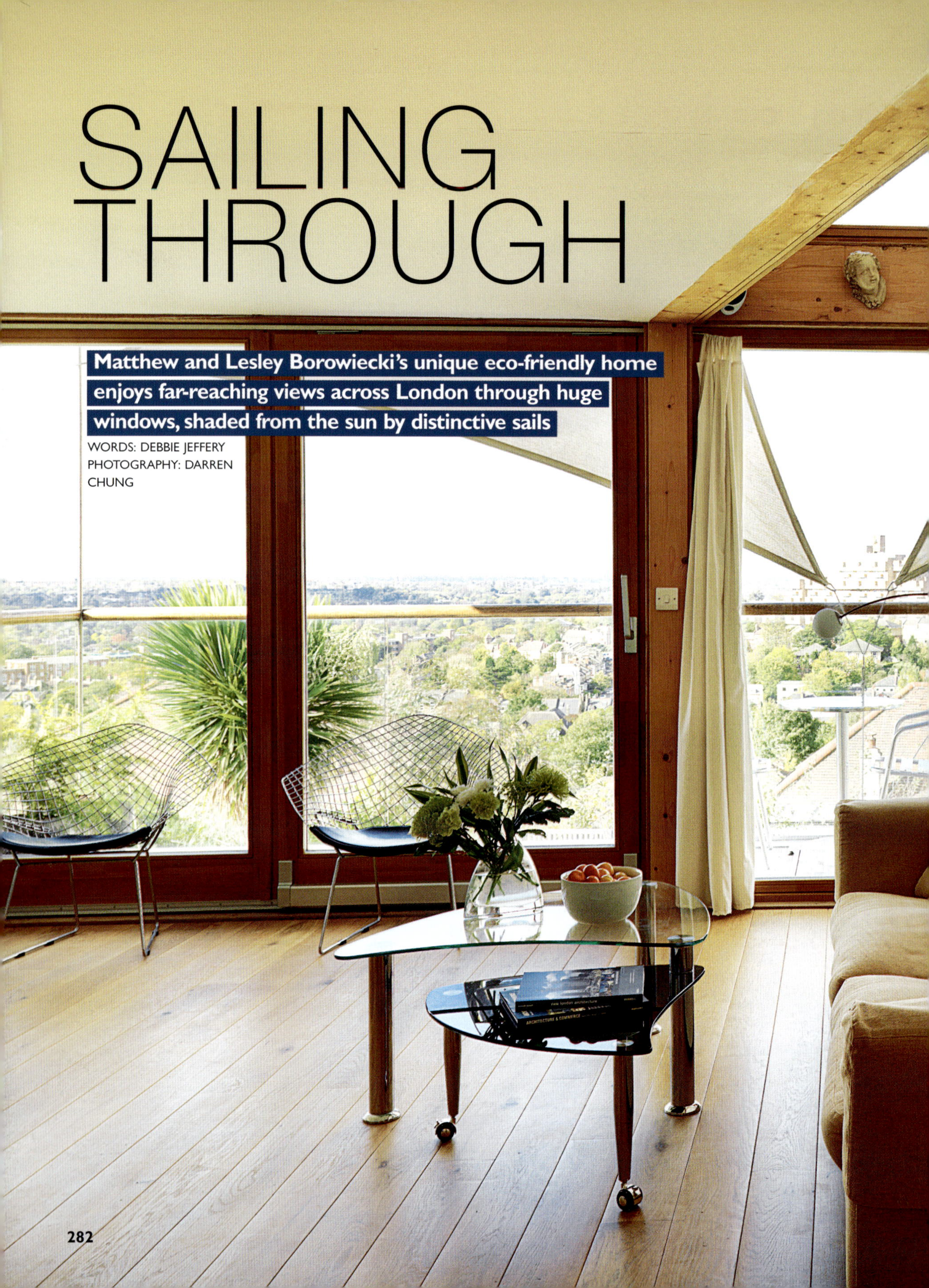

SAILING THROUGH

Above: The prefabricated components of the timber-frame kit lend themselves readily to Matthew's design. The solar water-heating system was made in Lithuania, including 4m² solar panels, the programmer and a 300-litre storage tank
Opposite: The rear of the house enjoys incredible views through massive windows of triple-glazed, argon-filled, low-E glass, shaded by distinctive sails

When Matthew and Lesley Borowiecki decided to build their own eco-friendly home, they arranged to import everything from Lithuania — including the timber frame, the kitchen, sanitaryware and even the tiles. The result is a stunning timber, steel and glass house, built in record time and fitted with some distinctive sun-screens which gave the new home its name: Sail House.

"I've actually lived in this part of South London for most of my life," says Matthew, whose family originally hails from Poland. "I used to pass by a bungalow high up on Forest Hill on my way to work, so when I saw that it had come up for sale I jumped at the chance to buy it and applied for planning permission to construct a replacement house there. The views of the city from up here are fantastic, and it's somewhere that I've always wanted to live."

Matthew and Lesley took a gamble and purchased the bungalow without any planning permission, convinced that they would be allowed to replace the small infill property with something altogether more substantial in a street of otherwise conventional 1920s villas.

In 2005, they applied for consent to demolish the bungalow which stood on the site and erect Sail House — a five bedroom, three-storey eco house, imported from Lithuania as a prefabricated timber-frame kit.

"We didn't want anything fussy, and the house is really quite a simple layout," Matthew explains. "It only appears to be two storeys from the front because it's built into the side of the hill, and inside it feels rather like being on top of a cliff at the seaside."

As an architect, Matthew was able to design his new 300m² home with input from the whole family — creating computer-generated 3D models to show them exactly how it would look. While the interior is contemporary and open plan, with white walls, exposed structural timbers and large amounts of glazing, the exterior has enormous gable windows under the eaves, shaded by extraordinary fabric 'sails'. There are also opening roof vents to help keep the house cool in summer.

For recently married Matthew and Lesley, this is the first time they have shared a home. The couple also live with Matthew's son, Ben, who has just taken his A-levels, and Lesley's children, Nathan, who works in media, and Bethany, who's studying architecture.

"The whole house has been designed around the family," says Lesley. "The children's rooms are all on the ground floor with their own spearate entrance. This means the ground floor has the potential to become a self-contained apartment in the future."

The house is built into the side of the hill over three storeys, with the main entrance on the first floor where the kitchen and open plan living/dining areas are. The children's rooms are on the ground floor while the master bedroom is at the top of the house, and there are additional studio spaces for working at home.

Left: Everything in the black and white kitchen was imported from Lithuania, right down to the floor tiles
Above: Despite its contemporary look, the use of natural materials and changes in ceiling height mean the house is full of character. Potentially dark corridors are filled with natural light thanks to their glazed doors, all of which were imported with the kit

"I've known one of the owners of Janes Homes for many years," says Matthew. "When we discovered that the company was about to start offering bespoke, timber-frame kit houses from Lithuania, we decided to allow our house to be the prototype. Prices are far lower over there, and Lesley and I went on three trips to Lithuania and shopped for everything we needed — right down to the door handles and kitchen appliances."

Virtually everything was imported, and co-ordinating the deliveries proved to be one of the most difficult elements of the project. Matthew needed to arrange for the road to be closed when the trucks arrived, also hiring a crane to lift the huge glulam timbers and prefabricated infill panels into place.

"Fortunately the deliveries didn't all come at once, but we had to make sure we ordered carefully because taking things back to a builders' merchant in Lithuania wasn't really an option," laughs Lesley. "Importing the timber frame, fixtures and fittings saved us around 20 per cent on UK prices, but it did mean that we needed to be really organised when everything was delivered."

The Borowieckis used Lithuanian labour to assemble their prefabricated Lithuanian house — although the cost of accommodating the men in London meant they didn't make any significant savings for this element of the build. However, the whole project took just six months to complete and went extremely smoothly, despite the sloping nature of the site.

The family found it satisfying to watch as the main structure of their new home was erected in just four days. Everything had been packed onto the trucks in reverse order so that, once unpacked, the materials were in the correct sequence to minimise both time and effort.

One advantage of prefabricated construction is that there's only around five per cent waste, whereas on most building sites about 20 per cent of the materials end up being thrown away.

"WE WENT ON THREE TRIPS TO LITHUANIA AND SHOPPED FOR EVERYTHING WE NEEDED — RIGHT DOWN TO THE DOOR HANDLES AND KITCHEN APPLIANCES."

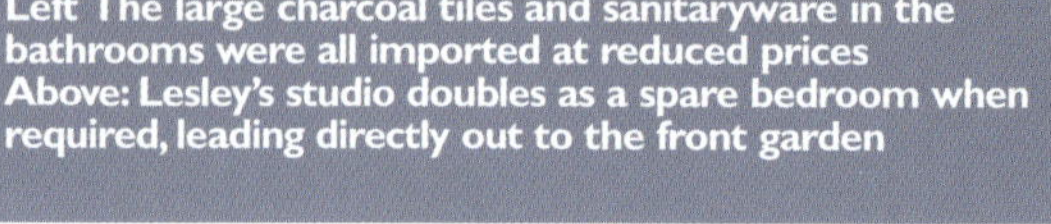

Left The large charcoal tiles and sanitaryware in the bathrooms were all imported at reduced prices
Above: Lesley's studio doubles as a spare bedroom when required, leading directly out to the front garden

"WE HAVE OVERHANGING EAVES AND THE TRIANGULAR SAILS, WHICH SHADE THE HOUSE FROM THE SUN WHEN IT GETS EVEN LOWER."

"We were working during October, when there were quite high winds, and at one point we did worry whether we could actually continue," Matthew recalls. "We were also up against it because hiring a crane costs thousands of pounds each day, and the road could only be closed for a limited time. The men worked until ten o'clock at night to finish, though, and the build attracted quite a crowd of onlookers."

The eco-credentials of the build are just as impressive as its apearance. The timber frame of the house was made using sustainably farmed wood and is massively insulated with triple-glazed, argon-filled windows. Large solar panels on the south-facing slope of the roof provide around 60 per cent of the family's hot water, and the Borowieckis also harvest rainwater from the roof to use in the garden. Underfloor heating can be controlled by room thermostats and most of the lighting that has been used throughout the house is low-energy LED.

Coloured display lights, white lighting and features such as rope lights and hanging fluorescent tubes create a vibrant effect in the main living space. "With so much glass we rarely need to turn on any artificial lights during the day," says Lesley, an artist. "The house was orientated so that it gets morning light in the kitchen and evening light in the living room."

The panoramic views from the house are truly incredible: the Borowieckis can see for miles across South London and as far as the city and the West End. This was the main reason for positioning their living room up on the first floor, where the balcony makes a perfect vantage point for watching the city lights at night.

"The problem with so much west-facing glass is that it could become very warm indoors as the sun sets in the evening," remarks Matthew. "We have overhanging eaves and the triangular sails, which are such a feature of the house, to help shade the house from the sun when it gets even lower. They're strung on halyards and can be put up and down using a block and tackle system, exactly like the sails on a boat. If it's a very windy night we can bring them indoors to store them — it's rather like being on board a ship!" ∎

PROJECT NOTES

FACT FILE

Names: Matthew and Lesley Borowiecki
Professions: Architect and artist
Area: South London
House type: Three storey, five bedroom detached eco house
House size: 300m²
Build route: Kit company
Finance: Private and mortgage
Construction: Timber frame
Build time: Oct '05 – May '06
Land cost: £300,000
Build cost: £350,000
Total cost: £650,000
Value on completion: £1,000,000
Cost/m²: £1,167

COST SAVING
35%

COST BREAKDOWN

Groundworks	£100,000
House build and frame	£180,000
Doors, windows, balconies and stairs	£22,000
Internal finishes (kitchen, bathrooms etc.)	£40,000
Freight from Lithuania	£8,000

USEFUL CONTACTS

Architect Matthew Borowiecki Architects: 07976 154751 mattborowiecki.co.uk **Timber frame kit, glazing, solar water-heating system, solid oak floors and joinery, glass balustrades, aluminium decking, glass table, coffee table, leather dining chairs, sanitaryware supply** Janes Homes: 020 7378 7391 janeshomes.co.uk **Artwork** Lesley Borowiecki: 020 8314 4014 borowiecka.co.uk **Coolaroo shade sails** Forsyth 4: 01564 784852 forsyth4.co.uk **Sofa, shelving** John Lewis: 0845 604 9049 johnlewis.com **Electric oven and extractor** Bosch: 0844 892 8979 bosch.co.uk **Taps and fittings** Hansgrohe: 0870 770 1972 hansgrohe.co.uk **Telescope** Scopes 'n' Skies: 0845 634 9192 scopesnskies.com **Sanitaryware** VitrA: 01235 750990 vitra.co.uk

SHADING A HOUSE FROM THE SUN

While Lesley and Matthew have used enormous textile 'sails' in order to prevent their house from overheating, a more conventional approach is to construct a 'brise-soleil', literally meaning 'sun breaker' in French. Designs vary, but in their basic form brise-soleils are made up of a horizontal projection that extends from the sunniest façade of the house. This prevents buildings which incorporate large amounts of glazing from overheating during summer. Louvres are often built in to the shade to prevent the high summer sun from falling on the house façade. They also allow low winter sun to enter the house, providing some passive solar heating.

MIXING UP TRADITIONAL LEVELS

The children's bedrooms are located on the ground floor, partially buried in the hillside. Lesley also has her studio on this level, which doubles as a spare room. The middle floor accommodates the kitchen, a cloakroom and the living/dining room with its balcony. An internal door links to the integral garage. The master bedroom and en suite are situated on the top floor with a mezzanine level above the living room, used as a study and separate bathroom. A void above the kitchen allows light to filter through the house.

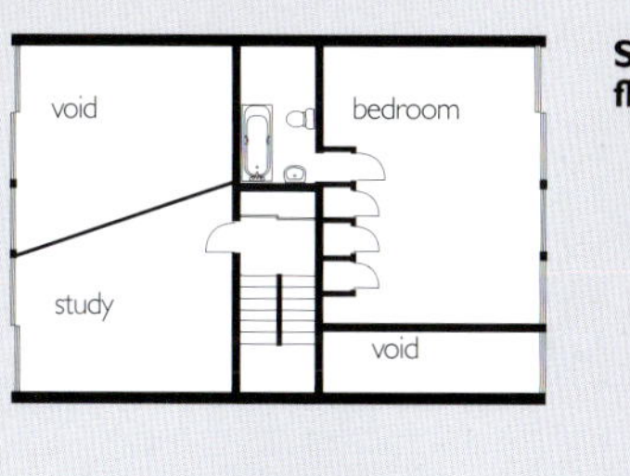

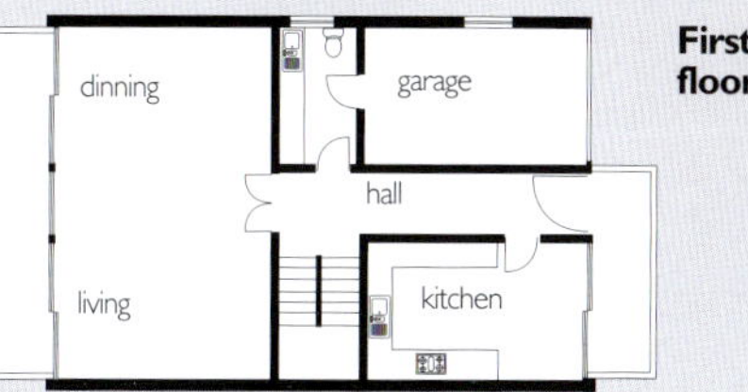

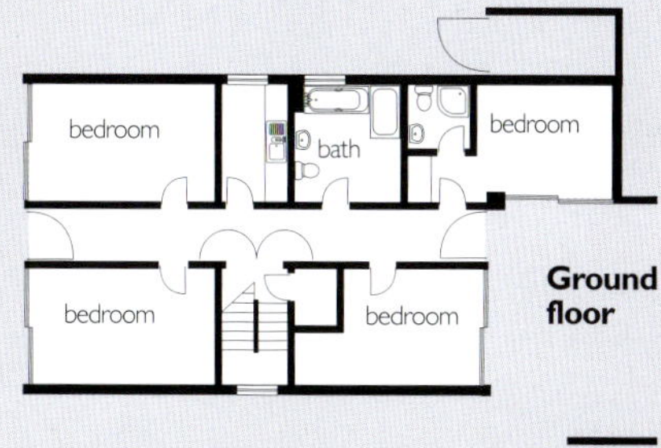

ON THE PANEL

Beccy and Steve Kestin's unique energy-efficient home was built using Structural Insulated Panels (SIPs) – chosen for their fast construction time and airtightness – ensuring the property is superbly insulated, despite its extensive use of glazing

WORDS: DEBBIE JEFFERY
PHOTOGRAPHY: NIGEL RIGDEN

When Beccy and Steve Kestin decided to start a new life in Cornwall they took on two immense challenges. The first was to start up a mussel farm – Cornish Mussels – which they now run together, and the second was to build a brand new, eco-friendly home on the site of a bland 1950s bungalow.

"We'd been living in Bristol, where Steve was working at the university and I was a primary school teacher," Beccy explains. "We wanted to move down to Cornwall, and when we decided to start up a mussel farm we needed to wait some time before we could begin harvesting and selling the mussels. Only then did we turn our attention to where we were going to live."

Keen to find a country home with enough land for machinery, the couple purchased a dilapidated bungalow on an elevated five-acre site, one mile outside a village near Falmouth. "The bungalow had already been extended, so was quite spacious, but there was no insulation and everything needed doing," says Steve. "But we wanted to take on a renovation project."

Once Beccy and Steve had moved into the property, the full extent of the renovation work became apparent, and they accepted that they would ultimately be left with just four poorly insulated external walls. Over the next few months they also realised the potential of their magnificent south-facing plot and were determined to build a new home to replace the existing bungalow.

Retired architect Geoff Carter was recommended to the couple and they explained to him their dream of creating a light, modern house incorporating plenty of glass. "We were all on the same wavelength from the start," says Beccy, "and we asked Geoff to design something which would make the most of the views."

When their plans for a four bedroom, two-storey house were duly approved, they began the preparations. "Our brief had been fairly specific and included a large conservatory for growing exotic plants," says Steve. "Until we were given the green light by the planners we hadn't really considered how the house would be built, however, and we were unsure which route to take."

Originally the Kestins considered constructing their new home in rendered solid lightweight blockwork, but the builder, who had years of experience building in Cornwall,

A contemporary open-tread ash staircase, with stainless steel handrails and glass panels, was chosen for the impressive double-height, extra-wide hallway

Above: The upper landing overlooks a double-height conservatory, and can be closed off using folding sliding doors
Above left: The master bedroom opens out onto a roof terrace through sliding glass doors and enjoys far-reaching views down over The Lizard. Light and privacy are balanced with the vertical 'slit' windows

"YOU WOULD THINK THAT SO MUCH GLASS MEANS THAT IT'S BOILING IN SUMMER AND FREEZING COLD IN WINTER, BUT IT REMAINS AT AN EVEN TEMPERATURE ALL YEAR ROUND"

commented that this method might not be the best option for their exposed coastal site and so they began exploring alternative options. "That's when we found out about SIPs and realised that they could make life easier in so many ways," Beccy recalls.

Structural Insulated Panels (SIPs) are a pre-engineered building system – long established in Scandinavian countries – which were first introduced to the UK in the 1970s. SIPs form a strong, lightweight structure which is fast to erect, thanks to the large components, and offers fantastic thermal performance.

"When we discovered how fast the shell could be built and how well insulated the house would be we approached Build It Green, a company which specialises in the supply and construction of SIPs," continues Steve. "Our builder also recommended a belt-and-braces approach by building an outer leaf of rendered blockwork in order to create a cavity construction — saying that, even Cornish rain couldn't jump a cavity!"

The architect's drawings were transformed into three-dimensional computer models by Build It Green, which gave the Kestins a detailed understanding of how their house would be built. "You could see the positions of all the panels and glulam beams," says Beccy. "The finished house is identical to the model."

Steve and Beccy vacated the old bungalow and moved into two mobile homes parked in their field while the work began. A local builder demolished the 1950s bungalow and prepared new, steel-reinforced foundations and a concrete slab for the load-bearing wall and roof panels, which were erected in just one month using glulam timber roof beam supports.

The main contractor, Peters & Jane, then completed the build and proved invaluable, ensuring that the project came in both on time and within budget. Steve acted as joint project manager – mainly keeping an eye on the quality of finishes – but tackled some of the physical work too, including landscaping the garden with granite boulders and completing the sections of flat roofing.

"The local tradesmen were fantastic, and we've become firm friends with both our architect and builder. In fact, the only major delay was caused by having to wait

White high-gloss units are topped with black granite in the limestone-floored kitchen

for some of the specialist glazing to arrive," recalls Steve. "Without the glass link the house wasn't weatherproof, and we couldn't continue fitting out the interiors, causing a three-month delay."

The house has been roofed in zinc, and incorporates an extraordinary amount of glazing — including an imposing two-storey conservatory which can be closed off when required. This glazed space captures heat from the sun, which is then redistributed around the house by the heat recovery system, and creates the perfect environment for Steve's exotic plants.

"We wanted an open plan kitchen/living room on the ground floor, which opens directly into the conservatory through sliding doors," says Beccy. "The double-height entrance hall also opens into the main living area, and is one of the features people comment on because it's 2.5 metres wide with a glazed roof, and gives a real feeling of space." This hallway is overlooked by a galleried landing, where glass doors can be pulled across to open or close off the upper conservatory, depending on the time of year.

Further folding, sliding doors lead out from the couple's bedroom onto an enclosed roof patio.

A heat recovery and ventilation system ensures that the house maintains a comfortable temperature, reclaiming heat from stale air which is used to warm fresh air brought in from outside. Oil-fired underfloor heating (which may be powered by a heat pump in the future) has been laid beneath the limestone and ash floors, but is only really needed on particularly cold days — ensuring that the new house is extremely economical to run.

"We never set out to build a green house," admits Steve, "but the more we discovered about SIPs, the more we realised that they would be the perfect choice for us. The build wasn't without its problems, but the SIPs construction was definitely the quickest and easiest part of the whole project."

After living in the '50s bungalow and then in mobile homes, the Kestins were particularly grateful to move into such a comfortable new home. "You would think that so much glass means that it's boiling in summer and freezing cold in winter," says Beccy, "but in fact the rooms remain at an even temperature all year round. It means that you can walk around indoors wearing a T-shirt any month of the year, which is one of the benefits of such a highly insulated home." ■

PROJECT NOTES

BRINGING LIGHT FROM ABOVE

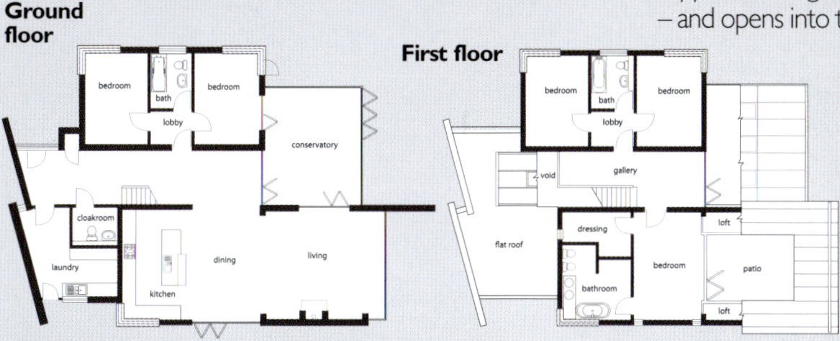

Ground floor

First floor

A 2.5 metre-wide, double-height entrance hallway is topped with a glass roof – flooding the area with light – and opens into the open plan kitchen/dining/living room, with a TV snug, ground floor bedroom and bathroom accessed via a separate lobby. Upstairs, the landing overlooks the upper conservatory. There is a guest bedroom and bathroom, a study and the master suite, which opens onto a sheltered outdoor terraced area set into the roof.

COST SAVING
22%

COST BREAKDOWN

Demolition and site clearance	£1,200
Reinforced slab and footings	£12,800
Scaffolding	£1,000
Floor insulation	£2,100
Structural insulated panels	£59,000
Zinc roof, soffits gutters	£17,879
GRP flat roofs	£800
Velfac corner windows	£13,000
Conservatory and sliding doors	£74,000
External rendering	£17,000
Underfloor heating	£4,000
Plumbing	£8,500
Electrics	£11,500
Plasterboard and plastering	£7,000
Limestone flooring	£17,000
Sanitaryware	£7,500
Kitchen units, appliances and granite	£15,000
Hearth	£700
Heat recovery unit and fittings	£3,500
Staircase	£8,250
Lighting design and supply	£5,000
Central vacuum system	£1,000
Patio	£1,632
Deck	£1,500
Fees	£26,000
Main contractor	£43,000

FACT FILE

Names: Beccy and Steve Kestin
Professions: Mussel farmers
Area: Cornwall
House type: Four bedroom detached house
House size: 270m²
Build route: Builder and specialist subcontractors
Finance: Private
Construction: Structural insulated panels (SIPs), blockwork, zinc roof
Build time: Jan '06 – March '07
Land cost: £305,000
Build cost: £360,000
Total cost: £665,000
Current value: £850,000
Cost/m²: £1,333

WHAT EXACTLY ARE SIPS?

Structural Insulated Panels (or SIPs) are made like a sandwich, with a filling of insulating foam (either expanded or extruded polystyrene) inserted between two sheets of structural board, such as plywood or oriented strand board (OSB). The layers are bonded together ensuring the panels are extremely robust. SIPs replace several components of conventional building such as studs and joists, insulation, and vapour and air barriers. As such they can be used for many different applications including the exterior wall, roof and floor. SIPs have been around for over 50 years internationally, but have only become commonplace in the UK over the last eight years or so. They create a house so airtight that most people need to specify whole-house mechanical ventilation; Beccy and Steve opted for a system from Villavent.

"WE NEVER SET OUT TO BUILD A GREEN HOUSE, BUT SIPS WERE PERFECT FOR US"

USEFUL CONTACTS

Structural Insulated Panels Build It Green: 0870 200 0358 **Main contractor** Peters & Jane: 01326 280624 **Aluminium windows** Velfac Ltd: 01223 897100 **Heat recovery and ventilation system** Villavent Ltd: 01993 778481 **Underfloor heating** Continental Underfloor Heating: 0845 108 7001 **Zinc roofing** Salmon Roofing: 01932 875050 **Staircase** Stairflight Ltd: 01590 676911 **Kitchen** Maurice Lay: 0870 606 9606 **Limestone flooring** Varcum Marble: 01209 610777 **Lighting design** GIGB Lighting: 0845 402 0673 **Render contractor** R & K Swaine: 01872 870010 **Decorators** RH Jane: 01326 290043 **Scan woodburning stoves** Wendron Stoves: 01326 572878 **Folding sliding doors and conservatory** Sunparadise: 0870 240 7604

TUNNEL VISION

Jamie and Zoe McLintock have built a contemporary-style home in the heart of a tourist attraction — with stunning views of the surrounding coastline and historic tunnels

WORDS: VICTORIA JENKINS
PHOTOGRAPHY: WILLOUGHBY ANDREWS

Left: Jamie and Zoe (pictured left with Millie and Marley) built their new home on the Devon clifftops. The tunnels (left) are now a tourist attraction
Right: The living/dining/ kitchen area is on the first floor to make the most of the fantastic views

A t the tender age of just 24, Jamie and Zoe McLintock became the proud owners of five tunnels and a mile of North Devon coastline — and then proceeded to turn them into a tourist attraction. "The tunnels are historic and actually put Ilfracombe on the map as a tourist resort in Victorian times," says Jamie. "Before that it was just a fishing village."

Originally blasted through the cliff in 1823 by Welsh miners from across the Bristol Channel, the tunnels once belonged to Zoe's grandfather. "He had leased them from the Ilfracombe Sea Bathing Company in the 1960s before buying them," explains Jamie. "Zoe's father inherited them in 1980, and Zoe and I had always seen the potential for developing the area, so when she became pregnant in December 2001 we thought the time was right to leave our jobs and persuade her father to sell them to us."

Having sold two properties in Warwickshire to raise capital, the couple rented accommodation nearby, then spent the next few years rewiring four of the tunnels and improving and creating various facilities, such as lavatories, a cafe, a shop, beach bar and picnic garden.

Once the bulk of this work was done, the couple felt it

was time to have a home of their own. This was in 2003
and by then around 80,000 people per season were
visiting the tunnels and beaches. "The business was going
really well," says Jamie, "so it seemed like the perfect time
to self-build."

The site the McLintocks chose was on top of the
cliff — above the tunnels — and resembled an overgrown
allotment, but it came with planning permission for a
bungalow. "It had been on the market for five or six years
and many builders had turned it down as being non-
viable," says Jamie. "However, we never intended to build
a bungalow." For — dazzled by the fabulous views across
the sea to Lundy island and Wales 30 miles away — the
McLintocks had other ideas.

"We bought the plot in 2003 and as we both
came from a design background, we were able to put
together sketches and a comprehensive brief for an

architect," says Jamie. "We wanted a very contemporary house complete with a curved roof and a tower like a lighthouse, with an elliptical glass top to let in the light. We thought the architect would change our ideas, but all he suggested was moving the tower back a metre from the edge of the cliff. As it is the house is only eight metres from a 50-metre drop."

There is, however, a single trackway separating the house from the drop. "The architect put in for planning permission in April 2004 and within seven weeks it had been granted," says Jamie. "No objections were raised — surprisingly so,

"WE WANTED A VERY CONTEMPORARY HOUSE COMPLETE WITH A CURVED ROOF AND A TOWER LIKE A LIGHTHOUSE, WITH AN ELLIPTICAL GLASS TOP TO LET IN THE LIGHT"

The glass-topped tower is made of reclaimed bricks

"THE HOUSE WAS SITED DIRECTLY ABOVE THE FIFTH UNUSED TUNNEL WHICH WAS ONLY FIVE-AND-HALF-METRES BELOW OUR BASEMENT"

considering Ilfracombe is a Victorian resort and people here tend to be protective of this Area of Natural Beauty."

What made building their home viable was that they included a basement in the design and have maximised the site by incorporating balconies. "It has a front of 35 metres but the depth tapers from 15 metres to only nine metres," explains Jamie, who was project manager.

"We also wanted a tower. This was for two reasons: one was for it to look nautical, and the other was that, as we gave it a glass top, it can let in as much light as possible." The house is built of blocks and mortar and is steel framed, both to create the curve of the zinc titanium roof and also to tie it down. "Yes, the house has stunning views but it is also subject to gale-force winds," says Jamie. "There is a two-and-a-half-metre overhang on the roof to protect the balcony and the steel framing had to be built within the roof in order to stop the wind whistling upwards from the sea and taking it right off."

The couple faced their biggest problem early on, when they started digging out the basement. "When the single trackway had been carved into the hillside in 1920, the waste had been dumped onto our plot," says Jamie. "We found it was non-weathered soft shale which meant we had to pile-drive the foundations. The house was sited directly above the fifth unused tunnel which was only five-and-half-metres below our basement. We had to bridge it with lots of engineering work to make sure the house would not collapse into the tunnel."

Work began in June 2004 but within weeks had to stop until the following January while the engineers put bridging across the tunnel. "They had to do test bores to make sure they were on solid rock," says Jamie. "It was a worrying time. We had staged to have the money for the mortgage on a draw-down basis and now had to spend £60,000 up front on the foundations.

It took 16 months to complete the house, and the family moved in last July. Now more than 420m² in size (including the double garage with its own basement), the property sits on 525m² of land with its own private access to the beach.

"I suppose buying five tunnels, two beaches and then building a house surveying it all was rather a weird thing to do!" laughs Jamie. "It was very exciting but also exhausting, and sometimes I have to pinch myself to prove I didn't dream it all." ■

PROJECT NOTES

Jamie and Zoe have incorporated balconies to make the most of the view, adding a long overhang onto the roof to guard against strong winds

FLOORPLAN

Ground floor

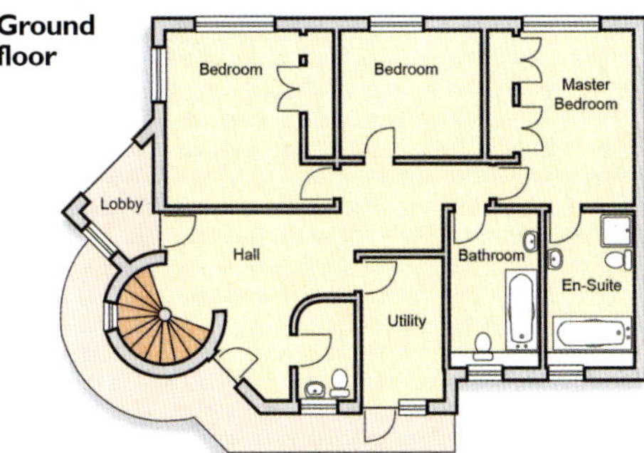

Basement

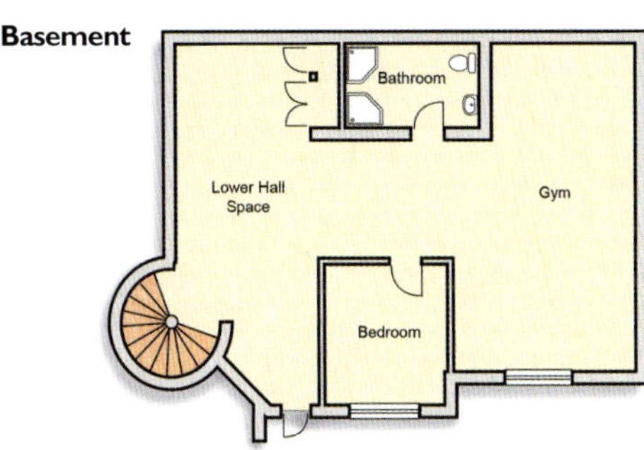

First floor

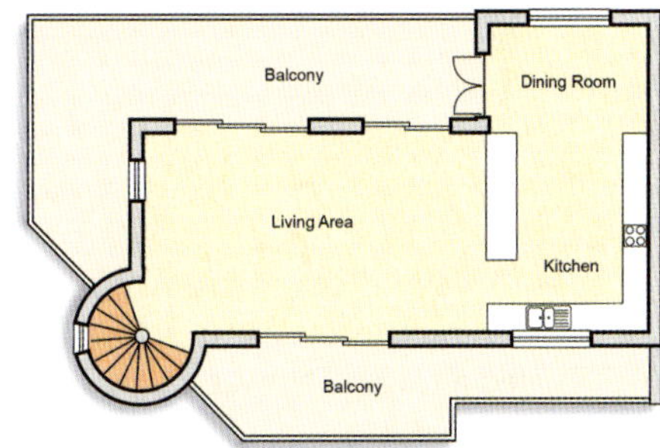

FACT FILE

Names: Jamie and Zoe McLintock
Professions: Self-employed tourist attraction and beach owners
Area: Ilfracombe, North Devon
House type: Contemporary coastal new build with four bedrooms
House size: 420m²
Build route: Selves as project managers plus architect
Finance: Private
Construction: Masonry plus steel frame
Build time: Three years
Land cost: £85,000
Build cost: £350,000
Total cost: £435,000
Current value: £1m
Cost/m²: £833

COST SAVING
56%

USEFUL CONTACTS

Builder Paul Prentice, now working full-time for Tunnels Beaches: 01271 879882
Kitchen Roundhouse Kitchens: 020 7428 9955
Oven Smeg: 0870 990 9907 **Induction hob, fridge, freezer, dishwasher** Neff: www.neff.co.uk **Floor tiles** Fired Earth: 0845 366 0400 **Bathroom tiles** Reed Harris: 020 8877 9774 **Limestone mosaic tiles** Mandarin Stone: 01225 460033
Bath and taps Traditional Contemporary Bathrooms: 01924 845000 **Basin** Kohler: 0870 850 5551

The open plan kitchen, living and dining rooms have all been situated on the first floor to make the most of the views and are surrounded by balconies. On the ground floor are three bedrooms and two bathrooms. The two floors are linked by a tower staircase. A basement contains games room, guest suite and gym.

Helen and John Morrison's striking new eco home has been partially buried in the ground and features a luxurious basement swimming pool — all built to last a lifetime

WORDS: DEBBIE JEFFERY   PHOTOGRAPHY: JEREMY PHILLIPS

When Helen and John Morrison decided to return to the pretty Kent village where they had lived some years before, they struggled to find a suitable house in the popular area. Eventually the couple purchased a run-down timber bungalow on the edge of the village, which they hoped to replace with a contemporary, eco-friendly home.

"The bungalow was erected during the First World War and used as a Red Cross first-aid hut. It was so full of holes that the place whistled when the wind blew," laughs John. "We spruced it up and it was fine as a temporary home — but we weren't particularly sad to finally watch it being demolished."

The couple lived in the old bungalow for almost two years while they waited for planning permission to be approved, and this enabled them to put together a very specific list of requirements for its replacement and to get a real feel for the north-facing site.

Located in the green belt, in an Area of Outstanding Natural Beauty, the new house is far removed from its leaky predecessor. Constructed using a strong,

Beetlebank is a contemporary home set in the heart of the Kent countryside, situated in a tranquil location overlooking farmland and the Medway Valley

lightweight steel frame and clad in a combination of green oak, reclaimed London stock bricks and huge sections of glazing, the contemporary building boasts some impressive eco credentials. The structure is massively insulated, and a geothermal heat pump serves the underfloor heating pipes, also providing hot water for the kitchen and bathrooms. Rainwater is recovered from the roof and used for watering the garden.

"The brief to our architect, Richard Reid, was to design a modern house which could take full advantage of the views and would incorporate green technology," says Helen. "The existing bungalow had a small basement reached by an external staircase, and we realised that sinking the new house into the ground would reduce its impact on the surroundings and give us the extra space we wanted."

In fact, half of the living accommodation has been buried below ground level, with a central atrium bringing natural light into the core of the basement. This contains a guest bedroom, bathroom and utility, a cinema/audio room and a fabulous indoor swimming pool and sauna.

"The pool was a vital part of the overall design and has totally changed our way of life," John explains. "Swimming before breakfast is a real luxury, and we've added

underwater speakers and a home cinema system in the pool area too."

At ground-floor level the living room opens through full-height glass doors onto a west-facing patio, while views down the Medway Valley over woods and fields can be enjoyed from the fully glazed east side of the room. The kitchen/dining area is open plan, with the master bedroom located to the south of the entrance hall, where the glazed lantern literally pops up out of the roof above the stairwell.

Originally the Morrisons had planned to include a study at first-floor level, reached by an external staircase. Realising how impractical this might prove, they decided instead on a separate contemporary oak box structure at ground floor level accessed by covered walkway.

Top left: The sitting room features a large brick fireplace and glass doors which can be pushed back to open the space directly to the garden
Below left: Oak cabinets are teamed with reconstituted stone worktops in the kitchen/diner
Above: Crisp white sanitaryware from West One Bathrooms creates a stunning contrast against dark stone tiling, with uplighters installed in the floor
Above middle and right: Glass balusters with steel handrails perfectly complement the stone-clad stair treads, kept light and open with glazed half-risers

"It's certainly a very unusual house," admits John. "We renamed it 'Beetlebank' to mark the fact that so much of the building is buried into the hill. People often wrongly assume that underground homes will feel dark and claustrophobic, but we've made sure that the basement level is warm and brightly lit — otherwise we simply wouldn't want to spend any time down there."

John and Helen's son Rob returned from France to take on the role of project manager for the build and worked with a construction firm headed by close family friend and qualified structural engineer, Rob Legon.

Building Beetlebank took around 18 months to complete and involved the entire family, with the Morrisons' two other sons – Mike and PJ – also lending a hand. Inevitably on such a complex build there were minor disputes with the occasional subcontractor, but ultimately everyone worked well together and thoroughly enjoyed being on site.

"Building this house from scratch has created opportunities for including eco features, and excavating the site was the perfect time to dig the three 50 metre-long trenches required for the geothermal heating," says John.

The house has been constructed with a flat roof, which will ultimately be planted with a layer of native wildflowers designed to minimise rainwater run-off, aid insulation and further camouflage the building.

Provision has also been made for the installation of photovoltaic (PV) cells above the atrium as a means of generating solar-power electricity, and for a wind turbine (subject to planning), which (they hope) will make Beetlebank virtually independent from the National Grid. The Morrisons are also considering the possibility of using their basement swimming pool as a heat sink at some

"PEOPLE WRONGLY ASSUME UNDERGROUND HOMES FEEL DARK AND CLAUSTROPHOBIC, BUT WE'VE MADE SURE THAT THE BASEMENT LEVEL IS WARM AND BRIGHTLY LIT"

"THE HOUSE WAS DEFINITELY DESIGNED AS A PARTY PAD, AND THE LAYOUT HAS PROVED ABSOLUTELY IDEAL FOR ENTERTAINING"

point in the future.

"We had to be mindful of our budget, and these technologies can cost an awful lot of money, so it was important that we didn't overspend on features which could easily be added later," Helen explains.

Predominantly natural materials have been chosen for the high-quality finish, including stone flooring laid over underfloor heating. The same golden crystalline oyster schist stone, with muted blue and red tones, has been used for the adjoining patios.

Fine oak joinery features in every room, with wardrobes, shelving and other furniture crafted by the same company who supplied the oak kitchen and reconstituted stone worktops.

Low-energy lighting was specified throughout the house and the huge expanses of glazing ensure that the interiors remain brightly lit while enjoying fabulous views across the neighbouring farmland.

"We wanted a virtually seamless connection between the indoor and outdoor spaces," John explains. "For us,

The basement swimming pool has underwater speakers and a cinema system to watch films or television as you swim...

the house is all about the location and the views.

"This house was definitely designed as a party pad, and the layout has proved absolutely ideal for entertaining. Now we have a sensational home, designed to our own specific requirements in the perfect setting," concludes John. "We've also made sure that it's a low-maintenance building. Hopefully we'll be living at Beetlebank for the rest of our lives." ■

PROJECT NOTES

Helen and John built the house to last into their old age, making it as low-maintenance as possible. Their son Rob acted as project manager

FACT FILE

Names: John and Helen Morrison
Professions: Surveyor and homemaker
Area: Kent
House type: Detached eco-friendly self-built house with basement
House size: 360m²
Build route: Building contractor and project manager
Finance: Private
Construction: Steel frame with oak and brick cladding
Build time: April '06 – Aug '07
Land cost: £400,000
Build cost: £750,000
Total cost: £1,150,000
Value on completion: £1,500,000
Cost/m²: £2,083

COST SAVING
23%

A BASEMENT STORY

The basement contains a guest bedroom, bathroom, utility room, cinema, sauna and swimming pool. On the ground floor there's a living room and open-plan kitchen/dining area, with two en suite bedrooms and an externally accessed study.

LIFETIME HOMES

As they plan to spend the rest of their lives here, Helen and John have very sensibly ensured their home is low-maintenance and built in features which will make life easier for them when they retire. This is very timely indeed: under new Government plans, by 2013 all self-builders will have to create new homes fit for an ageing population, including 16 requirements such as stairs wide enough for stairlifts and downstairs bathrooms.

However, though it may seem like an additional headache now, it really is just good common sense — the idea being to avoid building homes which will need costly adaptations as owners age.

Before it becomes compulsory, you would be wise to at least think about adding in features that will make life easier as you grow old and perhaps infirm – as far away as that may seem to be. It will certainly improve your home's appeal to future buyers.

Easy criteria to consider include creating wider corridors and doorways; adequate turning and circulation space for wheelchairs; windows low enough to be enjoy while seated; a reasonable route for a potential hoist from a main bedroom to bathroom; an entrance-level living room and bathroom, plus a space that could be used as a bedroom; and a wide car-parking space.

FLOORPLAN

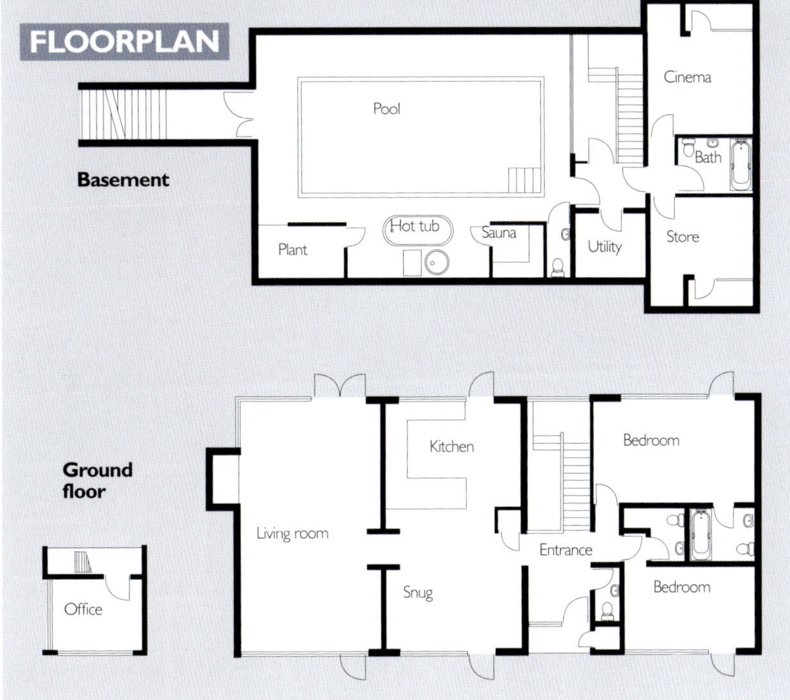

USEFUL CONTACTS

Project manager Robert Morrison, MDP Ltd: 07775 925379 **Architect** Richard Reid & Associates: 01732 741417 richardreid.co.uk
Builder and structural engineer RJ Legon Ltd: 01892 510010 **Kitchen, worktop, fitted furniture** Chamber Furniture: 01959 532553
Geothermal heating system Earth Energy Ltd: 01326 310650 earthenergy.co.uk **Sanitaryware** West One Bathrooms: 01342 822422

RIVERSIDE RETREAT

Mark Yeomanson and Maggie Samea have created a spectacular home that makes the most of its riverside location.

WORDS AND PHOTOGRAPHY: IMAGETEXT

A t a time when the rest of London and the Home Counties appeared to be 'escaping to the country', Maggie Samea and Mark Yeomanson decided to embark on a journey back from Devon – where they had just completed a barn conversion – to the Home Counties, an area familiar to both of them. "We missed being close to London," Maggie confides, "and as soon as we began to look at the cost of houses, we had no doubts that what we really wanted to do was another conversion or restoration. We were ready to launch into another project."

The problem in the London fringe areas is finding a site or a project that is worth the investment in terms of time, money and emotional drain. With developers snapping up most of the attractive sites, they had to look long and hard, turning down several likely-looking ideas before finally coming across an almost derelict chalet style bungalow on the bank of the River Thames at Shepperton.

The bungalow had been occupied by an elderly man for years and had become badly damaged by neglect and the elements. The garden was so overgrown that when they came to clear the site they discovered two cars in the grounds that they hadn't seen on their earlier visits.

The bungalow itself might have been a wreck but the old maxim about 'location being everything' certainly applied here. "How much is a view worth?" Maggie asks rhetorically. Just ten feet from the front of the property is the ever-changing panorama of one of the busiest stretches of the lower Thames with a constant stream of pleasure boats, rowers and waterfowl passing by.

"THERE'S SOMETHING WONDERFULLY RELAXING ABOUT BEING BESIDE FLOWING WATER AND THE RICH TAPESTRY OF RIVER LIFE SIMPLY ADDS TO THE SPECTACLE."

The spectacular
9.5m span that
houses the front
window is made
possible because
of the steel frame,
which has been
painted black.

The layout is very much focused on the views, with the red cedar decking that surrounds the exterior very much part of the living space.

"There's something wonderfully relaxing about being beside flowing water and the rich tapestry of river life simply adds to the spectacle," Maggie enthuses. "As soon as I saw where the bungalow was, I knew it would make a wonderful home. I could imagine how relaxing and enthralling it would be to sit and watch that view unfold over the course of the day." On a more practical basis Mark stated: "at least no one can build in front of us."

Being near to the river gave Mark a few doubts about the purchase, and it was not until after much research into the potential risks of flooding, erosion, subsidence and insurability that they decided to go ahead with the purchase.

The property purchase was to be by way of a sealed bid, always a difficult calculation, and Mark and Maggie had to calculate projected costs for all work on the site before they made their submission. For others facing this prospect, there could be a few lessons to be learnt from Maggie and Mark's approach, as Mark explains.

"Irrespective of the advertised guide price do not be tempted to bid more than what you think it is worth, and what the project could cost: taking into account a large provision for unforeseen problems that may arise at a later date. Our sealed bid was rejected and relegated to third place. But we were aware that a lot of developers are prepared to bid a high price to gain the opportunity to try and achieve large planning gains."

The steel staircase is very much in keeping with the open plan layout, with open risers and glass balustrading.

In the end the other parties failed to complete and the property was offered back to the couple. Mark has a very pragmatic approach to projects and he had almost forgotten it; but it was Maggie's intuitive feel that won the day.

"It was our intention to restore the property," Mark explains, "but the more we looked at the state of the structure and the projected costs, the more we realised that demolition and a new structure was the only realistic way forward."

The decision to level the site and start again was not one to take lightly. Mark and Maggie had bought the bungalow without any consideration for planning permission to demolish and design a brand new home.

"When we realised we would need to create a new dwelling and the reality of the situation started to dawn on us, there were a few sleepless nights, recalculating and assessing the situation," admits Mark. "We had no illusions as to the possible difficulties planning permission would present, but in reality the planners at Spelthorne Council were very helpful. I think they could see that the site would benefit from redevelopment. Of course they expected us to create something in keeping with the surroundings, but since almost every waterfront house in the area was different we were confident that this would give us plenty of scope in our design."

Considerations such as roof shape and height were to become the key issues. In many ways, these restrictions helped shape the final design and resulted in the glass frontage to the river creating a huge uninterrupted panoramic view. In fact they created two vistas, with the ground floor having an opening with an unsupported nine-

"THE MORE WE LOOKED AT THE STATE OF THE STRUCTURE, THE MORE WE REALISED THAT DEMOLITION WAS THE ONLY WAY FORWARD."

and-a-half metre span and the upstairs lounge leading out on to a nine metre balcony with an innovative glass floor and glass surround.

The requirements to raise the property to allow for flooding (even though this had never happened to the property) were laid down in legislation and were a condition of the planning permission.

After changing the design many times Mark, in conjunction with the architects, Pelta Associates of Chertsey, and Maggie's input on the practicality of the internal layout, the final plan was submitted and approved. Mark and Maggie had by this time decided that glass, steel, natural limestone and red hardwood cedar for the deck were going to be the key elements around which this contemporary house would evolve. The chalet style of the previous property had in part been retained but, within the format, Mark and Maggie have incorporated a fabulous range of innovative ideas and a stunning contemporary look.

As Maggie says, "With the concept of Mark's design being 'a seamless transition between the inside and outside space, utilising materials with an industrial quality', and having already used exposed timber in my barn project, the idea of using exposed steel was one that I embraced immediately in a modern building," Maggie explains. "When the steel frame was put up the rumours that the building was going to be a warehouse or a superstore were rife," she jokes.

Due to the complexity of the project a team incorporating an architect, engineers and a project management company were employed to bring the vision to reality. Even before the first piles on which the steel frame was to sit on were installed, Maggie and Mark had already sourced the major subcontractors and materials for the project.

"With the journey reaching its end, it's now time to sit back and enjoy what we have created," Maggie and Mark admit, "but we can't leave it there." Already, armed with the experience and possibly a raft of cost savings, they are looking for the next project to start some time in spring next year. ■

PROJECT NOTES

FACT FILE

Names: Maggie Samea and Mark Yeomanson
Professions: Company director and business consultant
Area: Middlesex
House type: Five bed, four bath chalet style self-build
House size: 331m² incl. garage
Build route: Builder and self-managed subcontractors
Construction: Steel frame with blockwork
Finance: Private
Build time: November '02 - May '04
Land cost: £499,000
Build cost: £1m
Total cost: £1.5m
House value: c.£1.8m
Cost/m²: £3,021

COST SAVING
17%

REPLACING BUNGALOWS

With virgin building plots rarer than ever, canny self-builders – and developers – recognise that bungalows are as ripe for replacement as they are for renovation. Each council has different guidelines, but it is usually possible to replace the bungalow with a dwelling of a larger size, often on more than one storey.

FLOOR PLAN

The layout is based entirely around the riverside views, with the main open plan living spaces on both floors to the front of the property, with two bedrooms on each floor to the rear.

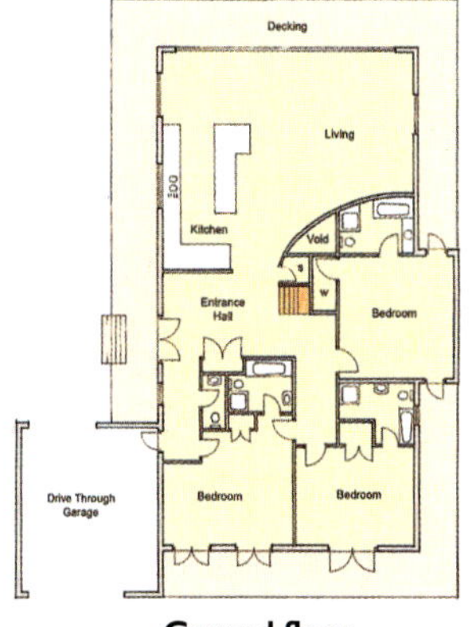

Ground floor

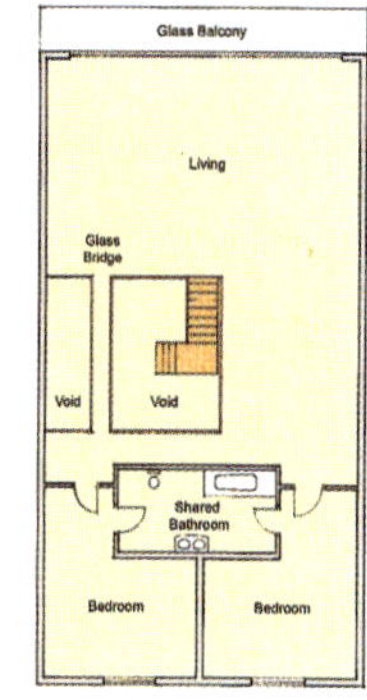

First floor

USEFUL CONTACTS

Architect Pelta Associates: 01932 561112 **Home automation** One Touch Solutions: 01483 302021 **Staircase and deck metalwork** Art Metal Industries: 01752 855100 **Main windows and doors** I-D-Systems: 01603 408804 **Bathrooms** DC dot Co: 01932 828152; **Internal glass, glass bridge, and glass balcony** Glazeguard: 01823 337755; **Kitchen** Miele: 01235 554455

OAKWRIGHTS®
Beautiful Homes, Uniquely Crafted
English Traditional • Barn Style • Contemporary

T.J.Crump OAKWRIGHTS Limited The Lakes Swainshill Hereford HR4 7PU
T: 01432 353353 F: 01432 357733 enquiries@oakwrights.co.uk www.oakwrights.co.uk

charnwood

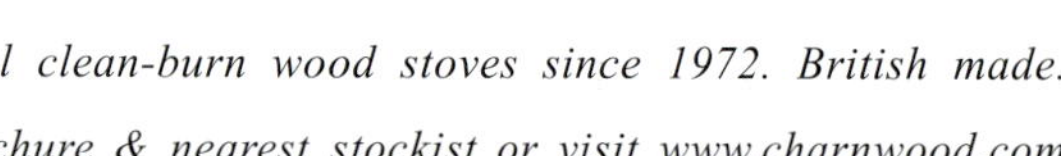

Designers & makers of exceptional clean-burn wood stoves since 1972. British made.
Telephone 01983 537780 for a brochure & nearest stockist or visit www.charnwood.com

Listen to RegaVent Whole House Ventilation

It's True!
Rega's unique WhisperFlow® technology ensures that even when operating at full 'Boost' mode (usually during the morning bathroom rush hour!) the system remains whisper quiet - unobtrusively and effectively venting stale and damp air and replacing it with air that's been gently warmed and filtered.

Low energy DC fans, insulated ducting and a high efficiency heat exchanger also ensure that energy usage and energy losses are kept to an absolute minimum.

And because RegaVent systems are designed and built here in the UK, to our own stringent quality assured standards, you can be sure that your RegaVent system will give you the optimum balance of a technical specification that's exactly right for the UK climate, coupled with low energy consumption - for lower heating bills!

* **Virtually silent operation**
* **Low energy DC electric motors**
* **Fully programmable**
* **Acoustically insulated ducting**
* **Filters reduce effects of respiratory allergies**
* **Reduces heating bills**
* **Can promote conditions for improved health**
* **Easy to install for DIYer or professional alike**
* **Conforms to Building regulations**
* **Full installation service available**

Tel: **01767 600499**   email: **sales@rega-uk.com**

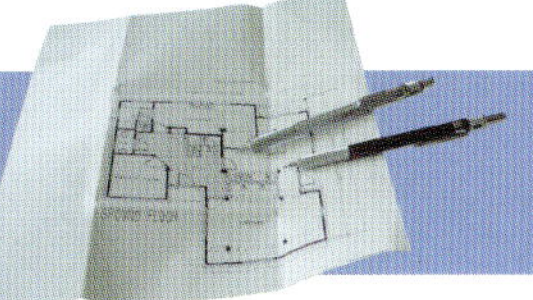

Rega Ventilation Limited
www.regavent.co.uk   email: sales@rega-uk.com
21/22 Eldon Way, Biggleswade, Beds SG18 8NH
Telephone: 01767 600499   fax: 01767 600487

BEST ECO HOUSE ROOF AWARD

ROOFKRETE WATERPROOFING IS SUSTAINABLE AND RECYCLABLE, WITH A 30 YEAR WARRANTY

THE ONLY PERMANENT WATERPROOFING FOR FLAT ROOFS AND BALCONIES

RoofKrete Waterproofing ltd

Roofkrete Waterproofing has won the 2009 AWARD from THE DAILY TELEGRAPH and HOMEBUILDING & RENOVATING MAGAZINE for the BEST ECO ROOF. This innovative eco-friendly home was built by Philip and Margaret Nierop. The design included several innovative solutions including a remarkable glass down pipe, and a Roofkrete membrane flat roof with a solar panel on top of the Roofkrete. The house boldly combines natural materials and manmade materials creating a striking focal point in the interior via exposed glulam posts and beams. The construction was a timber frame with a combined roof of zinc at the perimeter and Roofkrete Waterproofing in the centre of the building with a Solar Panel resting on the Roofkrete . The designers/owners Philip and Margaret Nierop specified Roofkrete because it did not decay like bitumen/asphalt or single ply roofing, and the Roofkrete is sustainable, recyclable, fire-proof, and will Last the life-time of the building!

Telephone: 07970 455050 Email: service@roofcrete.co.uk Web: www.krete.co.uk
Address: RoofKrete Waterproofing Ltd, Lower Woodlands, Lustleigh, Newton Abbot, Devon TQ13 9TG
Krete Sustain Systems Ltd, Sustain House, 367 Hale Road, Hale Barns, Altrincham WA15 8TB

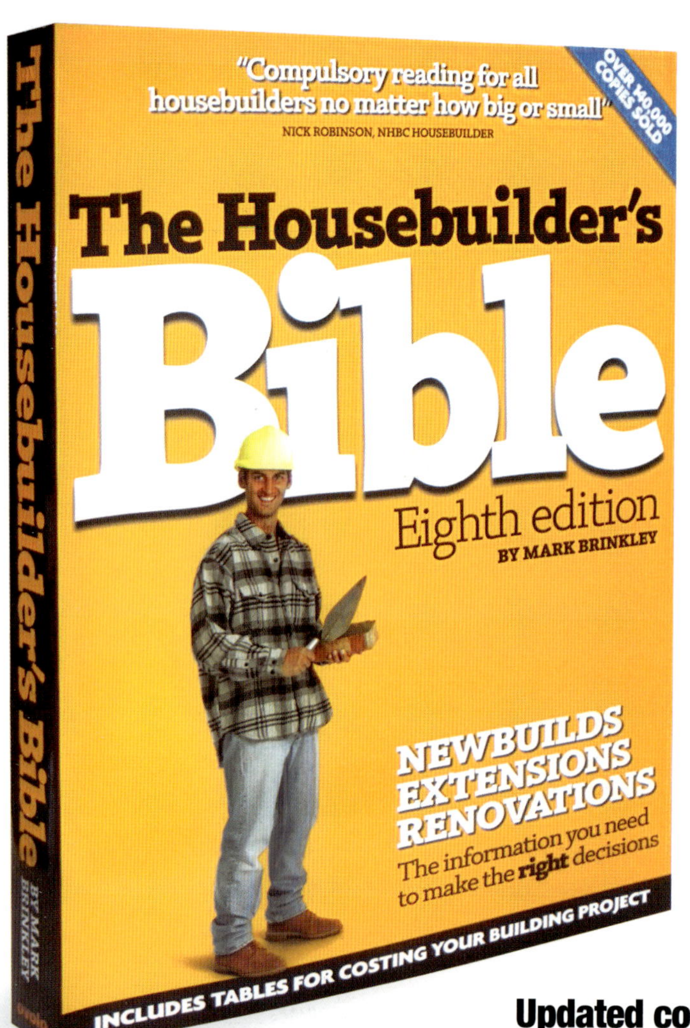

THE HOUSEBUILDER'S BIBLE

ISBN **978 1 905959 150**

Whether you're a first-time selfbuilder or seasoned professional this book tells you how to succeed at housebuilding. It explains everything you need to know about managing a build, buying and using materials, finding and employing the right people and doing it all without the pitfalls. Written in a highly readable style this eighth edition is fully updated and takes account of recent changes in fuel and property prices - including the new 'Code for Sustainable Homes'.

The story of a new benchmark house

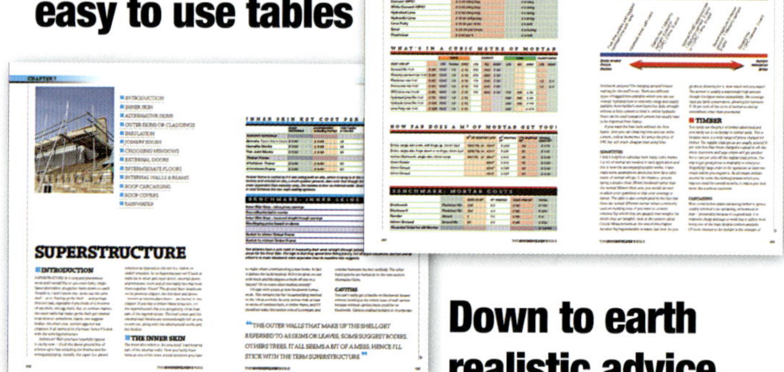

Updated costings in easy to use tables

Down to earth realistic advice

Large or small projects covered in detail

Great books from

All the best books available online at

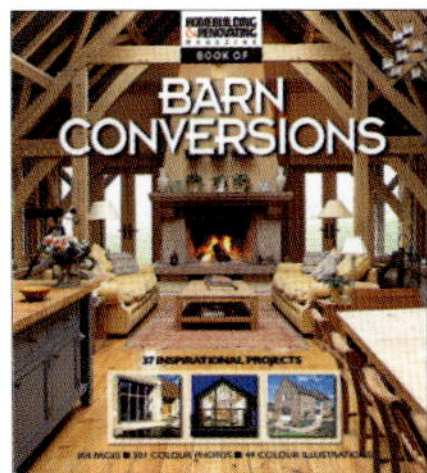
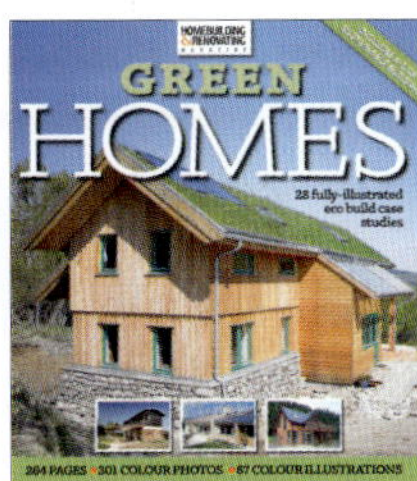
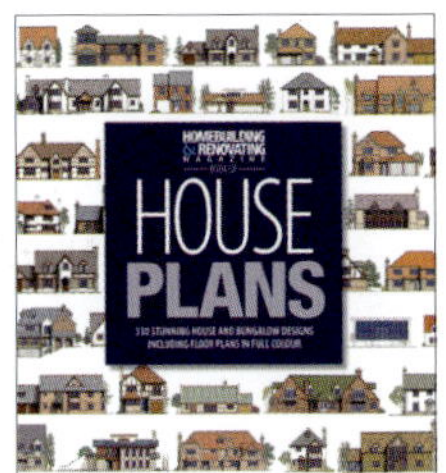

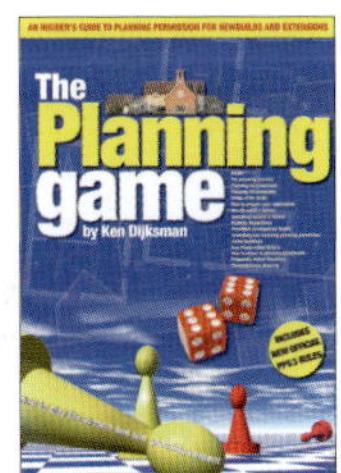

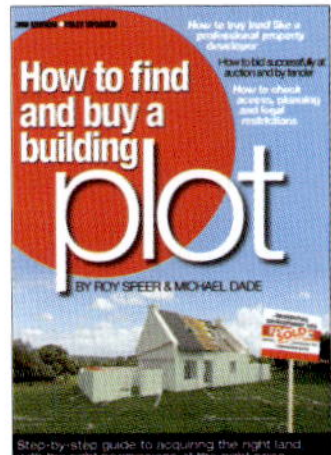

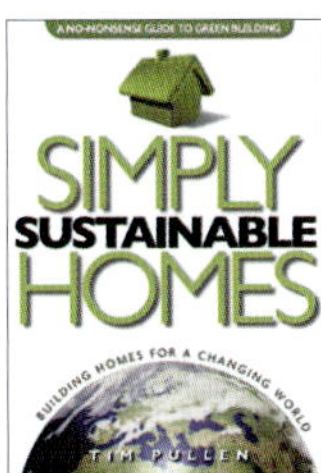
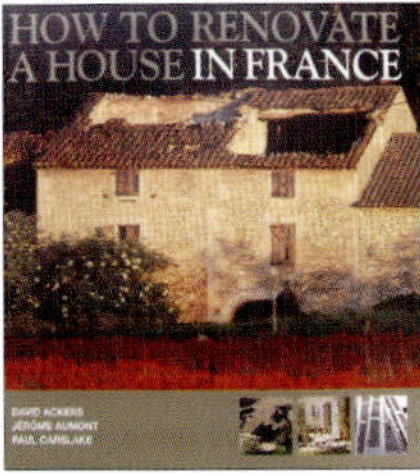
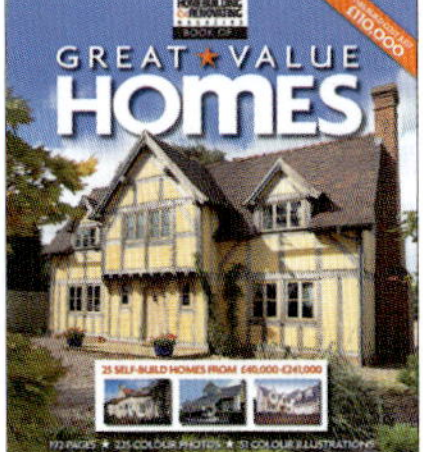
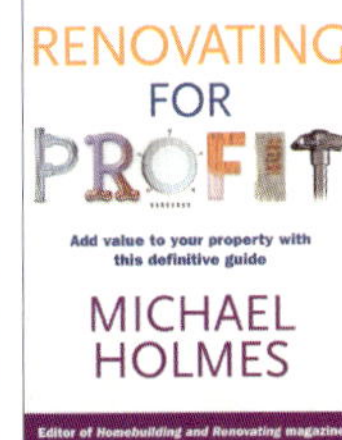

HOW TO GET PLANNING PERMISSION

ISBN **978 1 905959 129**

This new edition of the best-selling book on planning consent is used by public and professionals alike. Fully updated and completely re-designed it is ideal for anyone looking at newbuilds, extensions, loft conversions or any home improvement. The book features process flow charts, draft letters and many informative illustrations - all designed to take the stress out of applying for planning consent.

Expert advice presented in a clear and easy-to-follow style

Fully illustrated with photos and tables

Flow charts show how the system works

the H&R bookshop

www.homebuilding.co.uk/bookshop

Subscribe to Britain's best selling self-build magazine

- Home to the UK's leading self-build and renovation experts

- Inspirational design ideas for converting and renovating classic, rustic and contemporary builds

- Fully-costed readers' projects across all styles and budgets

- Expert project advice

- Independent guides and reviews

- Hear about new products and features first

Visit subscribetoday.co.uk
To subscribe or preview the latest issue online